TORTURE BEHIND BARS

TORTURE BEHIND BARS

Role of the Police Force in India

JOSHUA N. ASTON

OXFORD
UNIVERSITY PRESS

OXFORD

UNIVERSITY PRESS

Oxford University Press is a department of the University of Oxford.
It furthers the University's objective of excellence in research, scholarship,
and education by publishing worldwide. Oxford is a registered trademark of
Oxford University Press in the UK and in certain other countries.

Published in India by
Oxford University Press
22 Workspace, 2nd Floor, 1/22 Asaf Ali Road, New Delhi 110002, India

ISBN-13 (print edition): 978-0-19-012098-6
ISBN-10 (print edition): 0-19-012098-3

ISBN-13 (eBook): 978-0-19-099002-2
ISBN-10 (eBook): 0-19-099002-3

Typeset in Berling LT Std 9.5/13.8
by Tranistics Data Technologies, Kolkata 700091
Printed in India by Rakmo Press, New Delhi 110 020

The book refers to Jammu and Kashmir as the state of J&K, before
it was reorganized into the union territories of Jammu & Kashmir and
Ladakh in October 2019.

TORTURE BEHIND BARS

Role of the Police Force in India

JOSHUA N. ASTON

OXFORD
UNIVERSITY PRESS

OXFORD
UNIVERSITY PRESS

Oxford University Press is a department of the University of Oxford.
It furthers the University's objective of excellence in research, scholarship,
and education by publishing worldwide. Oxford is a registered trademark of
Oxford University Press in the UK and in certain other countries.

Published in India by
Oxford University Press
22 Workspace, 2nd Floor, 1/22 Asaf Ali Road, New Delhi 110002, India

First Edition published in 2020

ISBN-13 (print edition): 978-0-19-012098-6
ISBN-10 (print edition): 0-19-012098-3

ISBN-13 (eBook): 978-0-19-099002-2
ISBN-10 (eBook): 0-19-099002-3

Typeset in Berling LT Std 9.5/13.8
by Tranistics Data Technologies, Kolkata 700091
Printed in India by Rakmo Press, New Delhi 110 020

The book refers to Jammu and Kashmir as the state of J&K, before
it was reorganized into the union territories of Jammu & Kashmir and
Ladakh in October 2019.

'It is said that no one truly knows a nation until one has been inside its jails. A nation should not be judged by how it treats its highest citizens, but its lowest ones.'

— **Nelson Mandela**

CONTENTS

TABLES, FIGURES, AND APPENDICES

Tables

Figures

Appendices

ABBREVIATIONS*

ACHPR	African Charter on Human and Peoples' Rights
ACHR	American Convention on Human Rights
ACHR	Asian Centre for Human Rights
ACP	assistant commissioner of police
Addl DGP	additional director general of police
AFSPA	Armed Forces (Special Powers) Act
AFSPA (A&M)	Armed Forces (Assam and Manipur) Special Powers Act, 1958
AFSPA (J&K)	Armed Forces (Jammu and Kashmir) Special Powers Act, 1990
AFSPA (P&C)	Armed Forces (Punjab and Chandigarh) Special Powers Act, 1983
AHRC	Asian Human Rights Commission
APCOCA	Andhra Pradesh Control of Organised Crime Act
APP	additional public prosecutor
ARCHR	Arab Charter on Human Rights
Art./Arts	Article/Articles
BSF	Border Security Force

* This list consolidates abbreviations used in the book. There may be instances of duplication of an abbreviation by virtue of a difference in its full form. Readers are advised to refer to the list contextually.

CAT	Convention against Torture and Other Cruel, Inhuman or Degrading Treatment or Punishment
CBI	Central Bureau of Investigation
CED	International Convention for the Protection of All Persons from Enforced Disappearance
CEDAW	Convention on the Elimination of Discrimination against Women
CERD	Committee on the Elimination of Racial Discrimination
CGSPSA	Chhattisgarh Special Public Safety Act
CID	Crime Investigation Department
CJI	chief justice of India
CMS	Centre for Media Studies
CoI	Constitution of India
CP	commissioner of police
CPC	Code of Civil Procedure
CRC	Convention on the Rights of the Child
CrPC	Criminal Procedure Code
CRPF	Central Reserve Police Force
DGP	director general of police
DM	district magistrate
DSP	district superintendent of police
Dy IGP	deputy inspector general of police
ECHR	European Convention on Human Rights
EEVFAM	Extrajudicial Execution Victim Families' Association
EUCAT	European Convention against Torture and Other Cruel, Inhuman or Degrading Treatment or Punishment
FIR	First Information Report
FOP	Friends of Police
FTCA	Federal Tort Claims Act
GC	Geneva Convention**
HRC	Human Rights Committee

** Denotes the specific convention and not the entire Geneva Conventions as a whole.

IACPPT	Inter-American Convention to Prevent and Punish Torture
IB	Intelligence Bureau
ICC	international criminal court
ICCPR	International Covenant on Civil and Political Rights
ICESCR	International Covenant on Economic, Social and Cultural Rights
ICRC	International Committee of the Red Cross
ICRMW	International Convention on the Protection of the Rights of Migrant Workers and Members of their Families
IGP	inspector general of police
IHL	international humanitarian law
IHRL	international human rights law
INTERPOL	International Criminal Police Organization
IO	investigating officer
IPC	Indian Penal Code
IPS	Indian Police Service
MCOCA	Maharashtra Control of Organised Crime Act
NCRB	National Crimes Record Bureau
NGO	non-governmental organization
NHRC	National Human Rights Commission
NIA	National Investigation Agency
NPC	National Police Commission
NPM	National Preventive Mechanism
NSA	National Security Act
OP-ICCPR	Optional Protocol to the International Covenant on Civil and Political Rights
OP-CAT	Optional Protocol to the Convention against Torture and Other Cruel, Inhuman or Degrading Treatment or Punishment
para.	paragraph
PHRA	Protection of Human Rights Act
PIL	Public Interest Litigation
POT Bill	Prevention of Torture Bill
POTA	Prevention of Terrorism Act

PSHRC	Punjab State Human Rights Commission
SAARC	South Asian Association for Regional Cooperation
SAP	Special Armed Police
sec./secs	section/sections
SHRC	State Human Rights Commission
SIT	special investigation team
SP	superintendent of police
TADA	Terrorist and Disruptive Activities Act
TII	Transparency International India
UAPA	Unlawful Activities (Prevention) Act
UDHR	Universal Declaration of Human Rights
UN	United Nations
UN OHCHR	United Nations Office of the High Commissioner for Human Rights
UNCAT	United Nations Convention against Torture and Other Cruel, Inhuman or Degrading Treatment or Punishment
UNHCR	United Nations High Commissioner for Refugees
UNHRC	United Nations Human Rights Council
UPR	Universal Periodic Review

सत्यमेव जयते

Dr Kiran Bedi   Raj Nivas
Lieutenant Governor   Puducherry

FOREWORD

The United Nations Convention against Torture and Other Cruel, Inhuman or Degrading Treatment or Punishment (UNCAT) defines the term 'torture' as:

> any act by which severe pain or suffering, whether physical or mental, is intentionally inflicted on a person for such purposes as obtaining from him, or a third person, information or a confession, punishing him for an act he or a third person has committed or is suspected of having committed, or intimidating or coercing him or a third person, or for any reason based on discrimination of any kind, when such pain or suffering is inflicted by or at the instigation of or with the consent or acquiescence of a public official or other person acting in an official capacity.

Article 5 of the Universal Declaration of Human Rights declares torture as unacceptable.

Torture behind bars is certainly a serious violation of human rights of any individual by the law keepers, namely, the police force and the armed forces. Joshua Aston's scholarship has attempted to highlight a very serious issue, especially in a vast country like India, where the largest democracy of the world thrives.

Custodial violence is undoubtedly a serious issue in India, and the role of police and the nature of policing in the country is most of the

time questionable. As custodial violence is a subset of torture and violation of human rights, the author has aptly analysed this serious crime
under the provisions of various international conventions dealing with
the protection of human rights and prevention of torture in any form
as well as the national provisions laid down by the Constitution of India
and other national legislations. We often hear about custodial violence
and torture, illegal detention, custodial deaths, use of third-degree
method, assaults, and fake encounters, which are reported by the
media. This book highlights a number of such cases that have blatantly
disregarded the law meant for upholding the human rights and dignity
of individuals and render protection from torture. The author has made
an elaborate and exhaustive study within these parameters.

The author has very rightly discussed the reforms required in the
Indian police system and how the government, the police, and citizens
need to work together to protect citizens from such encounters with
the police. The author has rightly highlighted and indicated torture and
ill treatment committed by police officials and the armed forces in the
form of custodial violence. This book is an outcome of perseverance,
patience, and a detailed research done by the author, which will serve
its purpose of recommendation to policymakers in the government,
police officials, various human rights organizations, and social activists
who aim to uphold the rights of individuals and protect them from
torture.

I am glad that Joshua Aston has come up with this idea, which is
very thoughtful and important, and this will prove to be a book depict-
ing the entire picture of the existing police system in the country.

All in all, I have no hesitation in saying that the book in concise
and is recommended reading for students, academics, and practitioners
interested in law and policy. I wish Joshua Aston all the very best and
success for this rich content and idea.

Kiran Bedi (IAS)
Lieutenant Governor
Puducherry

PREFACE

This book provides the complete scenario and status of torture that is taking place behind bars—that is, custodial violence—and the role and accountability of the police force in India. The book as a whole presents reading material for students and teachers but I would consider my labour to be fully rewarded if the book serves the need of the students for whom it is primarily meant.

The prohibition of torture is indeed absolute,[1] and this prohibition applies even during war or any other emergency situations or threats to the national security of any country of the world.[2] To consider torture as a practice of the past[3] is not true as it is still practised in this era of modernization and globalization, and that too with more meticulousness and sophistication. International humanitarian law (IHL) and international human rights law (IHRL) have contributed considerably

[1] Tobias Thienel. 2006 'The Admissibility of Evidence Obtained by Torture under International Law', *The European Journal of International Law* 17, no. 2: 349–67.

[2] Article 3: Freedom from Torture and Inhumane and Degrading Treatment or Punishment'. Available at http://www.equalityhumanrights.com/sites/default/files/documents/humanrights/hrr_article_3.pdf, accessed on 4 March 2014.

[3] Oona A. Hathaway. 'The Promise and Limits of the International Law of Torture'. Available at http://www.law.yale.edu/documents/pdf/International_Law_of_Torture.pdf, accessed on 4 March 2014.

in developing a global realization that elaborate and explicit laws are required and need to be accepted as a standard for treatment of people who have been deprived of their liberty by law to provide protection and safeguard against all forms of gross ill treatment.[4] As far as the international legal regime on torture is concerned, it is definitely an area of convergence between IHRL and humanitarian law, which strengthen each other in dealing with this ancient global practice of torture.

The IHL, with the help of the International Committee of the Red Cross (ICRC), permits and mandates visits to detention facilities and helps to remove anonymity or secrecy, thus proving to be effective in the prevention of torture. International humanitarian law thus has a very significant position as many human rights treaties and conventions have been developed based on it. These laws guarantee the right to protection and provide preventive mechanisms on torture. International human rights law has created a plethora of universal instruments, which provides a framework to enforce it. The United Nations Convention against Torture and Other Cruel, Inhuman or Degrading Treatment or Punishment Convention against Torture (UNCAT) has thus provided a full range of possibilities. The IHL is, however, considered as a weak and soft law as it has a very feeble enforcement mechanism, except the provision related to International Fact-Finding Commission under Art. 90 of Additional Protocol I (AP-I) of the Geneva Conventions. Contrary to this perception, IHL has added value by evolving a notion of penal treatment to grave breaches of basic obligations under the Geneva Conventions (I, II, III, and IV) and its Additional Protocols (I and II), as it overtly mentions torture as an essential component in the meaning of grave breaches. On the other hand, IHRL ensures the right to reparation (compensation), which facilitates the recovery process and speeds up healing by supporting the victim's sense of justice. The perpetual existence of torture in various parts of the world is due to the absence

---

[4] Walter Kälin. 1998. 'The Struggle against Torture', *International Review of the Red Cross*, No. 324. Available at http://www.icrc.org/eng/resources/documents/misc/57jpg5.htm, accessed on 17 July 2017.

of real political will to prevent torture, which has resulted in legal gaps.[5]

Although there is a robust and comprehensive international legal framework to address the issue of torture and provide a model of solutions, namely, the United Nations (UN) conventions, declarations, and resolutions, regional frameworks such as those of the European Union, the African Union, and of various national responses have not proved to be much useful in preventing torture and protecting the rights of victims. This has created a legal gap, which multiplies with the ever-increasing crime rates, resulting in impunity and lack of command responsibility.

This book analyses the context of torture, ill treatment, and crimes committed by the police in the form of custodial violence, in the light of the reports of the UN Special Rapporteur on Torture and Other Cruel, Inhuman or Degrading Treatment or Punishment, UNCAT, the European Commission, the Asian Human Rights Commissions, the National Human Rights Commission (NHRC), the National Crime Record Bureau, police journals, international and national non-governmental organizations (NGO), and other independent reports.

The book also takes into account various international standards provided by the Universal Declaration of Human Rights (UDHR), the International Covenant on Civil and Political Rights (ICCPR), and the European Convention for the Prevention of Torture and Inhuman or Degrading Treatment or Punishment, recommendations of UN Rapporteur on Torture as well as legislations and recommendations of the Indian judiciary and statutory commissions such as the Gore Committee, the Ribeiro Committee, the Justice Hegde Commission, the Justice Malimath Committee on Reforms of Criminal Justice System, and the Veerappa Moily Commission, which have proposed an effective legal response to address the issue of torture and custodial violence. It looks at the special nature of torture that takes place on the grounds of race, gender, and minority status, keeping in tune with the principles and protection provided under the Convention

---

[5] Kälin. 1998. 'The Struggle against Torture'.

on the Elimination of Discrimination against Women (CEDAW), the UN Declaration on the Rights of Minorities, and Committee on the Elimination of Racial Discrimination (CERD).

Further, this book provides a detailed overview of the police system, its structure and functions, and its role in preventing crimes, and its participation in committing crimes, namely, custodial violence and related crimes. It elaborately discusses the role and accountability of the police in India. Although this book briefly touches upon the role of the armed forces in the country, the primary focus of the book remains on the Indian police system.

The instrument that governs the Indian police force is the archaic Indian Police Act of 1861 and any discussion on police reforms in India eventually directs towards the demand for replacing this act. British colonizers drafted the Indian Police Act of 1861 as a direct consequence of the first war for independence to ensure that the police functions under the rule of the politicians and powerful executives and follows an authoritarian approach towards the public. Hence here is a strong need to amend or replace the Indian Police Act.

Moreover, the Criminal Procedure Code (CrPC), the Indian Evidence Act and the Indian Penal Code (IPC) also need to undergo amendments to suit present requirements of the justice system of India, to be more citizen friendly, and to aim at protecting the rights of citizens and prevent torture by the police and the armed forces. The structure of the police force is strictly hierarchical, and decision making is centralized with a few high-ranking police officers. Postings and transfers are commonly interfered in by political influence. Thus, there needs to be a better law to prevent such misuse of law at the hands of politicians and other government agents.

This book provides a detailed discussion on the various recommendations of a number of committees constituted to reform the police system and administration in order to provide a better system of governance. Since 1971, there have been five major reform committees, namely, the Gore Committee, the National Police Commission (NPC), the Riberio Committee on Police Reforms, the Padmanabhaiah Committee on Police Reforms, and the Malimath Committee on Reforms of Criminal Justice System. But these recommendations were never paid heed to because of the politicization of the police, and hence many significant and important recommendations were never addressed.

For preventing crime and maintaining law and order in any society, the support of the community is a sine qua non. Thus the book highlights another reform that could be followed to provide better policing—neighbourhood or community policing. This should be encouraged in order to reduce the existing gap between the police and the public. Neighbourhood policing should be encouraged only in the context of helping the citizens from being treated inhumanly.

It is thus necessary and the need of the hour to reform and replace the current police act with a new law for the police system in India so that violations of human rights do not take place at the hands of police personnel and to ensure that the police have a greater sense of responsibility, accountability, and efficiency towards the protection of the public.

The research on this crucial and important issue in the country and its transformation into a book form would not have been possible without the help and support of several people whose contribution is immense. I would like to express my deep sense of gratitude to Kiran Bedi, Honourable Lt Governor, Union Territory of Puducherry, for her unstinted encouragement and for writing a foreword to book. I would like to express my sincere gratitude to Bimal N. Patel, Director of Gujarat National Law University, for being a great support. I extend my sincere thanks to my student Nadim Khan who has been of great assistance for this research and has contributed significantly to this book. I am grateful to the team at Oxford University Press for their professionalism and support in completing this project. My immense gratitude goes to my parents and brother who have always been unconditional in their support and encouragement.

INTRODUCTION

Torture is now absolutely and without any reservation prohibited under international law whether in time of peace or of war. ... [T]he prohibition of torture can be considered to belong to the rules of jus cogens. If ever a phenomenon was outlawed unreservedly and unequivocally it is torture. ... If there was some disagreement [in the General Assembly] in respect to [the Convention against Torture and Other Cruel, Inhuman or Degrading Treatment or Punishment], it had to do with the methods of control and implementation. There was no disagreement whatsoever on the fact that torture is absolutely forbidden.[1]

Overview

Custodial violence refers to violence that is experienced physically, psychologically as well as emotionally in the custody of law and lawful authority, which includes enforced disappearance, illegal detention, torture, extrajudicial execution, and various other forms of cruel, inhuman, and degrading treatments and punishment. Custodial violence involves specific situations such as those where

[1] P. Kooijmans. 1986. '1st Report on Torture and Other Cruel, Inhuman or Degrading Treatment or Punishment', in *Customary International Law and Torture: The Case of India*, by A. Mark Weisburd (1st Special Rapporteur on Torture for the UN Commission on Human Rights), UNHRC Resolution 1985/33, UN Doc E/CN4/1986/15 1.

custody itself is prima facie unlawful or does not have any authority of law, which is a violation of rights originating at the moment of invoking custody, and this continues post custody too, for instance, crimes of illegal detention and enforced disappearance by state or agents of state, that is, public authorities. Another specific situation is when the custody itself is lawful but the standards of custodial practices are not followed post custody. Thus violation of rights starts at some point of time post detention custody and this may continue during custody.

The role of the police and the nature of policing have become the focus of debate and controversy among politicians, media, and the public. With the police often being the major violator of human rights and the culprit in custodial violence, Indian policing is often perceived to be in a state of crisis. Major misuse of power and cause of injustice to the people have weakened the public confidence in police. There has been little agreement on what the police should do and not do, and this is the reason why there is a huge commotion in the structural foundation of the entire police system in India.

Legal Instruments against Torture in India

The crime rate in India is much higher as compared to other nations, especially when it comes to violation of human rights and human dignity. The ever-escalating trajectory of the crime rate also questions the role and status of the police system and the overall administration of law, order, and justice in the country. There lies a huge responsibility with the police force of the country to curb crime. As per the Indian Constitution, members of the police force are public servants and a police station is considered as public property. Therefore, the duty and the conduct of a police officer must conform to the law of the land, respect basic human freedom, and obey as well as maintain law and order in the country. However, time and again, we observe a contrasting character where members of the police are involved in custodial violence, torture, inhuman treatment, handcuffing prisoners, use of third degree methods, and so on, which are often demonstrated and practised by the police force during their official duties.

Relevant Provisions under the Indian Constitution

The CoI is based primarily on the principle and concept of equality among all citizens irrespective of their status, gender, caste, or creed and social, economic, and political justice.[2] The Constitution also guarantees some exclusive rights for persons who are under institutional custody besides other rights including fundamental rights. The concept of equality and the provision for protection against torture or any other arbitrary behaviour forms the basis of the Indian Constitution. Thus each and every citizen of the country has the right to equality and protection before law.[3] This can be in the form of reasonable, right, and fair conduct and protection from any kind of arbitrary treatment.[4] In addition, the Supreme Court of India has also acted towards supporting protection from such treatment and has discouraged the death penalty, which denotes an act of arbitrary treatment.[5] Thus, protection of the rights of the citizens of this country is the first and foremost duty of the government or any of its representatives.

Besides providing the right to equality and protection from arbitrary treatment, the Constitution also guarantees another exclusive freedom to citizens, namely, freedom of movement, association, assembly without arms, and so on,[6] but these freedoms can be restricted by law in certain conditions such as upholding integrity, sovereignty, security, public order, morality, and decency and while maintaining friendly relations with foreign states.[7] The Constitution also guarantees protection against self-incrimination, double jeopardy, and ex post facto laws. This means that no person in the country can be forced or compelled to provide any testimony against himself.[8] Forced or compelled testimony is not only limited to confessions or statements but

---

[2] Constitution of India (CoI), Preamble.
[3] CoI, Art. 14.
[4] *Maneka Gandhi* v *Union of India*, AIR 1978 SC 597.
[5] *Mithu* v *State of Punjab*, AIR 1983 SC 473.
[6] CoI, Art. 19(1).
[7] CoI, Art. 19(2).
[8] CoI, Art. 20(3).

also includes incriminatory statements.[9] The right to life and personal liberty as guaranteed by the Constitution establishes that nobody's life and liberty can be taken away and nobody can be deprived of their right to life and personal liberty unless there is a procedure that has been established by law.[10] The Supreme Court of India has further interpreted the 'procedure established by law' as 'due process of law' and thus stated that as per Art. 21 of the Constitution, the procedure of law must be fair, just, and reasonable and not arbitrary, cruel, or whimsical, which thus provides a triangular relationship between Arts 14, 19, and 21.[11] The Constitution also guarantees protection against detention, which includes the right to be informed about the grounds for detention and the right to consult and to be defended by a lawyer of choice. But it is also the duty of the detaining authority to produce the detained person before the competent magistrate within 24 hours of detention or arrest. However, such right to protection is not given to any enemy or alien during war and in case of preventive detention laws. Moreover, such preventive detention is time bound, that is, it should not be for more than three months.[12] The Constitution also states that the rights guaranteed under Arts 20 and 21 must not be suspended even during emergency.[13]

Although 'torture' is not defined per se in the CoI, the Constitution emphasizes the fundamental rights of its citizens and provides for respect and human dignity. Article 21 of the CoI provides that 'no person shall be deprived of his life or personal liberty except according to procedure established by law'. This can be interpreted as a guarantee to live life with dignity, free from any kind of torture or cruel, inhuman, and degrading treatment or punishment. Further, Art. 22 of the Constitution provides protection against arrest and detention in certain cases and provides guarantee against detention or custody without proper information on the grounds for arrest. It also provides

---

[9] *Nandini Satpathy v Dani (PL) and Another*, 1978 SCC (2) 42.

[10] CoI, Art. 21.

[11] *Maneka Gandhi v Union of India*.

[12] CoI, Art. 22.

[13] CoI, Art. 359.

that such detained persons have the right to consult a lawyer and defend themselves. Article 22 further states that the arrested and detained person is required to be produced before a magistrate within 24 hours of the arrest. Article 20(3) provides that the accused person shall not be forced into self-incrimination, that is, to be a witness against himself.

Other Legal Provisions

There are a number of sections in other legislations in the country that directly or indirectly have provisions against any kind of torture including custodial violence. However, there is no express or explicit legislation against torture till today. The following are some of the provisions which indirectly deal with the prohibition of torture.

- Section 54 of the CrPC, 1973, grants the arrested person the right to have himself medically examined. Under sec. 164 of CrPC, making a confession is a voluntary action and it is made in front of a metropolitan or judicial magistrate. Section 162 of CrPC provides that no statement of a witness or any person during an investigation recorded by a police officer can be used for any purpose other than to contradict his statement before the court.
- Sections 330 and 331 of the IPC provide for punishment for injury inflicted for extorting confession. Section 330 provides for causing a simple injury, while sec. 331 provides for causing grievous injury or harm to any person. Further, the crime of custodial violence or torture against prisoners can be brought under secs 302, 304, 304A and 306.
- Under the Indian Evidence Act, 1872, secs 25 and 26, a confession made to a police officer is not admissible in evidence. Section 24 of the act provides that a confession made by an accused person is irrelevant in a criminal proceeding if the making of the confession appears to the court to have been caused by any inducement, threat, or promise.[14]

[14] Sec. 24, The Indian Evidence Act, 1872.

Status of India under the International Legal Framework in Prohibition of Torture

Although India has signed the UNCAT, it is still not a party to the convention even after 30 years of signing it. The Supreme Court of India has, in many instances and occasions, laid down guidelines to recognize and protect the rights of victims of torture and custodial violence. Further, it has discussed the responsibility of the government to provide adequate legal protection by reforming the criminal justice system, especially the police force. Even though India is not a party to CAT, it is a party to the ICCPR and the Convention on the Rights of the Child (CRC), which provide the right to protection against torture and custodial violence. In view of this, it is relevant to explore and analyse efforts made by India in order to fulfill international commitments. The Malimath Committee recommends changes in the criminal justice system to improve the competence and credibility of the investigating agency.[15] In addition, it recognizes the legal and constitutional rights of the accused including the state obligation to adhere to the due process of law; speedy, independent, and impartial trial; restraint on torture and forced testimony; and legal aid.[16]

The Scenario of Custodial Violence in India

The seriousness of custodial violence can be assessed from the astonishing data of the past eight years, during the period from 1 April 2001 to 31 March 2009, which reported 1,184 deaths in police custody. More recently, the reports of the Asian Centre for Human Rights (ACHR) and the NHRC, which were presented in the Indian Parliament in 2018, showed more shocking data on custodial deaths. There were 1,674 cases of custodial deaths between 1 April 2017 and 28 February 2018, among which 1,530 deaths were in judicial

---

[15] Ministry of Home Affairs. 2003. *Report of the Committee on Reforms of Criminal Justice System*, para. 3.12. New Delhi: Ministry of Home Affairs, Government of India.

[16] Ministry of Home Affairs. *Report of the Committee on Reforms*, para. 4.2.

custody and 144 in police custody.[17] The analysis of this data reveals that the number of custodial deaths has increased to five deaths per day during 2017–18 in contrast to four deaths per day during the period 2001–10. The top five states in India that led the list of custodial deaths in police custody from 2001 to 2009 have been identified as Maharashtra followed by Uttar Pradesh, Gujarat, Andhra Pradesh, and West Bengal. In less than a year, that is, from April 2017 to February 2018, 365 cases of custodial deaths were registered in the state of Uttar Pradesh, which topped the list, followed by 127 in West Bengal, 118 each in Punjab and Maharashtra, 107 in Madhya Pradesh, and 102 in Bihar.[18] The major reasons for these deaths were torture and custodial violence, which occurred within the first 48 hours of custody.[19] The former director general of police (DGP) and Intelligence Bureau (IB) officer K.S. Subramanian acknowledged in an interview that torture chambers and terror cells exist in India, especially to deal with 'terrorist-related cases and the police may feel incentivized to describe people as terrorists and kill them for professional reasons and career advancement.' He also gave information about the killing of farmers in anti-Naxalite operations.[20] The Prevention of Terrorism Act (POTA), 2002, has been severely criticized of being misused towards

[17] Sankalita Dey. 2018. 'In 2017–18, There Were 5 Custodial Deaths Per Day in India, Says Report', *The Print*, 28 June. Available at https://theprint.in/governance/in-2017-18-there-were-5-custodial-deaths-per-day-in-india-says-report/75654/, accessed on 15 March 2019.

[18] Press Trust of India (PTI). 2018. '1680 Cases of Custodial Deaths Registered by NHRC in 10 Months', *Times of India*, 14 March 2018. Available at https://timesofindia.indiatimes.com/india/1680-cases-of-custodial-deaths-registered-by-nhrc-in-10-months/articleshow/63299768.cms, accessed on 15 March 2019.

[19] Asian Centre for Human Rights (ACHR). 2009. *Torture in India 2009*. Available at http://www.achrweb.org/press/2009/IND0209.html, accessed on 21 October 2017.

[20] Adnan Alavi. 2009. 'India's Own Abu Ghraib: The Week's Story on Secret Torture Chambers', 11 July 2009. Available at http://www.twocircles.net/2009jul10/indias_own_abu_ghraib_weeks_story_secret_torture_chambers.html, accessed on 21 October 2017.

selectively targeting and projecting a particular community as terrorists. There are also various reports alleging that the Government of Gujarat has abused POTA for terrorizing Muslims. Out of a total of 287 cases registered by the end of 2003, 286 cases were concerned with Muslims only, while one case was against a Sikh. The reports have also alleged that 245 persons were illegally detained for a period ranging from 3–25 days, before showing them as arrested. Suspects under POTA have been tortured repeatedly, including the use of electric shock to their genitals.[21]

As per the statement of Justice A.S. Anand, former chief justice of India (CJI) on 13 August 2001, custodial violence is perhaps one of the worst crimes in a civilized society and is a matter of concern for many reasons. Custodial violence, including torture and, in more extreme situations, death in lock-ups, strikes a heavy blow at the rule of law. This has raised a demand that the powers of the executive should not only be derived from law but also be limited by law. Transparency of action and accountability are two possible safeguards to prevent any abuse of the power in arresting a citizen. Section 7 of the Police Act of 1861 empowers the higher police officers to 'dismiss, suspend or reduce any officer of the subordinate ranks whom they shall think remiss or negligent in discharge of his duty or unfit for the same.' Even lesser punishments can be awarded. Section 29 of the act provides that any police officer if found violating the rules and regulations, including any police officer who shall offer any unwarrantable personal violence to any person in his custody, shall be punished with three months rigorous imprisonment. But in reality, these clauses have never been enforced for taking action against the police personnel for violating rules and committing violence, more particularly custodial violence. The Indian police in the present time find themselves handicapped not only in their numerical strength but also in terms of the inadequate infrastructural facilities available, for instance, lack of modern weaponry and equipment, transport, and communication networks. They

---

[21] Zakia Jowher and Mukul Dube. 2004. 'POTA in Gujarat and Its Meaning for India', 15 August 2004. Available at http://www.sacw.net/Gujarat2002/Dube_Jowher15August2004.html, accessed on 21 October 2017.

also require need-based training, which is of utmost importance in making the Indian Police force a more efficient and effective instrument of law enforcement.

The late Justice V.R. Krishna Iyer termed torture and prison justice in India as a 'virgin area of jurisprudence', which is significant to ensure the guarantee of rights inside prisons. He ruled that imposition of inhuman treatments and brutal restrictions and subjecting inmates to torture are not laws.[22] The Supreme Court has already ruled out the use of third degree torture methods and outlawed 'third degree' and 'compelled testimony'.[23] Justice E.S. Venkataramiah held that any form of torture or cruel treatment that is degrading and inhuman is contrary to human dignity and opposes the right to live, and hence it is forbidden under Art. 21. No such behaviour that amounts to torture, ill treatment, and inhuman and degrading treatment can be legitimized under law and can never be proved as reasonable. Article 21 of the CoI also guarantees the right to protection against torture or any kind of cruel, inhuman, or degrading treatment and absolutely follows Art. 5 of the UDHR and Art. 7 of the ICCPR.[24] Justice Chinnappa Reddy too voiced his opinion that no person, whether he is inside or outside the prison, can be stripped off his rights, and everyone is protected by virtue of the principles of right, just, and fair means. Article 32 of the Constitution ensures and provides the remedy to intervene and protect people from torture and is considered to be important.[25] Justice Ranganath Misra opined that the courts are under a huge obligation to ensure that detainees' right to freedom from torture is honoured and protected at all the times during the detention.[26] Justice A.S. Anand held that in cases where there has been confirmed violation of the fundamental right to life of a citizen by public servants, monetary or pecuniary compensation is the only suitable remedy on grounds of the

---

[22] *Sunil Batra* v *Delhi Administration*, AIR 1978 SC 1675.

[23] *Nandini Satpathy* v *Dani (PL) and Another*.

[24] *Francis Coralie Mullin* v *Administrator, Union Territory of Delhi*, 1981 SCC (1) 608.

[25] *Sunil Batra* v *Delhi Administration*.

[26] *Sheela Barse* v *State of Maharastra*, AIR 1983 SC 378.

vicarious liability of the state for the actions of its servants or agents. This resulted in the evolution of a novel principle of application of international law in Indian courts, which upheld the legitimacy of the right to reparation despite India's reservation to it, in cases of illegal detention under Art. 9(5) of the ICCPR.[27]

The Supreme Court in the early 1980s evolved the concept of constitutional torts and ensured the right to compensation for violation of right to life and freedom by agents of the state. For the first time, it awarded monetary compensation under the writ jurisdiction under Art. 32 of the Constitution in a case of illegal detention of a prisoner named Rudul Shah, who had been kept in illegal detention for over 14 years even after his acquittal. The right to compensation was recognized by the Supreme Court in cases of grave violations of the right to personal liberty.[28] In another case, the Supreme Court considered enforced disappearance akin to custodial death and held the state responsible to pay compensation for the enforced disappearance of a person while he was in police custody.[29] In a case of custodial death in the state of Odisha, the Supreme Court awarded compensation and laid down the rule for award of compensation by enlarging its jurisdiction under Art. 32 of the Constitution and that of high courts under Art. 226 of the Constitution.[30]

The Supreme Court has also provided guidelines for the armed forces when they act in aid of a civil power. It has ruled that third-degree methods to extract information or confession should not be used; no person, especially women and children, should be ill-treated; and there should not be any kind of torture or harassment with any civilian.[31] After one of the major events of torture, the NHRC reported in an affidavit that from 2007 to 2012, it had received 1,671 complaints

---

[27] *Shri D.K. Basu* v *State of West Bengal,* AIR 1997 SC 610.

[28] *Rudul Shah* v *State of Bihar,* AIR 1983 SC 1086.

[29] *Sebastian M. Hongray* v *Union of India,* AIR 1984 SC 1026.

[30] *Smt. Nilabati Behera alias Lalit Behera* v *State of Orissa & Ors.,* 1993 2 SCC 746.

[31] *Naga People's Movement of Human Rights* v *Union of India,* AIR 1998 SC 431.

or information regarding fake encounters. It made this admission in response to the alleged, unaddressed extrajudicial killings in Manipur. The NHRC further reported, 'The commission in the last five years has awarded monetary compensation to the tune of Rs 10.51 crore in 191 cases'.[32] The NHRC awards compensation in the range of Rs 5–10 lakh to the kin of victims if, after the inquiry, it comes to the conclusion that the encounter was fake. In response to the shocking attitude of the government of the militancy-affected state of Manipur where over 1,500 alleged fake encounter killings had taken place between 1980 and 2010, a bench of Justices Aftab Alam and Ranjana P. Desai asked during the last hearing of the case, 'Is there a war going on within? Is this the attitude and orientation of a state to say that if they are killing my men, we will kill them?'[33] Two organizations—Extrajudicial Execution Victim Families' Association (EEVFAM) and Human Rights Alert—based in Manipur submitted the petition for the investigation of such killings and fake encounters in September 2012, listing 1,528 extrajudicial killings. In its investigation, the NHRC was forced to 'address the larger question of the role of the State Police'.[34] The bench of Justices Aftab Alam and Ranjana P. Desai examined the committee's report, which said that none of the six cases reported qualified to be encounters and that they were fake.[35] The Supreme Court then

---

[32] Dhananjay Mahapatra. 2012. '191 Fake Encounters in Last Five Years, NHRC Tells Supreme Court', *Times of India*, 5 December. Available at http://timesofindia.indiatimes.com/india/191-fake-encounters-in-last-five-years-NHRC-tells-Supreme-Court/articleshow/17486080.cms, accessed on 15 December 2017.

[33] Mahapatra. '191 Fake Encounters in Last Five Years, NHRC Tells Supreme Court'.

[34] *Extra Judl. Exec. Victim Families Assn. & Anr.* v *Union of India & Ors.*, Writ Petition (Crl.) 129 of 2012 and Writ Petition (C) No. 445 of 2012; judgment dated 14 July 2017.

[35] PTI. 2013. 'Six Cases of Encounters in Manipur Not Genuine: Panel to SC', *Economic Times*, 4 April. Available at https://economictimes.indiatimes.com/news/politics-and-nation/six-cases-of-encounters-in-manipur-not-genuine-panel-to-sc/articleshow/19377147.cms?from=mdr, accessed on 2 November 2019.

reacted very strongly to the state of affairs of the Armed Forces (Special Powers) Act (AFSPA) and sharply questioned how an army man could enter any home, commit rape, and then say that he enjoys immunity as the actions have been done in the discharge of official duties.[36] Further, on 26 November 2018, Justices Madan Lokur and Uday Umesh Lalit passed the decision that the continuing mandamus must continue and the independence and integrity of the Special Investigation Team (SIT) and the judges dealing with the case would be maintained and the death and killing of people by the army, the paramilitary forces, and the Manipur forces would be investigated by the SIT.[37]

Regarding torture and violence committed by the police force, the NHRC raised a concern in 2018 that cases of fake encounters have been on the rise. The NHRC reported that 2,955 complaints of encounter deaths had been registered with it between 1 April 1998 and 31 March 2018.[38] In Uttar Pradesh alone, 1,100 encounters have taken place in which 49 people were killed and 370 injured. The Supreme Court too has raised serious concern on the issue of encounter deaths.[39]

The Law Commission of India has made a special note that the victims of custodial crimes, torture, injury, or death generally belong

[36] *Times of India.* 2011. 'Can Army Kill, Rape & Enjoy Immunity: SC Poser to Govt', *Times of India,* 17 June. Available at http://timesofindia.indiatimes.com/india/Can-army-kill-rape-enjoy-immunity-SC-poser-to-govt-/articleshow/8883883.cms?intenttarget=no, accessed on 15 December 2017.

[37] *Lourembam Deben Singh & Ors.* v *Union of India & Ors.,* Writ Petition (Criminal) No. 205 of 2018. Available at https://www.sci.gov.in/supremecourt/2018/30415/30415_2018_Judgement_12-Nov-2018.pdf, accessed on 28 March 2019.

[38] ACHR. 2018. *The State of Encounter Killings in India.* Available at http://www.achrweb.org/programme/torture-in-india/the-state-of-encounter-killings-in-india/, accessed on 26 December 2018.

[39] *The Hindu.* 2019. 'U.P. Police Encounter Deaths a Serious Issue, Says Supreme Court', 14 January. Available at https://www.thehindu.com/news/national/other-states/up-police-encounter-deaths-a-serious-issue-sc/article25991249.ece, accessed on 28 March 2019.

to the vulnerable groups.[40] The 152nd report of the Law Commission of India acknowledged that there is a necessity of the police for the maintenance of law and order and respect of law. However, the report also emphasized that use of torture and third-degree methods during investigation and interrogation cannot be justified or permitted in a civilized nation like India.[41]

In November 2017, the Ministry of Law & Justice, Government of India, proposed a draft bill focusing on the prevention of torture in any form in the country—Prevention of Torture Bill (POT Bill), 2017, which had been crafted by the Law Commission of India in its 273rd report and recommended ratification of CAT. A report was submitted to the Ministry of Law & Justice in October 2017 by the Law Commission of India, proposing the inclusion of 'torture' as a crime by amending secs 330 and 331 of the IPC. Proposals were also shared with state governments for their views and suggestions, but most states have been silent on this matter as the bill recommends jail term for public servants convicted of torture. Moreover, the report recommended making amendments in the CrPC, 1973, and the Indian Evidence Act, 1872, to incorporate provisions for compensation and burden of proof. But there has been no progress in this matter till date.[42]

[40] 13th Law Commission of India. 1994. *152nd Report on Custodial Crimes*, para. 1.5. New Delhi: 13th Law Commission of India.

[41] 13th Law Commission of India. *152nd Report*, para. 1.6.

[42] PTI. 2018. 'Prevention of Torture: Most States Silent on Bill to Punish Public Servants', *Indian Express*, 30 December. Available at https://indianexpress.com/article/india/prevention-of-torture-most-states-silent-on-bill-to-punish-public-servants-5515999/, accessed on 28 March 2019.

I

INTERNATIONAL LEGAL FRAMEWORK IN PROHIBITION OF TORTURE AND CUSTODIAL VIOLENCE

There is enough data to prove that torture has been and is being practised in India on a large scale in spite of an elected government in power and the necessary legislations in place. The use of torture during interrogation at police stations is a routine practice. The perpetrators of torture mostly include the members of the police force, the military and paramilitary forces, governmental officials, and health professionals. The perpetrators also include co-detainees who act under the orders of the officials in the police system or the government. And this continues to happen in spite of the fact that India is party to a considerable number of international conventions and treaties such as the UDHR, the CRC, and the ICCPR.

The international legal framework against torture as enshrined under various international, regional, and local/national instruments, including the UDHR, the ICCPR, the International CAT, and the CRC. India acceded to the ICCPR on 10 April 1979 and the CRC on 11 December 1992. However, India has not signed the Optional Protocol (1966) I and II (1989) to the ICCPR.[1]

---

[1] United Nations Office of the High Commissioner for Human Rights (UN OHCHR), 'Ratification Status for India'. Available at https://tbinternet.ohchr. org/_layouts/TreatyBodyExternal/Treaty.aspx?CountryID=79&Lang=EN, accessed on 28 September 2017.

The ICCPR is a major torchbearer of the rights enunciated in the UDHR, and like the latter, it also ensures the right to life and protection against arbitrary deprivation of life;[2] prohibits torture or cruel, inhuman treatment and degrading punishment; and provides everyone protection against such practices and treatment.[3] The CAT provides a detailed structure for the mechanism to redress human rights violation and to protect against torture and custodial violence, providing a comprehensive definition of the term. It tries to remove ambiguity around the interpretation and application of the term 'torture'[4] and calls for nations to criminalize torture,[5] urging them to enact legislation on the subject.[6] It further restrains nations to legitimize torture in the name of any exceptional circumstances or necessity such as war, threat of war, internal instability, and public emergency[7] and further lays down the procedure for states to adopt in such cases. It calls for states to exercise their jurisdiction over such crimes of torture committed within their territory[8] and prohibits nations to extradite any criminal if s/he is likely to be subjected to torture on extradition.[9] It emphasizes on international cooperation for ensuring justice to the victims of crimes of torture.[10] It makes a system of mandatory registration of complaints, impartial investigation, and adjudication of crime of torture.[11] In addition to the provision for criminal redress of torture, states are obliged to make legal arrangements for a system of adequate compensation and rehabilitation for victims of torture.[12]

---

[2] ICCPR, Art. 6(1).
[3] ICCPR, Art. 7.
[4] CAT, Art. 1.
[5] CAT, Art. 4.
[6] CAT, Art. 2.
[7] CAT, Art. 2.
[8] CAT, Art. 5.
[9] CAT, Art. 3.
[10] CAT, Art. 9.
[11] CAT, Art. 13.
[12] CAT, Art. 14.

Role of International Humanitarian Law and International Human Rights Law in Prohibition of Torture

The IHL and IHRL are two distinct bodies of law but complementary to each other. Both aim to protect the lives, health, and dignity of individuals, with IHL applicable in armed conflicts and IHRL at all times. IHL is based on the Geneva Conventions, the Hague Convention, and the Additional Protocols. On the other hand, IHRL includes a number of regional treaties.

The definition of torture, under IHL and IHRL, contains three major characteristics:[13]

a. The act must be one by which severe pain or suffering, whether physical or mental, is inflicted on a person.
b. The act must be intentionally inflicted.
c. The act must be instrumental for purposes such as
   i. obtaining from the individual or a third person information or a confession,
   ii. punishing him/her for an act he/she or a third person has committed or is suspected of having committed,
   iii. intimidating him/her or a third person,
   iv. coercing him/her or a third person, or
   v. for any reason based on discrimination of any kind.

The key definitions and provisions under IHL that prohibit torture and other forms of ill treatment are provided in Art. 4 of the 1907 Hague Regulations, respecting the Laws and Customs of War on Land, the four Geneva Conventions of 1949, Art. 75(2)(a)(ii) of the Additional Protocol I of 1977, and Art. 4(2)(a) of the Additional Protocol II of 1977.

Under IHRL, the prohibition on torture is included in Art. 5 of the 1948 UDHR, Art. 7 of the 1966 ICCPR, the 1984 CAT, and Art. 37(a) of the 1989 CRC.

---

[13] International Committee of the Red Cross (ICRC). 2014. 'Prohibition and Punishment of Torture and Other Forms of Ill-Treatment', Advisory Service on International Humanitarian Law. Available at https://www.icrc.org/en/document/prohibition-and-punishment-torture-and-other-forms-ill-treatment (accessed on 30 September 2017).

International Legal Framework against Torture

To protect and prevent torture, the UN has enforced various international frameworks against torture under a number of international and regional instruments. These include the UDHR, CAT, and the CRC, and among the regional instruments, the European Convention on Human Rights 1950 (ECHR), the European Convention against Torture and Other Cruel, Inhuman or Degrading Treatment or Punishment (EUCAT), the American Convention on Human Rights 1969 (ACHR), the Inter-American Convention to Prevent and Punish Torture, 1985 (IACPPT), the African Charter on Human and Peoples' Rights (ACHPR), and the Arab Charter on Human Rights (ARCHR) are some of the important ones.

The International Convention against Torture and Other Cruel, Inhuman, or Degrading Treatment or Punishment

The CAT was concluded in New York and was adopted, signed, and opened for signature, ratification, and accession by the General Assembly Resolution No. 39/46 of 10 December 1984. It came into force on 26 June 1987 following the 20th ratification under Art. 27(1) of the CAT, and as on 15 June 2014, the CAT has 155 parties, 81 signatories, and 70 ratifications[14] On 14 October 1997, the permanent representative of India to the UN Kamlesh Sharma[15] signed the CAT.[16]

The international community conceived the CAT on the basis of the fundamental human rights principle, which is enshrined under the Charter of UN by proclaiming equal and inalienable human rights

[14] CAT, chapter IV. Available at https://treaties.un.org/Pages/ViewDetails. aspx?src=TREATY&mtdsg_no=IV-9&chapter=4&Lang=en#EndDec, accessed on 10 January 2018.

[15] Permanent Representative of India to the United Nations. Available at http://en.wikipedia.org/wiki/Permanent_Representative_of_India_to_the_United_Nations, accessed on 10 January 2018.

[16] National Human Rights Commission (NHRC). *Annual Report (1997–98)*. Available at http://nhrc.nic.in/ar97_98.htm#cat, accessed on 10 January 2018.

as the foundation of freedom, justice, and peace, and human dignity as the fountain of all human rights.[17] The CAT draws its authority directly from states' inherent duty 'to promote universal respect for, and observance of, human rights and fundamental freedoms'[18] and to guarantee freedom and protection from torture or cruel, inhuman, or degrading treatment or punishment.[19] It aims at making the global fight against torture and other cruel, inhuman, or degrading treatment or punishment effective.[20]

Definition of Torture   The definition of torture as given in the CAT provides a detailed one and describes torture from four perspectives. These perspectives are the nature of injury, class and categories of victims, class and categories of perpetrators, and the nature of motive. Therefore, the word 'torture' is defined as follows:[21]

1. An intentional act of a public officer or a person in his/her official capacity or by any person at the instigation of or consent or acquiescence of a public official.
2. Such act is inflicted on a person or a third party.
3. Such act must result in 'severe pain or suffering' including physical or mental sufferings.
4. Such act must be committed with the motive of
   a. extracting information or confession from him or a third person;
   b. punishing him/her or a third person for any act done or suspected to be done;
   c. intimidation and coercion; or
   d. any other motive based on discrimination on any ground.
5. *Exception*: Pains or sufferings caused only inherent in or incidental to lawful sanctions are not considered torture.

---

[17] CAT, Preamble.
[18] CAT, Preamble and UN Charter, Art. 55.
[19] CAT, Preamble; UDHR, Art. 5; and ICCPR, Art. 7.
[20] CAT, Preamble; UDHR, Art. 5; and ICCPR, Art. 7.
[21] CAT, Art. 1(1).

The aforementioned definition of torture does not distinguish between citizens and foreigners or aliens, and hence all natural persons are entitled to protection under the provisions of the CAT. It further gives permission to state parties to adopt wider definitions of torture in any international instrument or national legislation.[22] This narrows down the scope of application of the provisions for protection of torture under the CAT at the domestic or national level. However, in exceptional circumstances of internal disturbance, war or threat of war, public emergency, or political instability in a state, state parties cannot justify torture.[23] Further, torture also cannot be justified by an order of any public authority or command.[24]

State's Obligations   All state parties have an obligation under the CAT, and as per this obligation, state parties must undertake effective steps in the form of legislative, administrative, judicial, or other actions and initiatives for preventing torture within their respective territorial jurisdictions.[25]

Prohibition of Expulsion, Return, or Extradition in Certain Circumstances   State parties must not 'expel, return or extradite' any person to a state, where it has firm grounds to believe that he/she would likely be subjected to torture, including factors such as 'gross, flagrant, or mass violation of human rights'.[26]

Crimes of Torture, Attempt, Abetment, and Conspiracy   State parties to the CAT are required to enact or modify criminal law, and while doing this, they should remember the serious nature of the crime and should include all acts of torture including attempt, abetment, participation, and conspiracy as crimes punishable under the national law.[27]

---

[22] CAT, Art. 1(2).
[23] CAT, Art. 2(2).
[24] CAT, Art. 2(2).
[25] CAT, Art. 2(3).
[26] CAT, Art. 3.
[27] CAT, Art. 4.

Exercise of Jurisdiction within Its Territory and on Board of a Ship or Aircraft Registered in that State   State parties are required to take necessary steps to claim the jurisdiction over the crimes of torture mentioned previously when:

a. the crime has taken place in the territory of or ship or aircraft registered in the state;
b. the suspect(s) is a national of the state; or
c. the affected person(s) is a national of the state.[28]

State parties can further undertake steps to enlarge their jurisdiction over extraditable offences committed by a person present in its territory.[29]

Duty to Detain, Investigate, and Inform in Case of Criminal Prosecution or Extradition of a Foreigner/Alien Suspect Found within Its Territorial Jurisdiction   In certain circumstances where an alien suspect is found within the territorial jurisdiction of a state party, it should detain the person or make sure that the person is present until the completion of extradition or the prosecution process, only after examining the circumstances and on being satisfied about the necessity of such action. The state party should make a preliminary enquiry into the matter and assist the detained person in communicating immediately with the representative of the state to which the person belongs or has a habitual residence in. Further, it has the duty to immediately notify the state concerned about such detention and its reasons thereof and also promptly share the preliminary report and convey its claim of jurisdiction to the state concerned.[30]

Duty to Ensure Fair Trial to Alien Suspects in Certain Circumstances   In cases where the state party decides not to extradite an alien suspect found on its territory, the case should be produced before an authorized forum, agency, or body for initiating prosecution proceedings for

[28] CAT, Art. 5.
[29] CAT, Art. 5(2).
[30] CAT, Art. 6.

the detained person. The decision of such a forum, body, or agency must be taken in the same way as it is carried out in any other serious crime by virtue of its national law. The required standard of evidence must not be less strict than that which applies to its nationals, and there should be fair treatment through the proceedings.[31]

Torture Deemed to Be an Extraditable Offence   Any offence committed under the CAT is deemed to be an offence covered by any extradition treaty, and it must be included in all existing and future extradition treaties that are negotiated between state parties. For extradition, the offence is required to be treated as if it has been committed within the territory of the state that is requesting for extradition, besides being committed at the place of occurrence. The convention provides rules for state parties that do not have any extradition treaties. These are as follows:

1. *Where extradition is subject to an extradition treaty*: In cases where no extradition treaty is signed between state parties, but the state party considering the request for extradition requires an extradition treaty, it may consider CAT as the basis for such extradition, which will be subject to the conditions laid down in the law of the requesting state.
2. *Where extradition is not subject to an extradition treaty*: In cases where no extradition treaty has been signed between the state parties and the party considering the request for extradition does not require an extradition treaty, it should recognize torture and other related offences as extraditable offences subject to the conditions prescribed under the law of the requesting state.[32]

Training to Law Enforcement Personnel   The convention states that all state parties should ensure that all information related to prohibition of torture should be included in the training programmes for the military and civil law enforcement officials, all staff of the medical

---

[31] CAT, Art. 7.
[32] CAT, Art. 8.

profession, public officers, and all other such personnel who are associated with the custody, interrogation, medical aid, or treatment of persons in custody. Further, the prohibition of torture should be included in their respective rule books or respective manuals so that they perform their duties and functions efficiently and under the CAT guidelines.[33]

Review of Interrogation Rules, Instructions, Methods, and Practices   State parties should maintain a method of periodic and systematic review of the aforementioned rules, methods, procedures, and practices; of arrangement and treatment in custody; and of keeping a check on the occurrence of any kind of torture in custody.[34]

Prompt and Impartial Investigation   State parties should ensure that the appropriate public authority initiates investigation in all cases where a prima facie case of torture is being committed within its jurisdictional limits, without any kind of delay and in an impartial and unbiased manner.[35]

Right to Complain, Protection of Victims and Witnesses, and Prompt and Impartial Investigation   Every victim of torture has the right to complain about any torture and to an impartial and timely investigation. The complainant and witnesses should also be provided sufficient protection by state parties.[36]

Right to Redress, Adequate Compensation, and Full Rehabilitation   Every victim of torture, or dependants in case of death, should have a legally enforceable right to redress, adequate compensation, and full rehabilitation.[37]

[33] CAT, Art. 10.
[34] CAT, Art. 11.
[35] CAT, Art. 12.
[36] CAT, Art. 13.
[37] CAT, Art. 14.

Statement Extracted by Torture Not to Be Admissible as Evidence in Any Proceeding except in Proceedings against the Accused of Torture State parties should ensure that any statement, confession, or information, proved to have been given because of torture must not be admissible as evidence in any proceeding, apart from proceedings against the accused or suspect of torture.[38]

Prevention of Cruel, Inhuman, and Degrading Punishments Not Amounting to Torture State parties are bound by the convention and have a duty to prevent every instance of cruel, inhuman, and degrading punishments not amounting to torture, if committed intentionally by a public officer, a person in his/her official capacity, or any person at the instigation of, consent, or acquiescence of a public official. The provisions of CAT under various articles are as follows: Art. 10 lays down the duty of state parties with respect to training of law enforcement personnel; the systematic and periodic review of interrogation rules, instructions, methods, and practices comes under Art. 11; the provision for prompt and impartial investigation is under Art. 12; and the right to complain, protection of victims and witnesses, and prompt and impartial investigation under Art. 13 are also applicable to cruel, inhuman, and degrading treatment or punishment.[39]

Constitution of Committee against Torture A Committee against Torture should be constituted comprising 10 elected human rights experts[40] to perform the following roles and functions.

1. *Receipt of Information on Act of Torture, Enquiry, and Recommendations*: The committee upon receipt of any trustworthy information disclosing systematic commission of torture within the territorial limits of a state party should
   a. request the state party to cooperate in the examination of the veracity of the information and to submit its observation report;

---

[38] CAT, Art. 15.
[39] CAT, Art. 16.
[40] CAT, Art. 17.

   b. commission one or more of the committee's members to conduct a confidential enquiry and to promptly submit an enquiry report;

   c. seek cooperation and permission from the party in question to conduct the enquiry, including making visit(s) to its territory;

   d. examine the enquiry report and transmit it to the party in question with its comments and suitable recommendations;

   e. maintain utmost confidentiality and seek cooperation of the involved party at every step of the proceeding; and

   f. consult the state party concerned for publishing the summary of the outcome in its annual report.[41]

2. *Declaration of Recognition of Jurisdiction of the Committee and Dispute Resolution*: On declaration by a state party recognizing the competence of the committee to receive and consider communications relating to the claim of a state party about non-compliance of CAT by another party, the following procedure should be adhered to:

   a. The undermentioned procedure of dispute resolution would apply only when such declaration is issued and deposited with the secretary-general of the UN by at least five parties.

   b. The committee should receive and consider such communication only if it is made by a party that has accepted the committee's competence by way of a prior declaration.

   c. The committee should not deal with communication if it is made with reference to a party without a prior declaration by the said party.

   d. The party claiming non-compliance of CAT by another party may issue a written communication bringing the matter to the notice of the party in default.

   e. The party in default should within a period of three months issue a written explanation or clarification in response to the communication, including actions such as domestic law, procedures, and remedial measures undertaken, planned, or in existence.

---

[41] CAT, Art. 20.

    f. Either of the state parties is entitled to move the committee by issuing a notice to the committee and other party if the dispute remains unsettled even after six months of the receipt of the initial communication through the aforementioned procedure.

    g. The committee should entertain and deal with the matter in accordance with the general practices of international law, provided that parties have exhausted all the local remedies, except where the exercise of local remedy is unduly prolonged or unlikely to yield effective relief to the victims.

    h. The committee should hold closed-door meetings during examination of the allegations.

    i. The committee should promote amicable settlement of dispute by making its good offices available to the parties or by appointing an ad hoc conciliation commission.

    j. The committee may require state parties to produce all the material information related to the dispute.

    k. The state parties to the dispute are entitled to representation and to make written or oral submissions before the committee.

    l. The committee should decide the matter and submit its final report within a period of 12 months of the notice.

    m. The committee should not comment on the merits of a case and limit its final report to the summary account of material facts and the terms of settlement owing to the amicable settlement between the parties through the good offices or ad hoc conciliation commission.

    n. The committee, in all circumstances other than what is mentioned earlier, should include written and oral submissions, in addition to the material facts and decision in its final report.

    o. The committee should transmit the final report to the parties involved.[42]

3. *Declaration of Recognition of Jurisdiction of the Committee to Deal with Communication by Victims*: On declaration by a state party recognizing the committee's competence to receive and consider

---

[42] CAT, Art. 21.

communications from victims or on their behalf with respect to the claim of violation of CAT, the committee will be authorized to apply the procedure of dispute resolution, only when such declaration is issued and deposited with the UN secretary-general by at least five parties.

The committee should disregard all anonymous communications, communications that are considered abuse of the right to submission, or any communication that is made contrary to CAT.

Further, before proceeding with the communication, the committee should find out that the matter referred to it has not been or is not being subjected to consideration by another parallel international procedure and the available local remedies have been exhausted by the individual, except where the exercise of local remedy is unduly prolonged or unlikely to yield effective relief to the victims. Then the committee should inform any such communications to the party in question. Thereafter, the committee should hold close-door meetings during examination of the allegations. The state party should submit a written explanation or clarification to the committee within a period of six months, clarifying the matter, including remedial measures that have been undertaken to address the grievance. The committee should transmit its views to the individual and state party.[43]

Optional Protocol to CAT

The Optional Protocol to CAT (OPCAT) was adopted on 18 December 2002 and came into force on 22 June 2006 after the 20th ratification/accession in accordance with Art. 28(1). Till date, 75 states have signed and 73 parties have acceded or ratified OPCAT.[44] The main aim for OPCAT was to have a method of conducting regular visits by

---

[43] CAT, Art. 22.

[44] OPCAT, chapter IV. Available at https://treaties.un.org/pages/ViewDetails.aspx?src=TREATY&mtdsg_no=IV-9-b&chapter=4&Lang=en, accessed on 18 January 2018.

independent international and national organizations to detention and prison facilities or any other facility where people are kept in custody in order to check whether there is any kind of torture or other cruel, inhuman, or degrading treatment or punishment taking place in these facilities.[45]

Constitution of a Subcommittee The OPCAT constituted a Subcommittee on Prevention of Torture and Other Cruel, Inhuman or Degrading Treatment or Punishment of the Committee against Torture (the Subcommittee on Prevention), which functions according to the framework of the UN Charter and UN norms by ensuring confidentiality, impartiality, non-selectivity, universality and objectivity as its guiding principles.[46] On the other hand, the OPCAT also provides guidelines for state parties to establish, appoint, and manage National Preventive Mechanisms (NPM), which should include one or more domestic visiting organizations.[47] Initially, the Subcommittee on Prevention comprised 10 members, which was later exceeded to 25 after the 15th accession.[48]

Visit to Place of Detention by International and National Preventive Mechanisms State parties should permit the Subcommittee on Prevention and NPMs to visit such places where the detained and imprisoned persons are kept or placed in private or public custodial settings, within their jurisdiction and control, by virtue of an order of a public authority (judicial, administrative, or other authority), or at its instigation or with the consent or acquiescence of the said authority, so as to facilitate strengthening the protection of detainees against torture or cruel, inhuman, and other degrading treatment and punishment.[49]

[45] OPCAT, Art. 1.
[46] OPCAT, Art. 2.
[47] OPCAT, Art. 3.
[48] OPCAT, Art. 5.
[49] OPCAT, Art. 4.

Mandate of the Subcommittee on Prevention   The mandate of the Subcommittee on Prevention[50] is to perform the following functions:

a. To visit places of detention within the jurisdiction and control of state parties
b. To make suitable recommendations to state parties with respect to protection of detainees in line with CAT
c. To guide and aid state parties in establishing NPMs
d. To keep a direct or confidential contact with NPMs
e. To offer and provide NPMs training, technical assistance and capacity-building support
f. To guide and aid in the needs assessment and means evaluation required for strengthening the protection of detainees
g. To recommend to and share observations with state parties in order to capacitate NPMs
h. To cooperate with UN organs and mechanisms and other international, regional, and national bodies concerned

State's Obligations towards the Subcommittee on Prevention   The obligation of state parties is to facilitate the Subcommittee on Prevention in fulfilling its objective and mandate.[51] In particular, state parties should have the following duties:

a. To receive and allow access to places subject to visit by the subcommittee as per OPCAT
b. To give every information as and when requested by the Subcommittee on Prevention, which is necessary for needs and means assessment, and suggest adoption of certain measures to safeguard detainees
c. To promote and facilitate liaison between the Subcommittee on Prevention and NPMs
d. To scrutinize recommendations and discuss means and steps for the realization of such recommendations

---

[50] OPCAT, Art. 11.
[51] OPCAT, Art. 12.

Programme of Periodic Visit by the Subcommittee on Prevention   The Subcommittee on Prevention should introduce periodic visits to state parties to ensure fulfillment of its established mandate. Such visits should be notified to state parties after consultations so that required arrangements could be made on time. The visit must be conducted by at least two members, who may be accompanied by experts, where necessary. A follow-up visit may be planned after periodic visits.[52]

Access to Information and Detainees   The Subcommittee on Prevention should be guaranteed free access to information regarding the number of detainees, place and location of detention facilities, and treatment and condition of detainees and unhindered access to all places of detention facilities during their visit by the state parties. Further, the subcommittee should have the liberty to choose places for visit and detainees for interviews and have the opportunity to conduct private interviews of detainees and such other persons who are acquainted with the necessary information. However, state parties may object to such visits on critical and convincing grounds of national defence, public safety, natural disaster, or severe disorder but not on the grounds of declared emergency.[53]

Bar on Sanction against Persons or Organizations in Certain Circumstances   Sanction cannot be ordered, applied, permitted, or tolerated against any person or organization for communicating with the Subcommittee on Prevention and sharing any information with its delegates, whether the information so communicated or shared was correct or incorrect. Further, they should not be subjected to any prejudicial treatment. The Subcommittee on Prevention should maintain the highest degree of confidentiality.[54]

Establishment of NPMs   State parties are required to set up, designate, or manage as many autonomous NPMs as required at the

[52] OPCAT, Art. 13.
[53] OPCAT, Art. 14.
[54] OPCAT, Art. 15.

national level[55] and make sure that there is functional autonomy, including autonomy to NPM personnel. State parties should also ensure that NPMs possess necessary competency and professional capabilities and should take steps for adequate resource allocation.[56]

Powers of NPMs   The powers and authority of NPMs[57] are as follows:

a. To inspect the treatment and conditions of detainees in detention facilities regularly
b. To recommend means and steps to improve treatment and conditions of detainees and to check torture and other cruel, inhuman, or degrading treatment or punishment on the basis of CAT and other UN norms
c. To present proposals or remarks on existing or draft laws

Access to Information and Detainees   State parties should guarantee free access to NPMs for gathering information regarding the number of detainees, place and location of detention facilities, and treatment and condition of detainees. They should also ensure that NPMs have unhindered access to all places of detention facilities. Further, state parties should guarantee that NPMs have the freedom to choose places for visit and detainees for interviews and afford them the opportunity to conduct private interviews of detainees and such other persons who are acquainted with the necessary information. NPMs should have the right to liaise, share information, and meet with the Subcommittee on Prevention.[58]

Bar on Sanction against Persons or Organizations in Certain Circumstances   Sanction cannot be ordered, applied, permitted, or tolerated against any person or organization for communicating and

---

55 OPCAT, Art. 17.
56 OPCAT, Art. 18.
57 OPCAT, Art. 19.
58 OPCAT, Art. 20.

sharing any information with the NPM, whether the information so communicated or shared was correct or incorrect. Further, they should not be subjected to any prejudicial treatment. NPMs should maintain the highest degree of confidentiality.[59] The state party concerned is expected to scrutinize recommendations given by the NPM and discuss with it all the means and steps for the realization of such recommendations.[60]

The International Convention of Civil and Political Rights (ICCPR)   The ICCPR was adopted on 19 December 1966 and came into force on 23 March 1976. It has been signed by 74 states and 168 states are party to it. India acceded to it on 10 April 1979[61] but had reservations to the provisions related to the right to self-determination under Art. 1, the right to compensation to the victim of unlawful arrest or detention under Art. 9(5), and the rights of aliens in matters of expulsion under Art. 13.[62] Thereafter, two optional protocols to the ICCPR have been adopted till date which are: (a) Optional Protocol to the International Covenant on Civil and Political Rights (OP-ICCPR-I) and (b) Second Optional Protocol to the ICCPR Aiming at the Abolition of the Death Penalty (OP-ICCPR-II). OP-ICCPR-I was adopted on 16 December 1966 and came into force on 23 March 1976, and 115 states are party to it till date.[63] OP-ICCPR-II was adopted on 15 December 1989 and came into force on 11 July 1991,

---

[59] OPCAT, Art. 21.

[60] OPCAT, Art. 22.

[61] ICCPR. Available at https://treaties.un.org/pages/ViewDetails.aspx?src=TREATY&mtdsg_no=IV-4&chapter=4&Lang=en, accessed on 20 January 2018.

[62] Essays, UK. 2018. 'India's Reservations and Declarations to Core Human Rights Conventions International Law Essay'. Available at http://www.ukessays.com/essays/law/indias-reservations-and-declarations-to-core-human-rights-conventions-international-law-essay.php, accessed on 20 January 2018.

[63] Optional Protocol to ICCPR. Available at https://treaties.un.org/pages/ViewDetails.aspx?src=TREATY&mtdsg_no=IV-5&chapter=4&Lang=en, accessed on 20 January 2018.

and till date, 37 states have signed and 81 states have become party to it.[64] However, India is still not a party to both these optional protocols.[65]

The ICCPR, just like the UDHR, ensures equal rights for every man and woman so that they enjoy all the rights guaranteed by it. It also guarantees the right to life and protection against arbitrary deprivation of life[66] and further prohibits torture in the form of cruel, inhuman treatment or degrading punishment. It also provides every individual protection against such treatment.[67] Furthermore, the ICCPR provides a right to effective judicial remedy for redressing violation of civil and political rights that are recognized by the ICCPR.[68]

As mentioned earlier, the ICCPR guarantees the right to liberty and protects individuals from arbitrary arrests or detention. Besides, it also provides some conditions of arrests in the form that a person can only be deprived of liberty according to the procedure established by law and not otherwise; the individual must be informed about the reasons of arrest and charges; the individual arrested must be produced immediately before the judicial authority; and the person being arrested is entitled to a time-bound trial and can be released if charges are not proved.

The person being arrested is entitled to challenge the legality of his/her detention before an appropriate court of law and has the right to enforce compensation in case the detention has been illegal.[69]

---

[64] 'Second Optional Protocol to the International Covenant on Civil and Political Rights, Aiming at the Abolition of the Death Penalty'. Available at https://treaties.un.org/doc/Publication/MTDSG/Volume%20I/Chapter%20IV/IV-12.en.pdf, accessed on 20 January 2018.

[65] 'Core International Human Rights Treaties, Optional Protocols & Core ILO Conventions Ratified by India'. Available at http://nhrc.nic.in/documents/india_ratification_status.pdf, accessed on 20 January 2018.

[66] ICCPR, Art. 6(1).

[67] ICCPR, Art. 7.

[68] ICCPR, Art. 3.

[69] ICCPR, Art. 9.

The ICCPR also ensures that all detainees are treated compassionately and with respect.[70]

The ICCPR further ensures the right to equal treatment before judicial and quasi-judicial forums, and every individual charged and tried by such a forum is entitled to a fair and public hearing. It provides for every individual to be treated as innocent until the charges against him/her are proved[71] and further prohibits forceful confession.[72]

Enforcement and Suspension of Rights during Public Emergency As per Art. 6 of the ICCPR, state parties can suspend the rights given under the ICCPR, except the right to life and protection against arbitrary deprivation of life in case of a public emergency. Further, Art. 7 provides protection against torture or other cruel, inhuman, or derogatory practices or punishments and Art. 8 ensures protection against slavery besides various other rights that are protected under Arts 11, 15, 16, and 18.[73]

Constitution of the Human Rights Committee The ICCPR set up the Human Rights Committee (HRC), which consists of 18 members.[74] The HRC works as the treaty monitoring body[75] and can request state parties to submit their reports on the status of implementation of the ICCPR in their respective countries. The committee also scrutinizes and considers these reports that are sent by the secretary-general of the UN, and it then gives its observations, comments, and recommendations on the report submitted to the state party concerned.[76]

---

[70] ICCPR, Art. 10(1).

[71] ICCPR, Art. 14(1) and 14(2).

[72] ICCPR, Art. 14(3)(g).

[73] ICCPR, Art. 4(2).

[74] ICCPR, Art. 28.

[75] UNHCHR. 'Civil and Political Rights: The Human Rights Committee', Fact Sheet No. 15 (Rev 1). Available at http://www.ohchr.org/Documents/Publications/FactSheet15rev.1en.pdf, accessed on 20 January 2018.

[76] ICCPR, Art. 40.

Dispute Resolution: Declaration of the Competence of the HRC   In case a state party declares that another state party has not complied with the provisions of CAT and recognizes the competence of the HRC to receive and consider communications related to such claims of non-compliance, the subsequent procedure[77] is required to be followed:

a. The undermentioned procedure of dispute resolution would apply only when such declaration is issued and deposited with the UN's secretary-general by at least 10 parties.

b. The party claiming non-compliance of CAT by another party may issue a written communication bringing the matter to the notice of the party in default.

c. The party in default should issue a written explanation or clarification owing to the written communication, within a period of three months, including actions such as domestic law, procedures, and remedial measures undertaken, planned, or in existence.

d. Either state party is entitled to move the committee by issuing a notice to the committee and other party, if the dispute remains unsettled even after six months of the receipt of the initial communication through the aforementioned procedure.

e. The committee should entertain and deal with the matter in accordance with the general practices of international law provided that the parties have exhausted all the local remedies, except where the exercise of local remedy is unduly prolonged or unlikely to yield effective relief to the victims.

f. The committee should hold closed-door meetings during examination of the allegations.

g. The committee should promote amicable settlement of dispute by making its good offices available to the parties.

h. The committee may require state parties to produce all the material information related to the dispute.

i. The state parties to the dispute are entitled to representation and make written or oral submissions before the committee.

[77] ICCPR, Art. 41.

j. The committee should decide the matter and submit its final report within a period of 12 months of the notice.

k. The committee should not comment on the merits of a case and limit its final report to the summary account of material facts and the terms of settlement owing to the amicable settlement between the parties through the good offices.

l. The committee, in all circumstances other than what is mentioned earlier, should include written and oral submissions, in addition to the material facts and decision in its final report.

m. The committee should transmit the final report to the parties involved.

Appointment of Ad Hoc Conciliation Commission   In certain circumstances when a dispute remains unsettled by the HRC and the state parties are satisfied about the circumstances, the former may then appoint an Ad hoc Conciliation Committee with the consent of the parties to the dispute for a friendly dispute settlement. The Ad hoc Conciliation Commission consists of five members and is agreed by the parties to the dispute. In case the parties do not reach an agreement about the composition of the members, then the members are elected by the HRC members through secret ballot by a majority of two-thirds votes. In such dispute cases, the conciliation process is required to be completed within a period of 12 months after which a final report needs to be submitted to the chairperson of HRC for onward information to the state parties concerned. This report includes the status of the proceedings of conciliation if it is not completed within the said duration. The report should also include if the settlement has been reached amicably, the material facts and outcome of the settlement, and terms and conditions of the settlement. Alternatively, the final report should contain findings vis-à-vis all the issues, views of the commission, and written and oral submissions. Thereafter, the state parties to the dispute are required to communicate with and inform the chairperson of the HRC whether they have accepted or rejected the report and the decision within a period of three months.[78]

---

[78] ICCPR, Art. 42.

The OP-ICCPR-I was adopted for enlarging the scope of the HRC vis-à-vis communications by victims.[79] The parties to OP-ICCPR-I recognize and accept the competence of the HRC to receive and consider communications from victims about violation of their rights by a state party.[80] A communication can be submitted by the victim in writing to the HRC only after he/she has tried all possible remedies in his/her country at the local level.[81] In such cases, the HRC should ignore all kinds of anonymous communications; communications that abuse the right to submission; and communications that are contrary to the ICCPR.[82] The HRC is required to find out if the matter related to the communication received from the victim is being considered or tried by any other parallel procedure at the international level and if the victim has tried all sorts of local remedies. However, the HRC can accept the communication of victims in cases where the local remedy has been prolonged or delayed unduly.[83] After this, the HRC needs to inform the state party concerned about any such communication, and the state party is required to give a written explanation or clarification to the committee within a period of six months about the remedial measures undertaken for the grievance redress of the victim.[84] The HRC then conducts closed-door meetings during the investigation and examination of the allegations and inform the views of the committee to the individual victim concerned as well as the state party after completing the investigation.[85]

The Universal Declaration of Human Rights

The UDHR states that all human beings are born free and are equal in dignity and rights.[86] It is hence the basis of standards of human life.

[79] OP-ICCPR-I, Preamble.
[80] OP-ICCPR-I, Art. 1.
[81] OP-ICCPR-I, Art. 2.
[82] OP-ICCPR-I, Art. 3.
[83] OP-ICCPR-I, Art. 5.
[84] OP-ICCPR-I, Art. 4.
[85] OP-ICCPR-I, Art. 5.
[86] UDHR, Art. 1.

The UDHR thus ensures the right to life, liberty, and security to every individual;[87] provides the right to protection against torture or any kind of cruel, inhuman, or degrading treatment or punishment;[88] and protects against arbitrary arrests and detention.[89] The UDHR promotes equal access to human rights and liberty to all persons without any sort of discrimination on the grounds of race, colour, sex, religion, language, political, national or social origin, birth, property, or any other criteria. It also prohibits any discrimination or distinction based on any person's country status or any limitation of sovereignty.[90]

The Convention on the Rights of the Child, 1989

The CRC recognizes the need for special protection and care, including suitable legal protection to the rights of children.[91] It lays down state obligations and guarantees protection of every child against torture or any other cruel, inhuman, or degrading treatment or punishment; imprisonment for life term without release; and capital punishment. It forbids any unlawful or arbitrary deprivation of liberty and states that the exercise of arrest, detention, or imprisonment should be a choice of last resort only and that too for an appropriate and the shortest span. In all circumstances, arrest, detention, or imprisonment should only be made as per the law and not otherwise, and every such child must be treated in a dignified, humane, age-appropriate, and need-based manner. The CRC further states that children under institutional custody must be kept separated from adults except if it is required in the best interests of the child. Children are also entitled to maintain contact with their family members through visits and correspondence. Every such child is also entitled to the right to quick access to legal and other assistance and the right to challenge the legality of actions that deprive them of their liberty. Such cases should be produced before a

---

[87] UDHR, Art. 3.
[88] UDHR, Art. 5.
[89] UDHR, Art. 9.
[90] UDHR, Art. 2.
[91] CRC, Preamble.

competent, independent, and impartial court or authority, which should provide a speedy and timely decision on such cases.[92] The CRC further enforces a duty on state parties to take suitable measures for promoting the psychological as well as physical recovery and social reintegration of a child victim of any form of abuse, neglect, or exploitation; torture or any other form of cruel, inhuman, or degrading treatment or punishment; or armed conflict. Such recovery and reintegration steps should take place in an environment that fosters the health, self-respect, and dignity of the child.[93]

International Convention for the Protection of All Persons from Enforced Disappearance

The International Convention for the Protection of All Persons from Enforced Disappearance (CED) was adopted at New York on 20 December 2006, and it came into force on 23 December 2010 after the 20th instrument of ratification/accession to the secretary-general of the UN in pursuance of Art. 39. It has been signed by 98 States; 60 States have ratified it and are party to this convention as of 17 July 2019.[94] India signed the convention on 6 February 2007 but has not ratified it.[95] The major aims of this convention are the abatement of enforced disappearance, to fight impunity, to guarantee the right against enforced disappearance, and to provide justice and reparation/compensation.[96]

The convention prohibits enforced disappearance in all circumstances, and such acts cannot be justified on the basis of any exceptional circumstances such as war, threat of war, public emergency, and/or internal political instability.[97]

---

[92] CRC, Art. 37.

[93] CRC, Art. 39.

[94] CED. Available at https://treaties.un.org/pages/ViewDetails.aspx?src=IND&mtdsg_no=IV-16&chapter=4&Lang=_en, accessed on 18 July 2019.

[95] CED, accessed on 23 January 2018.

[96] CED, Preamble.

[97] CED, Art. 1.

As per the convention, 'enforced disappearance' is defined as such situations where arrest, detention, abduction, or any other form of detention is done by the servants/personnel of the state or by anyone by virtue of the authority, support, or acquiescence of the state, without any acknowledgement of the arrest or by concealment of the victim's fate or whereabouts and by denying such a person the protection of law.[98] When enforced disappearance takes place on a large scale or in a systematic way, then such act must be considered as crime against humanity and should be dealt as per the relevant international law.[99]

State's Obligations The Convention provides the following set of obligations for state parties:

1. *Recognition of Offence of Enforced Disappearance and Other Offences Related to Children*

State Parties should ensure and recognize acts of enforced disappearance as an offence under their respective national penal codes.[100]

Further state parties should check and penalize offences against children, particularly,[101]

a. the wrongful removal of children subjected to enforced disappearance, children of disappeared parents or legal guardians, or children born during detention; and

b. the fabrication, concealment, or destruction of information about the identity of such children.

2. *Recognition and Imposition of Criminal Responsibility of the Public Authority and Command Head*

The act of enforced disappearance cannot be justified on grounds that it was under the order or instruction of a public, civil, military, or other

---

[98] CED, Art. 2.

[99] CED, Art. 5.

[100] CED, Art. 4.

[101] CED, Art. 25(1).

authority. State parties should undertake steps to impose criminal liability on the following:[102]

    a. Persons responsible for the commission, abetment, soliciting, inducement, or conspiracy of; attempt to; and participation in the commission of crime of enforced disappearance

    b. Superiors or command having knowledge or intentionally disregarding information about the commission or planning of commission of offence of enforced disappearance by their subordinate(s)

    c. Superiors or command responsible for controlling or checking actions done as a part of the commission of enforced disappearance

    d. Superiors or command who have failed to undertake reasonable steps necessary to exercise power to check or repress the commission of the crime of enforced disappearance

    e. Superiors or commands who have failed to report or refer the matter to authority concerned for enquiry, investigation, and prosecution

  3. *Responsibility to Ensure Mitigating Circumstances in Order to Bring Back the Disappeared Persons*

State parties may create mitigating circumstances for the accused to contribute towards the return or recovery of the victims who are alive; to identify the persons responsible for the enforced disappearances; or to afford clarity in such cases. This does not affect other penal procedures that are concerned with the death or murder of a person so disappeared and enforced disappearance of vulnerable persons including women, minors, and persons with disabilities.[103]

Rule of Limitation   State parties should ensure a longer limitation period for criminal proceedings proportionate to the extent of seriousness of the crime. The period of limitation is measured from the

---

[102] CED, Art. 6.
[103] CED, Art. 7.

time the enforced disappearance ceases. State parties must guarantee the right to effective remedy to the victims of enforced disappearance during the limitation period.[104]

Exercise of Jurisdiction within Its Territory and on Board of a Ship or Aircraft Registered in that State   A state party should take necessary steps to claim jurisdiction over the crimes of enforced disappearance, when

a. the crime has taken place on its territory or on a ship or aircraft registered in the state,
b. the suspect(s) is a national of the state,
c. the affected person(s) is a national of the state, or
d. the alien suspect is present on its territory.[105]

Duty to Detain, Investigate, and Inform in Case of Criminal Prosecution or Extradition of a Foreigner/Alien Suspect Found within Its Territorial Jurisdiction   In circumstances where an alien suspect is found within the territorial jurisdiction of a state party, after examining the circumstances and on being satisfied about the necessity of the action, the state should detain such person or ensure his/her presence until the completion of the extradition or prosecution process. The state should make a preliminary enquiry into the matter and assist the detained person in communicating immediately with the representative of the state of his/her nationality or habitual residence. Further, the state is duty-bound to immediately notify the state/nation concerned about the person's detention and its reasons thereof. It should also share the preliminary report and convey its claim of jurisdiction to the latter immediately.[106]

Duty to Ensure Fair Trial to Alien Suspects in Certain Circumstances   In case where the state party decides not to extradite or surrender an alien

---

[104] CED, Art. 8.
[105] CED, Art. 9.
[106] CED, Art. 10.

suspect found on its territory, to the other state or the international criminal tribunal, it should present the matter before an authorized forum, agency, or body for initiating prosecution proceedings in its state. The decisions of such a forum, body, or agency must be taken in the same way as it is carried out in any other serious crime by virtue of its national law. The required standard of evidence must not be less strict than that which applies to the nationals of the state, and the state must ensure fair treatment to the detained person at all times during the proceedings.[107]

Enforced Disappearance Deemed Not to Be a Political Offence but an Extraditable Offence   An offence under the CED is not a political offence. It is rather considered to be an offence covered by any extradition treaty and should be included in all existing and future extradition treaties being negotiated between state parties. For the purpose of extradition, the offence should be treated as if it has been committed not only at the place of occurrence but also within the territory of the requesting state. Further, the convention has laid down the following rules that are applicable between state parties that do not have any extradition treaty:[108]

1. *Where extradition is subject to an extradition treaty*: In such circumstances where there is no extradition treaty between the state parties, and the state party considering the request for extradition requires an extradition treaty, it may consider the CED as the basis for such extradition, subject to the conditions laid down in the law of the requesting state.

2. *Where extradition is not subject to an extradition treaty*: In such circumstances where there is no extradition treaty between the state parties and the state party considering the request for extradition does not require an extradition treaty, it should identify enforced disappearance as an extraditable offence, subject to the conditions as prescribed under the law of the requesting state.

---

[107] CED, Art. 11.
[108] CED, Art. 13.

3. *Rejection of Extradition in Certain Circumstances*: In certain circumstances, the receiving state may reject the request of extradition, when there is a possibility that the person so extradited will
be prosecuted and harmed on the grounds of his/her sex, race,
religion, nationality, ethnic origin, political belief, or membership
to a particular social group.

**Right to Complain, Protection of Victims and Witnesses, and Prompt
and Impartial Investigation**   Every victim of enforced disappearance
has the right to make a complaint and the right for an impartial and
timely investigation. The complainant, witnesses, relatives of disappeared person(s), defence counsel, and other persons participating in
the investigation of such offences should be given protection by state
parties. Authorities can initiate investigation without a formal complaint
where there is firm grounds to believe that there has been an enforced
disappearance. The investigating authority should be given the required
powers and means to fulfill its mandate efficiently, including the power
to access documents, information, and detention facilities. Further, state
parties should also ensure that the investigation is carried out without
any interference and should also take steps to prevent the exercise of
influence, especially by the suspect through ways such as intimidation,
threat, or reprisal to the complainant, witnesses, victim(s), relatives of
victims, defence counsel, and persons taking part in the investigation.[109]

Duty to Cooperate and Provide Mutual Legal Assistance   State parties
have the duty to cooperate with each other under the CED, provide
mutual legal assistance, and furnish evidence in penal proceedings,
subject to the existing domestic laws and treaties of mutual legal
assistance.[110] Further, such cooperation and mutual assistance should
be extended for assisting the victims; in the search and release of the
victims; or in case of death, in exhuming, identifying, and returning
their mortal remains.[111]

[109] CED, Art. 12.
[110] CED, Art. 14.
[111] CED, Art. 15.

Prohibition of Expulsion, Return, or Extradition in Certain Circumstances   State parties should not 'expel, return or extradite' any person to a state, where it has firm grounds to believe that the person would likely be subjected to enforced disappearance, including factors such as 'gross, flagrant, or mass violation of human rights'.[112]

Prohibition on Secret Detention and Maintenance of Register of Detainees   The convention strictly prohibits any person being subjected to secret detention.[113] The CED mandates state parties to maintain a register(s) of detainees, which should be available for scrutiny by the court, authority, or institution concerned. The register should have details such as identity of detained persons; date, place, and time of detention; identity of the detaining officer; identity of officer authorizing or ordering detention; grounds for detention; authority responsible for supervision of detention; location for detention facility; date and time of admission to the facility; identity of authority responsible for supervision of the facility; status of health of detainee; reasons of death and location of the mortal remains in case of death in custody; date and time of release or transfer of detainee; location of new facility and identity of authority responsible for transfer.[114]

Legislative Measures to Regulate Detention   The convention imposes an obligation on state parties for bringing legislative regulation to set out governing principles and practice with respect to detention. This includes:[115]

a. defining and enumerating conditions required to be fulfilled before issuing a legitimate order of detention;
b. indicating and listing authorities that are competent and authorized to issue an order of detention;
c. ensuring that a detainee is placed in a legitimately recognized and supervised facility;

[112] CED, Art. 16.
[113] CED, Art. 17(1).
[114] CED, Art. 17(3).
[115] CED, Art. 17(2).

d. ensuring every detainee the means and opportunity to communicate with and be visited by family, counsel, and/or any preferred person;

e. ensuring access to the detention facility by the authorities or organizations concerned, with or without judicial sanction; and

f. entitling a relative, representative, or counsel in all circumstances the opportunity to approach a suitable judicial forum on behalf of the victim, for deciding the legality of such detention.

Access to Information about Detention by a Victim's Relative, Counsel, and Representative   The state party should ensure that the victim's relatives, counsel, and representative have access to information including date, time, and place of detention; identity of officer authorizing or ordering detention; authority responsible for supervision of detention; whereabouts of the detained person; date and time of admission to the detention facility; identity of the authority responsible for supervision of the facility; status of health of detainee; reasons of death and location of the mortal remains in case of death in custody; date and time of release or transfer of detainee; location of new facility; and identity of authority responsible for transfer. The CED ensures that adequate arrangements are made by state parties for the protection of the victim's relatives, counsel, and representative as well as the persons taking part in the investigation.[116]

Denial of Right to Information in Certain Cases and Judicial Remedy to Obtain Information   The right to information mentioned earlier may be curtailed by law in extreme necessity and exceptional circumstances, only in conditions when the detained person is under the protection of law and judicial control and if the transmission would negatively affect the privacy or safety of the detained person or hinder a criminal investigation. State parties should also ensure that the relatives, counsel, or representative of the victim have the right to timely and efficient judicial remedy to acquire information as mentioned earlier, and this right cannot be suspended or restricted in any circumstance.[117]

[116] CED, Art. 18.
[117] CED, Art. 20.

Collection of Medical and Genetic Data and Its Transmission for Search, Prosecution, and Reparation   Personal data such as medical and genetic information should be collected and transmitted for purposes such as search of disappeared persons; use in appropriate criminal proceeding; and claim of reparation. Such collection, processing, storage, and use of personal data should not violate human rights, liberty, and human dignity of the persons concerned.[118]

Release of Detainees   The state party should take the necessary steps to make sure and verify that the detainee is actually released. It should also guarantee that the physical integrity of the released person is secured and the person is fully capable of enjoying his/her rights.[119]

Steps to Check and Sanction Delay, Obstruction, Failure to Maintain Necessary Records, and Denial or Supply of Wrong Information   State parties should take steps to check and sanction for:[120]

a. delaying or impeding the right to information and the right to judicial remedy in case of denial of information,
b. failure to record information or correct information about the detention in the detention register, and
c. denial of information or supplying wrong information about the detention.

Training of Law Enforcement Personnel   State parties should ensure that the training programme for the civil and military law enforcement personnel, medical professionals, public officers, and all other such personnel associated with custody, interrogation, medical aid, or treatment of persons in custody should cover necessary education and information on the CED for the purpose of prevention of enforced disappearance by aforementioned authorities and officials.

---

[118] CED, Art. 19.
[119] CED, Art. 21.
[120] CED, Art. 22.

The programme should also stress the benefits of prevention and investigation of enforced disappearance and recognize the critical need of resolving cases of enforced disappearance. Further, state parties should prohibit orders or instructions authorizing or encouraging enforced disappearance and also ensure that any subordinate who refuses to obey such illegal order should not be penalized for breach of command. Moreover, if the authorities mentioned earlier have the knowledge or suspicion that enforced disappearance has occurred or being planned, they should report to their superiors and/or the authority empowered to review or remedy.[121]

Rights of Victim(s)   Any disappeared person or any person who has suffered direct harm due to such enforced disappearance is entitled to the following rights as provided by the CED:[122]

a. The right to know the facts concerning the circumstances of his/ her enforced disappearance, the progress and outcome of the investigation, and the fate of the disappeared person(s)
b. A legally enforceable right to reparation; prompt, fair, and adequate compensation covering material and moral damages; restoration, rehabilitation, and satisfaction, including the restoration of dignity and reputation; and guarantee of non-repetition
c. The right to establish, join and participate in organizations involved in investigation, release, return, and assistance of victims of forced disappearance
d. State parties to undertake all suitable steps to search, locate, and release disappeared persons and in case of death, locate, respect, and return their mortal remains
e. State parties, in addition to their obligation to investigate, to take suitable steps with respect to the legal status of the disappeared person who has not been found and released and that of his/her relatives in areas such as social welfare, financial matters, family laws, and property rights

[121] CED, Art. 23.
[122] CED, Art. 24.

State Obligations towards Child Victims State parties have certain specific obligations towards children, including the following:[123]

a. To undertake essential steps to search for and identify child victims and to return or reunite such children with their families of origin

b. To cooperate with and assist other state parties in such search, identification, and location of children

c. To enact a suitable law and establish an adoption mechanism and other placement arrangements; to establish a procedural order for systematic and periodic review; to have a procedural mechanism for the invalidation of adoptions or placements carried out during enforced disappearance in order to secure the best interest of children; and to ensure that children enjoy the right to preserve or reestablish their name, nationality, and family

d. All state actions vis-à-vis the above categories of children to be guided by considerations such as the best interests of the children; the children's right to express free views; and taking into account such views according to the age and maturity of the children

Establishment of the Committee on Enforced Disappearance The CED established the Committee on Enforced Disappearance, consisting of 10 elected human rights experts,[124] which perform specific roles and functions and apply the following procedures:

1. *Declaration of Recognition of Jurisdiction of the Committee to Deal with Communication by State Parties*: On declaration by a state party recognizing the committee's competence to receive and consider communications relating to the claim of a state party about non-compliance of the CED by another party, the procedure laid down under the CED for dispute resolution should be followed.[125]

2. *Declaration of Recognition of Jurisdiction of the Committee to Deal with Communication by Victims*: On declaration by a state party recognizing the committee's competence to receive and consider

---

[123] CED, Art. 25.

[124] CED, Art. 26.

[125] CED, Art. 32.

communications from victims or on their behalf relating to the claim of violation of the CED provision, the committee should disregard all anonymous communications, communications that are considered abuse of the right to submission, or communication that is contrary to the CED. The committee, before proceeding with the communication, should find out that the matter referred to it has not been or is not being subjected to consideration by another parallel international procedure and that the available local remedies have been exhausted by the individual, except where the exercise of local remedy is unduly prolonged. In such circumstances, the committee should transmit any such communication to the party in question and request to take interim steps to stop irreparable loss to the victim. The committee should hold closed-door meetings during examination of the allegations. The state party should submit a written explanation or clarification to the committee. The committee should transmit its views to the individual and state party.[126]

3. *Urgent Request by Victims to the Committee*: On receipt of an urgent request by a victim about a disappeared person being sought and found, the state party should transmit its recommendations to the state party concerned, including interim steps such as finding out the location of and protecting the disappeared person.[127]

4. *Receipt of Information about the Commission of Enforced Disappearance, Enquiry, and Recommendations*: Upon receipt of any trustworthy information disclosing the commission of enforced disappearance within the territorial limits of a state party, the committee should assign one or more committee members to conduct an enquiry and make visit(s) to its territory and promptly transmit its findings to the party in question along with its comments and suitable recommendations.[128]

5. *Receipt of Information on Widespread and Systematic Commission of Enforced Disappearance*: Upon receipt of any trustworthy information

---

[126] CED, Art. 31.

[127] CED, Art. 30.

[128] CED, Art. 33.

disclosing that an act of large-scale, widespread organized crime of enforced disappearance within the territorial limits of a state party has occurred, the committee should urgently bring it to the notice of the General Assembly of the UN via the Secretary General.[129] Such commission of widespread and systematic enforced disappearance should be considered as a crime against humanity.[130]

The Geneva Conventions, 1949: Prohibition of and Protection against Torture and Other Cruel, Inhuman, and Degrading Treatment during Armed Conflicts

The Geneva Convention for the Amelioration of the Condition of the Wounded and Sick in Armed Forces in the Field, 1949 (GC-I), the Geneva Convention for the Amelioration of the Condition of Wounded, Sick and Shipwrecked Members of Armed Forces at Sea, 1949 (GC-II), the Geneva Convention Relative to the Treatment of Prisoners of War, 1949 (GC-III), and the Geneva Convention Relative to the Protection of Civilian Persons in Time of War, 1949 (GC-IV) along with Protocol Additional to the Geneva Conventions of 12 August 1949, relating to the Protection of Victims of International Armed Conflicts, 1977 (AP-I) deal with armed conflict of an international character.

GC-I and GC-II prohibit the killing of, causing injury to, and torture of sick and wounded and shipwrecked members of the armed forces and other protected persons. They ensure respect, protection, humane treatment and care, and non-discrimination in all situations to the sick and wounded and all other protected persons.[131] GC-III prohibits physical or mental torture and all kinds of coercion of prisoners of war for obtaining information; further, it prohibits any kind of threat, insult, or exposure to obnoxious or prejudicial treatment of any kind on the refusal to provide information.[132] It also strictly prohibits collective punishment for individual acts, corporal punishment, and torture or

---

[129] CED, Art. 34.
[130] CED, Art. 5.
[131] GC-I and II, Art. 12.
[132] GC-III, Art. 17.

cruelty of all kinds.[133] GC-IV prescribes a mandatory duty to the high contracting parties to especially exercise restraint in taking steps that result in bodily pain or the killing of persons protected under GC-IV. It also prohibits murder, torture, corporal punishment, mutilation, medical or scientific experiments, and brutal treatment.[134]

AP-I binds high contracting parties to ensure certain minimum guarantees to all persons protected under GC-I, II, III, and IV, including prohibition of violence to life, health, or physical or mental well-being; all forms of torture (physical and psychological); corporal punishment; and mutilation.[135] It also ensures fundamental guarantees such as humane treatment; non-discrimination on the grounds of racial, sexual, linguistic, religious, political, national, social, or class identities or on the basis of wealth, birth, colour/complexion, opinion, or other status; and the right to respect, honour, convictions, and religious practices.[136]

Grave Breach: Forbidden under GC-I, II, III, and IV   Grave breaches under GC-I, II, III and IV are similar with very minor differences and mainly comprise all illegal acts against protected persons or properties, as detailed further.

The grave breaches under GC-I and GC-II include the following:

1. intentionally causing death; torture, inhuman treatment, or conducting biological trials and tests; intentionally inflicting serious pain, suffering, grave bodily injury, or harm to the health of protected persons[137] such as the wounded and sick, medical personnel, chaplains of armed forces,[138] members of armed forces performing auxiliary roles in hospitals,[139] in case of GC-I while hospital personnel, crew of hospital ship,[140] in case of GC-II,

---

[133] GC-III, Art. 87.
[134] GC-IV, Art. 32.
[135] AP-I, Art. 2(a)(ii), 2(a)(iii), and 2(a)(iv).
[136] AP-I, Art. 75(1).
[137] GC-I, Art. 50.
[138] GC-I, Art. 4.
[139] GC-I, Art. 25.
[140] GC-II, Art. 36.

personnel of the ICRC, National Red Cross Societies, voluntary aid societies,[141] medical personnel of recognized societies of neutral countries,[142] and religious personnel;[143] and

2. unjustified, unlawful, unprovoked, and widespread devastation and misappropriation of protected properties such as medical units and establishments including buildings, material, stores, equipment,[144] property of registered aid societies,[145] in case of GC-I and establishment ashore,[146] in case of GC II, medical transport,[147] hospital ships,[148] and vehicles bearing the red Cross, Red Crescent, and recognized emblems of the armed forces.[149]

Further in GC-III and GC-IV, the following grave breaches were included: all illegal acts against protected persons or properties, such as intentionally causing death; torture, inhuman treatment, or conducting biological trials and tests; intentionally inflicting serious pain, suffering, grave bodily injury, or harm to the health of prisoners of war; forcing a prisoner of war to give service to a hostile power; power and intentional denial of the right to a fair trial[150] under GC-III while GC-IV focuses mainly on the civilian and includes those breaches which are intentionally inflicted on the civilians, such as unlawful deportation, transfer, or unlawful confinement of a civilian; taking hostage; forcing a civilian to give services to a hostile power; intentional denial of the right to a fair trial; and unjustified, unlawful, unprovoked, and widespread devastation and misappropriation of property.[151]

---

[141] GC-I, Art. 26.
[142] GC-I, Art. 27.
[143] GC-I, Art. 30.
[144] GC-I, Art. 31.
[145] GC-I, Art. 34.
[146] GC-II, Art. 23.
[147] GC-I, Art. 35.
[148] GC-I, Art. 20.
[149] GC-I, Art. 38.
[150] GC-III, Art. 130.
[151] GC-IV, Art. 147.

The Geneva Conventions, 1949: Protection against Torture and Other Cruel, Inhuman, and Degrading Treatment in Armed Conflict Not of an International Character

The Geneva Conventions also deal with non-international armed conflicts and provide basic minimum entitlements to all protected persons, especially non-combatant and hors de combat, such as: humane treatment; non-discrimination on grounds of racial, sexual, religious, class, national, and other identities; and prohibition or and protection against violence to life and person, in particular murder, mutilation, cruel treatment, and torture.[152] Additional Protocol to the Geneva Conventions of 12 August 1949, relating to the Protection of Victims of Non-International Armed Conflicts, 1977 (AP-II) requires high contracting parties to ensure minimum fundamental guarantees, as described earlier, to all protected persons under GC-I, II, III, and IV in armed conflicts of non-international character[153] in the same manner as mandated under AP-I in case of an armed conflict of international character.

The Convention on the Elimination of Discrimination against Women

The Convention on the Elimination of Discrimination against Women (CEDAW) is an international treaty that was adopted on 18 December 1979 by the UN General Assembly. It has been ratified by 189 state parties. The CEDAW defines discrimination against women as 'any distinction, exclusion or restriction made on the basis of sex which has the effect or purpose of impairing or nullifying the recognition, enjoyment or exercise by women, irrespective of their marital status, on a basis of equality of men and women, of human rights and fundamental freedoms in the political, economic, social, cultural, civil or any other field.'[154]

---

[152] GC-I, GC-II, GC-III, and GC-IV, Art. 3.

[153] AP-II, Art. 4.

[154] CEDAW. Available at https://www.un.org/womenwatch/daw/cedaw/, accessed on 4 April 2019.

State parties are committed to take steps towards ending discrimination against women in all forms which includes the following:

- Incorporating the principle of equality of men and women in their legal system, abolishing all kinds of laws that discriminate women and adopt laws towards prohibiting all kinds of discrimination against women
- Establishing tribunals and other public institutions for ensuring protection of women against discrimination in an effective manner
- Ensuring elimination of all acts of discrimination against women by persons, organizations, or enterprises

State parties to this convention, those who have ratified or acceded to the convention, are legally bound by its provisions. These state parties are also required to submit reports, at least every four years, detailing the measures taken by them in compliance with the convention obligations.

The CEDAW, which oversees the activities of the convention and its implementation by its state parties, in the 46th session in July 2010, has proposed to take necessary and appropriate steps to ensure the prosecution and punishment of the officials/security personnel who commit custodial violence, including acts of sexual abuse of women and girls, and to consider this as grave crimes.[155] Further, on 14 July 2017, the CEDAW updated the guidance to state parties as provided in General Recommendation No. 19 (GR 19) and General Recommendation No. 35 (GR 35). In spite of the development and growth made by GR 19, extensive gender-based violence and impunity across the world have persisted. Besides updating GR 19, GR 35 also strengthens state obligations in tackling violence against women as mentioned in GR 28 and GR 30 on women in conflict and post conflict respectively, and in GR 33 on access to justice.[156]

---

[155] CEDAW. 2010. 'Concluding Observations of the Committee on the Elimination of Discrimination against Women, 46th Session, 12–30 July 2010. Available at https://www2.ohchr.org/english/bodies/cedaw/docs/co/CEDAW-C-PNG-CO-3.pdf, accessed on 4 April 2019.

[156] Christine Chinkin. 'General Recommendation No. 35 on Gender-Based Violence against Women, Updating General Recommendation No. 19',

The International Convention on the Protection of the Rights of Migrant Workers and Members of Their Families

It was in the year 1990 that the UN General Assembly adopted the International Convention on the Protection of the Rights of Migrant Workers and Members of their Families (ICRMW). However, it finally came into force on 1 July 2003. The convention provides for the elimination of the exploitation of migrant workers throughout the entire process of migration and for the protection of the human rights of both documented and undocumented migrants. As of 6 March 2019, only 54 states have ratified this convention.[157] It took 13 years for this convention to come into force because it required a minimum of 20 states to ratify the convention before it could come into force. Unfortunately, there are other issues such as the fight against illegal migrants that are generally on the top of the agenda of these states.

The Committee on the Protection of the Rights of All Migrant Workers and Members of Their Families is a monitoring and a supervising body under this convention. This committee monitors the proper implementation of the convention in the member states. All state parties to this convention are required to submit their reports to this committee within one year of their ratification and are also obliged to send their periodic reports after every five years regarding the implementation of the convention in their states and their conformation to the convention. These reports also contain the present scenarios in the individual countries and the activities being undertaken to protect the rights of all migrant workers. After receiving the reports, the committee examines and gives its recommendations and also expresses its concerns to state parties in the form of 'concluding observations'. The committee holds two sessions in a year and meets in Geneva every year.[158]

LSE Women, Peace and Security Blog. Available at https://blogs.lse.ac.uk/vaw/int/cedaw/general-recommendation-no-35/, accessed on 4 April 2019.

[157] OHCHR, 'Status of Ratification'. Available at http://indicators.ohchr.org/, accessed on 4 April 2019.

[158] Committee on Migrant Workers. Available at http://www2.ohchr.org/english/bodies/cmw/, accessed on 3 April 2019.

Convention and Protocol Relating to the Status of Refugees

The 1951 Convention and the 1967 Protocol relating to the status of refugees are the most important international steps taken towards the protection of the refugees. Article 1 of the Refugee Convention defines 'refugee' as being any individual who is outside the country of his/her nationality or habitual residence who has a well-founded fear of persecution for reasons of race, religion, membership of a particular social group, nationality, or political opinion and is unable or unwilling to avail himself of the protection of that country or return to it.

This convention builds on Art. 14 of the UDHR of 1948 and recognizes the right of persons to seek asylum from persecution in other countries. The convention is legally binding, though there is no separate body that monitors compliance of state parties to the convention. The UN High Commissioner for Refugees (UNHCR), however, has been entrusted with supervisory responsibilities, but it does not have the right or authority to enforce the convention.[159]

Rome Statute of the International Criminal Court[160]

The Rome Statute is a treaty that set up the International Criminal Court (ICC),[161] a permanent court having jurisdiction on crimes of genocide, crimes against humanity, war crimes, and crimes of aggression.[162] The ICC has the power of exercising jurisdiction if a matter is referred to the prosecutor by a state Party; by the UN Security Council; *suo moto* by the prosecutor itself;[163] or by a declaration of a non-state accepting the ICC jurisdiction.[164]

---

[159] Convention and Protocol Relating to the Status of Refugees. Available at https://www.unhcr.org/protection/basic/3b66c2aa10/convention-protocol-relating-status-refugees.html, accessed on 4 April 2019.

[160] Adopted at Rome on 17 July 1998; came into force on 1 July 2002.

[161] Rome Statute, Art. 1.

[162] Rome Statute, Art. 5.

[163] Rome Statute, Art. 13.

[164] Rome Statute, Art. 12(3).

The Rome Statute considers commission of torture,[165] enforced disappearance of persons,[166] and other inhuman acts resulting in great sufferings or severe harm to human body, mind, or health[167] as crime against humanity, when done with the knowledge and in pursuance of a planned, organized, large-scale, and widespread attacks on civilian population. Accordingly, any premeditated causing of serious pain or suffering, physical and psychological, to anyone under detention or under the control of the accused is termed as torture. However, it excludes all pains or sufferings intrinsic or incidental to sanction imposed according to law.[168] Similarly, a state or a political outfit that makes an arrest, detention, or abduction of anyone or authorizes, gives aid, or consents to such an arrest, detention, or abduction, and thereupon refuses to recognize or provide information about such person's fate or location in order to intentionally deprive him/her of protection of law for a longer duration is considered as enforced disappearance of persons.[169]

Further the definition of 'war crimes' under the Rome Statute for the exercise of jurisdiction by the ICC includes planned, widespread, and grave breaches of the GC-I, II, III, and IV against protected persons and objects, including the commission of torture or inhuman treatment and biological experiments in case of an armed conflict of international character.[170] Similarly, in circumstances of a non-international armed conflict, war crimes would constitute a grave breach of Art. 3 of GC-I, II, III, and IV. Such crimes include violence to life and person, in particular murder of all kinds, mutilation, cruel treatment, and torture on anyone not participating in direct hostilities.[171]

The Rome Statute provides certain rights to the accused for ensuring fairness during investigation. Accordingly, an accused in no

---

165 Rome Statute, Art. 7(1)(f).
166 Rome Statute, Art. 7(1)(i).
167 Rome Statute, Art. 7(1)(k).
168 Rome Statute, Art. 7(2)(e).
169 Rome Statute, Art. 7(2)(i).
170 Rome Statute, Art. 8(2)(a)(ii).
171 Rome Statute, Art. 8(2)(c)(i).

circumstance should be forced to confess or give a self-incriminating testimony. Further, he/she must not be coerced; pressurized; threatened; tortured; or subjected to cruel, inhuman, or degrading treatment or punishment.[172] The Rome Statute also guarantees every victim the right to reparation, restitution, compensation, and rehabilitation based on the principles evolved by the ICC for determining the criteria for its coverage and may order the convict to provide reparation to be awarded through the Trust Fund for Victims. The rights and remedy under the Rome Statute are in addition to the rights of victims and other remedies available under national and international laws.[173] Further, the Rome Statute has power to award sentence up to 30 years of imprisonment as well as fines and forfeiture of property and assets.[174]

Regional Legal Framework

The Organization of American States

The USA enforced and implemented conventions and laws to fight torture and related crimes. The ACHR 1969 guarantees every person the right to have his/her physical, mental, and moral integrity respected, and it prohibits torture or cruel, inhuman, or degrading punishment or treatment.[175] The Organization of American States has also adopted a specific instrument on torture, viz., the IACPPT, 1985. The IACPPT defines torture as any act intentionally performed whereby physical or mental pain or suffering is inflicted on a person for purposes of criminal investigation, as a means of intimidation, as personal punishment, as a preventive measure, as a penalty, or for any other purpose. Torture shall also be understood to be the use of methods upon a person intended to obliterate the personality of the victim or to diminish his physical or mental capacities, even if they do not cause physical pain or mental anguish. The concept of torture

---

[172] Rome Statute, Art. 55.
[173] Rome Statute, Art. 75.
[174] Rome Statute, Art. 77.
[175] ACHR, Art. 5.

shall not include physical or mental pain or suffering that is inherent in or solely the consequence of lawful measures, provided that they do not include the performance of the acts or use of the methods referred to in this article.[176]

The convention also specifically states that any public official who carries out torture, who orders it, or fails to prevent it is guilty of a crime and that acting under orders is no defense to the crime. The convention provides for an absolute prohibition of torture that cannot be suspended under any circumstance.

The Inter-American Convention further requires the following:

- Police and other public officials are trained to prevent torture
- Allegations of torture are investigated and criminal prosecutions occur where appropriate
- Laws are passed to provide compensation for torture victims
- Statements extracted under torture are not admissible as evidence in legal proceedings
- States prosecute or extradite alleged torturers

The convention also requires the parties to it to take effective measures to prevent and punish other cruel, inhuman, or degrading treatment or punishment. While the convention does not contain a separate enforcement mechanism, the Inter-American Commission on Human Rights has an obligation to report on the practice of torture in member states, and the Inter-American Court has taken on jurisdiction of this treaty.

The European Union

The European Union (EU) has enforced various conventions with the aim of prohibiting and preventing the crime of torture and inhuman treatment of human beings. Among the various conventions here are some of the important ones that prohibit the act of torture and consider it as a grave crime. The ECHR 1950 prohibits torture or inhuman

---

[176] IACPPT, Art. 2.

or degrading treatment or punishment.[177] The EUCAT provides comprehensive regional instruments and legal arrangements to address the issue of torture within the EU. It established a European Committee for the Prevention of Torture and Inhuman or Degrading Treatment or Punishment, a non-judicial institution with a mandate to monitor the crimes of torture within the EU.[178] The committee is authorized to visit and inspect any place in order to monitor the provisions of this convention.[179] It is worth mentioning here that this convention puts a bar on reservation to any provision of the convention,[180] thereby making it mandatory and removing the space for selective implementation as every EU member is bound to accept application of all the provisions of this convention in its entirety.

Organization of African Unity

The ACHPR 1981, also known as the Banjul Charter, recognizes individual's rights to the respect of the dignity inherent in a human being and to the recognition of his/her legal status. It prohibits all forms of exploitation and degradation of humans, particularly slavery; slave trade; torture; and cruel, inhuman, or degrading punishment and treatment.[181]

The League of Arab States

The ARCHR, which was adopted on 22 May 2004 and entered into force on 15 March 2008, prohibits physical or psychological torture or cruel, degrading, humiliating, or inhuman treatment. It imposes a duty on state parties to protect every individual within their jurisdiction from such practices and to take effective measures to prevent them. It considers such acts as grave crimes and urges all parties to the charter to guarantee the right to redress and the right to rehabilitation and

---

177 ECHR, Art. 3.
178 EUCAT, Art. 1.
179 EUCAT, Art. 2.
180 EUCAT, Art. 21.
181 ACHPR, Art. 5.

compensation for the victims of torture within their legal and judicial systems.[182]

Right to Compensation against Illegal Deprivation of Liberty in the United States of America

In the US, the Federal Tort Claims Act, 1946 (FTCA) governs the state's liability for torturous acts of its employees or agents. Initially, it did not cover state's liability for damages in cases of violation of liberty, but subsequently the courts have evolved principles of right to compensation in cases of violation of Fourth Amendment rights.

In a first ever claim of this nature under the FTCA in the year 1971, when a petitioner claimed damages from the Federal Bureau of Narcotics, for the illegal conducts of its agents, who made a warrantless entry, search, arrest, manhandling in front of his wife and children, and threat to arrest the entire family, while acting under the colour of federal authority, the Supreme Court of USA reversed the order of the court of appeal and remanded the case back to the district court for trial. The Supreme Court of USA in this case enunciated the principle of federal cause of action under the Fourth Amendment. Justice Brennan while delivering the opinion of the bench invoked the Fourth Amendment as guaranteeing 'the right of the people to be secure in their persons, houses, papers, and effects, against unreasonable searches and seizures', which, he pointed out, shall not be violated. He upheld the petitioner's right under the FTCA, for which damages are recoverable upon proof of injuries resulting from the federal agents' violation of that amendment.[183]

A case on waiver of liability was discussed by the Supreme Court of USA, involving sexual assault and verbal threat to a prisoner/petitioner Kim Millbrook in the custody of the Federal Bureau of Prisons by correctional officers. The officers claimed waiver, which was declined. The court explained and enlarged the meaning of 'scope of employment' and propounded that acts or omissions of law enforcement officers arising within the scope of their employment, regardless of whether

---

[182] ARCHR, Art. 8.
[183] *Bivens v Six Unknown Federal Narcotics Agents*, 403 U.S. 388 (1971).

the officers are engaged in investigative or law enforcement activity, are executing a search, seizing evidence, or making an arrest.[184]

In another case before the Supreme Court of USA on Human Testing of Drugs, it invoked the Nuremberg Code of the United States Military Tribunal, used as a standard to establish and judge German scientists for experimenting on human subjects, and laid down the principle of 'voluntary consent' by making voluntary consent an absolute element for initiating, directing, and engaging in experiments on human subjects. It imposed an absolute, personal, direct, and non-delegable duty and responsibility upon each individual who initiates, directs, or engages in the experiment to ascertain the quality of the consent.[185]

Guantanamo Bay Detainees Case

In *Rasul*,[186] the legality of writ to *habeas corpus* to alien detainees held at Guantanamo Bay, Cuba, was discussed in the Supreme Court of United States of America. The case was filed in the backdrop of the 9/11 attacks and the military campaign of the US against al-Qaeda in Afghanistan. The petition was filed on behalf of two Australian citizens and 12 Kuwaiti citizens. The petitioners were captured outside the US during the armed conflict between the US and the al-Qaeda. Since 2002, they had been held by the US military at the naval base at Guantanamo Bay along with approximately 640 other non-American detainees captured abroad.

The US occupies and exercises complete jurisdiction and control over the 45 square miles base by virtue of a lease agreement of 1903, which recognizes Cuban sovereignty over the leased land.

The petitioners in their writ of habeas claim in 2002 questioned the legality of their detention at the Guantanamo Bay Base in the US District Court for the District of Columbia on the basis of their contention about their non-involvement as enemy combatants against the US or in any terrorist act. They alleged that they had neither been charged

---

[184] *Millbrook* v *United States*, 569 U.S. 10362 (2013).

[185] *United States* v *Stanley*, 483 U.S. 669 (1987).

[186] *Shafiq Rasul, et al.* v *George W. Bush, President of the United States, et al.* 542 U.S. 466 (2004).

with any wrongdoing nor been allowed access to a court or tribunal or consultation with a counsel. The district court dismissed them for want of jurisdiction, which was later affirmed by the court of appeals.

The question before the Supreme Court of USA was to determine whether US courts lack jurisdiction to consider writs of habeas corpus challenging the legitimacy of the detention of foreign nationals captured abroad and held in custody at the Guantanamo Bay Naval Base, Cuba. In other words, the task before the Court was to look into jurisdictional aspects of the habeas statute and not the ultimate sovereignty with regard to the conferment of a right to judicial review of an executive detention of aliens in a territory over which the US exercises plenary and exclusive jurisdiction. The court relied on the Common Law principles enunciated by Lord Mansfield (1759) that there was no doubt as to the court's power to issue writs of habeas corpus, even if a territory was not a part of the realm but the territory was under the subjection of the Crown. The Supreme Court of USA reversed the verdict of the court of appeals and the matter was remanded to the district court of first instance.

In *Boumediene*,[187] the Supreme Court relied on the principles laid down in *Rasul* and ruled de jure sovereignty to Cuba. It, however, affirmed that the US maintains de facto sovereignty over Guantanamo Bay and is hence subjected to the habeas jurisdiction. A 5–4 majority decided the case. Justice Kennedy, while delivering the judgment, laid down the following three-point rule for assessing extraterritorial habeas claims:

1. Detainees citizenship and status
2. The place of seizure and confinement
3. Restriction on the enjoyment of habeas rights

In *Al Maqaleh*,[188] the DC Circuit Court was confronted with a similar issue involving three detainees—foreign nationals captured outside Afghanistan and brought to and detained at the Bagram Theater

---

[187] *Lakhdar Boumediene, et al.* v *George W. Bush, President of the United States, et al.* 553 U.S. 723 (2008).

[188] *Al Maqaleh* v *Gates*, 605 F.3d 84 (D.C. Cir. 2010).

Internment Facility (also known as the Parwan Detention Facility)—who challenged their detentions through habeas corpus. The Bagram Theater Internment Facility was a temporary collection point having around 1,700 detainees. The District Court of Columbia, relying on the *Rasul* (2004) ruling of the Supreme Court of USA, ruled in favour of the petitioners by inferring Bagram akin to Guantanamo. In an appeal before the DC Circuit Court, the question of whether Bagram could be treated as part of the US was considered, that is, whether Bagram was de facto US soil, just as Guantanamo had been considered. The US government, in the appeal at the DC Circuit Court, argued that habeas rights do not cover enemy aliens in the active war zone at Bagram and invoked the Military Commissions Act of 2006, which restricted federal courts' jurisdiction in such cases. The detainees argued the protection under the Suspension Clause, which prohibits suspension of habeas corpus, except in the events of rebellion or invasion and to secure public safety. However, the court sided with the justification of the government and reversed the order of the District Court of Columbia and ruled that the writ of habeas corpus does not apply to aliens captured and held outside the sovereign territory of the US.

* * *

This chapter provided a detailed overview of various conventions that have been implemented to prevent torture and enforced detention in any form across the world. These conventions provide the major international framework to fight torture or any kind of inhuman, degrading, and cruel treatment towards any person. Besides the international framework enforced and enacted by the UN, some of the major regional frameworks that have been enforced are those by the EU, the African Union, the US, and the League of Arab States. Thus, it is very important for all the state parties of these conventions to work towards preventing torture and related crimes.

2

POLICING IN INDIA AND THE STATUS OF HUMAN RIGHTS

The right of a person is an interest that is protected by law, and thus it is the fundamental duty of the police to ensure that people living in a democratic society are free to enjoy their rights. Every human being has certain rights that are universal, natural, absolute, basic, and fundamental,[1] and the enjoyment of these rights becomes the foundation of freedom and liberty in the world. A right is also defined as the 'liberty of doing or possessing something for the infringement of which there is a legal sanction'.[2] But it has been noticed in our history that human beings have not been allowed to enjoy these fundamental rights because of various diverse political, social, economic, cultural, administrative, or fiscal actions and reasons. The improper use of power and authority by the police has time and again been found to be responsible for the denial of some of these rights, and while committing such acts, some of the law keepers do not even realize and understand that they are violating the human rights of the people for whose welfare and protection the very service of the police was created and maintained.

[1] Ed Sparer. 1984. 'Fundamental Human Rights, Legal Entitlements, and the Social Struggle: A Friendly Critique of the Critical Legal Studies Movement' *Stanford Law Review* 36, no. 1/2: 509–74.

[2] Definition of 'Right' as per *Watson's Law Lexicon*.

The Indian Police Act, 1861, under which the police functions today did not assign any role to the police of protecting human rights. Instead, it gave a very narrow and reactive role of maintenance of law and order and prevention and diction of crime.[3] The same act governed the police in India in 1919 when Brigadier General Reginald Edward Harry Dyer ruthlessly opened fire to an unarmed crowd at Jallianwala Bagh leaving several innocent people dead.[4] After Independence, the government completely ignored the human rights aspect of its citizens while enacting the police acts and granted arbitrary powers to the security forces, which can be termed as 'black laws'. This has been one of the major reasons for the frequent violations of human rights in the country. These laws include the National Security Act (NSA), the Terrorist and Disruptive Activities Act (TADA), the AFSPA, and the POTA.[5] But in some cases, for example, the use of the NSA, which provides for preventive detention, the law may be necessary in terrorist-affected areas in conditions when witnesses are not willing to come forward to provide evidence. However, even in such cases, the act must be used very cautiously and only by responsible and highly placed officials. But unfortunately, laws like the NSA and TADA have been extended to areas that are free from insurgency and terrorist activities.[6]

Status of Human Rights and Policing in India

Despite the declaration and adoption of human rights by the CoI, there are reports of violations of different types of freedoms and human rights

[3] S. Pachauri. 1999. *Prisoners and Human Rights*. New Delhi: APH Publication Corporation.

[4] Armed Conflict Timeline Index 1919–28. 'Jallianwala Bagh Massacre in India 1919'. Blog post. Available at http://www.onwar.com/aced/data/india/india1919.htm, accessed on 15 December 2017.

[5] 'POTA: The Latest Black Law'. Available at http://www.geocities.com/aipsg/charcha/May2002/alok_pota.htm, accessed on 21 December 2017.

[6] 'Human Rights and Human Rights Instruments'. Available at http://www.hri.ca/partners/sahrdc/india/fulltext.shtml, accessed on 21 December 2017.

every day in the country.[7] The media has frequently reported incidents of violation of human rights and complaints against the use of torture, third-degree method, illegal detention, custodial deaths, assaults, and fake encounters. There are numerous instances of reported custodial crimes and terrible cases of the use of third-degree methods, harassment, and misuse of power, position, and authority. These incidents give a glimpse into the serious violation of human rights at the hands of the police.[8]

Some of the very disturbing and terrible violations of human rights by the police, which were reported in newspapers and by various other human rights agencies, are listed here:

a. Dhananjoy Chatterjee, convicted of rape and murder, was executed by hanging on 14 August 2004, under questionable investigation by the Kolkata police.

b. Members of the family of a secretary to the Government of India were beaten up by the police in Delhi in 2001.

c. Vipin and Gogia were abducted by the police in Punjab in 1993.

d. Six members of a family in Thanjavur committed suicide due to police harassment in 2003.

e. A person in custody beaten up by the police in the Supreme Court premises in 2009.

f. Agitators in support of the Narmada Dam were handcuffed and paraded by police in Gujarat in June 2017.

g. Manjula Shette, an inmate of Byculla prison, murdered by the prison staff in 2018.

h. Two policemen were sentenced to capital punishment 13 years after the crime was committed—the assault and custodial death of a scrap dealer Udaykumar in 2005.

Apart from these, another grave incident came to light where, in 2007, a 20-year-old man hailing from Mohali was allegedly tortured

---

[7] 'Human Rights and the Indian Constitution'. Available at http://www.boloji.com/perspective/256.htm, accessed on 21 December 2017.

[8] V. James. 1999. *Human Rights and the Police in India*. New Delhi: APH Publication Corporation.

by the local police when he was brought to the police station. He was beaten by a cane, given electric shocks, and later abandoned in a village called Daun. After this case was reported, the Punjab State Human Rights Commission (PSHRC) recommended the Punjab government to pay Rs 25,000 to the victim as the commission determined that the nature of the injuries prima facie suffered by the victim warranted immediate interim relief.[9]

Arrest, Third-Degree Methods, and Custodial Crimes

Personal liberty and freedom of movement are the basic human rights as per the law of nature as well as rights guaranteed by the Constitution. But when a person is arrested, he is deprived of his rights. Hence, the decision of arresting someone has serious implications and consequences on that person and his family, and such actions need to be exercised with due caution and care. However, in reality, it is seen that an action of arrest undertaken by the police is routinely carried out on mere suspicion. These acts conducted by the police in India amount to serious and gross violation of human rights, which include illegal, arbitrary, and unwarranted arrests; illegal and unauthorized detentions; using handcuffs; parading the arrested person on the streets; and not producing the arrested person before a magistrate as per the law of the land.[10] It is also noticed that the persons arrested are not even aware of or informed about the reason for their arrest. Moreover, they are not even permitted to consult an advocate and are mostly subjected to third-degree torture and violence. This is really a serious violation of human rights at the hands of the law keepers.

[9] Times News Network, 'Torture Case: PSHRC comes to victim's aid', 7 February 2007. Available at https://timesofindia.indiatimes.com/city/chandigarh/Torture-case-PSHRC-comes-to-victims-aid/articleshow/1647526.cms, accessed on 25 December 2017.

[10] Human Rights Watch. Available at http://www.hrw.org/doc/?t=asia&document_limit=1860,20, accessed on 25 December 2017.

Unwarranted Summoning of People to the Police Station

In a country like India, the police is considered to be a representation of power and authority. This gives them the discretion to summon citizens they suspect to police stations for interrogation to obtain information on various issues related to law and order and to obtain evidence in any crime. But repeated summons to the general public/citizens to report at police stations violate their right of personal liberty and freedom of movement. These acts of summoning citizens and making them sit for hours or using power and treating them inhumanly on the pretext of getting information are serious violations of human rights and dignity. Thus there is an urgent need to find ways and make rules so that the police or security forces do not apply force or unnecessary, unauthorized, and illegal summons to the general public and treat them in an inhuman manner.

Bail and Not Jail

The CoI has provided and guaranteed certain rights and freedom such as the right to life, personal liberty, and freedom of movement. 'Bail and not jail' characterizes this underlying principle of these rights, which is also provided to citizens in the criminal justice system of India. Whenever a person is arrested or detained or some restriction or restrain is imposed on his personal liberty, he has a right to be considered for bail.[11] In case of any offence that is bailable, the person has a right to get the bail. On the other hand, when the offence is non-bailable, then the bail is at the discretion of the police authorities. But the actual scenario is totally different on the ground. It is often seen that there is no fair and just process of releasing the persons arrested under the provision of bail in non-bailable offences. The detained persons are mostly denied the right to get a bail in most cases.[12] Thus, there is an urgent need for the police to act in a manner that does not violate the human rights principles. They should not arrest persons only on mere

[11] CrPC, sec. 436.

[12] 'Right to Bail: The Class Bias'. Available at http://www.combatlaw.org/information.php?article_id=233&issue_id=9, accessed on 25 December 2017.

suspicion or doubt or for extracting information. Detained persons in bailable offences should be granted bail, while in non-bailable offences, the police should use their discretion to release the person, provided they are following the law. In the human rights perspective, the police needs to realize that the provision of granting bail was introduced so that the personal liberty of a person is upheld. Ensuring social security should be adopted as a priority activity of the police.

Handcuffing in India

In the criminal justice system prevailing in the country, handcuffing has been included as an important rule while arresting a person, detaining in police remand, or moving from one place to another during trial. This is done for security purposes as per the police and security forces. However, the Supreme Court of India had said that this act of handcuffing is a clear violation of Art. 21 of the Constitution. But this violation is always done as nobody from civil society or the legal professions addresses or opposes it. The case of Justice A.S. Bains who was brought to a magistrate in handcuffs is one of the most striking instances the country has seen. This act showed the arrogance and utter lack of decency of the police and the government of Punjab[13] Thus, handcuffing is certainly against human dignity. It violates human rights and adds to the degrading and ill treatment by the police forces of the country.

In the case of *Altamesh Rein* v *Union of India*, the Supreme Court of India laid down the guidelines for handcuffing, stating that handcuffs should only be used when the person arrested is violent, desperate, obstructive, rowdy, or likely to attempt suicide or escape and that handcuffs should not be used in routine arrests.[14] Further, the Supreme Court added that there should ordinarily be no reason to handcuff persons who hold a good position in society or in the

[13] 'Police and Human Rights'. Available at http://www.pucl.org/from-archives/Police/human-rights.htm, accessed on 28 December 2017.

[14] T. Mandeep. 2005. *Human Rights and Policing*. New Delhi: Commonwealth Human Rights Initiative.

case of professionals such as lawyers, doctors, jurists, writers, and journalists. The Supreme Court also said that such persons when handcuffed should not be made to walk through the streets, but this judgment was open to criticism as it gave the police the discretion of using handcuffs. But after this judgment, it has been noticed in many cases that offenders or criminals when arrested use this 'no handcuffing' rule as an advantage, and this has led to increased cases of criminals escaping from police custody. While using this rule to their advantage, the criminals are in turn committing another crime, of escaping, which is considered as an offence under the law in the country.[15] The crime of escaping from police custody is an offence that is bailable, and the punishment for this is not deterrent. Hence, more and more criminals have started using this tactic and are escaping from police custody. For such criminals, rules should be more stringent, and when they escape from custody, they should not be granted any kind of judicial concession in future. This has further led to the police forces becoming more stringent and ruthless due to which the line between the actual offenders of crime and the innocent ones is diminishing. The statistics in Table 2.1 show that criminals escaping from police custody has increased by five times due to the rule of 'no handcuffing'.

The statistics in Table 2.2 show the number of criminals escaping from police custody in 2016 in the country, which is too high.

Human Rights Commission and the Police

The NHRC in India is an autonomous statutory body, which was established on 12 October 1993 under the Protection of Human Rights Act, 1993 (PHRA; Act 10 of 1994).[16] It was formulated on the lines of the UDHR. The commission is always working towards the objective of providing and protecting the rights of every individual in society and ensuring that no person in the country is deprived of his/

---

[15] IPC, sec. 224.

[16] National Human Rights Commission, New Delhi, India, Official Website. Available at http://nhrc.nic.in/, accessed on 28 December 2017.

Table 2.1 Escape from Police Custody in Haryana, 1998–2000

	1988	1989	1990	1991	1992	1993	1994	1995	1996	1997	1998	1999	2000
Escape on the way to court	2	1	3	2	2	0	1	1	1	11	22	31	23
Escape from police custody from hospital	2	0	0	0	0	0	1	2	2	3	4	8	8
Escape from police custody	2	5	2	7	11	13	10	7	28	48	22	2	0
Escape from jails	0	0	0	0	1	0	0	0	0	2	19	19	38
TOTAL	6	6	5	9	14	13	12	10	31	64	67	60	69

Source: D. Singh. 2002. 'Handcuffing', *The Indian Police Journal* 49, no. 2.

Table 2.2 Escape from Police Custody in India, 2016

No. of Cases Registered (U/S 224, 225 B)	Total No. of Persons Who Escaped from Police Custody	Persons Who Escaped from Police Custody Lockup	Persons Who Escaped Outside Lockup	Escapees Rearrested Who Escaped		No. of Persons Chargedsheeted for the Offence of Escape
				From Lockup	Other than Lockup	
1,143	1,320	210	1,110	168	790	969

Source: Crime in India. 2017. '2016 Statistics', p. 533. NCRB, Govt. of India. Available at http://ncrb.gov.in/StatPublications/CII/CII2016/pdfs/NEWPDFs/Crime%20in%20India%20-%202016%20India%20-%202016%20Complete%20PDF%20291117.pdf, accessed on 24 February 2019.

her right, even at the hands of the security forces such as the police and the armed forces. The police, on the other hand, are in apprehension that the interference by the NHRC in their work creates problems in maintaining law and order, the enforcement of laws, and the investigation of crimes in the country. But this 'interference' has helped citizens in many cases to uphold their rights when the police have violated and subjected them to illegal detention and torture in custody. All these acts were committed by the police in violation of the principles and provisions given in the Indian Constitution, the Indian Police Act, the Code of Civil Procedure (CPC), the CrPC, and the guidelines of the NHRC and the UN.

Despite the success of the NHRC in many cases in dealing with the police and other authorities, it has faced many challenges. One of the major challenges is the lack of knowledge of the laws among the junior officials of the government and other such organizations. The NHRC investigates many cases of human rights violations in the country and receives plenty of complaints. But it does not have much to do towards the NHRC's aims and objectives other than recommending remedies or asking for compensation from the government—both national and state governments and other authorities. The NHRC does not have the power to act on human rights violation cases committed by private parties.

Thus, the police forces or other security forces need to be more cautious, should be more accountable for their acts, should adhere to the laws of the country and the CoI, and should not violate the human rights of the citizens of this nation.

* * *

The human rights of every citizen are the fundamental rights that are provided by the CoI, Thus violating these rights and depriving individuals of their rights to life and personal liberty by the police and armed forces are serious issues that need to be addressed immediately. The police personnel need to undergo some reform in terms of their rules and regulations as well as their attitudes and behaviour. Such reform of behaviour should be introduced at the individual as well as departmental level so that the persons joining the police force are sound, courteous, aware of social and constitutional norms, and morally strong in their attitude and character. Some training and workshops should be arranged for the police so that their teamwork, group behaviour, and attitude towards the community is improved. There should be programmes where the police and the community are brought together so that their bond becomes strong and the police personnel develop a courteous attitude and not an authoritative one. This kind of relationship between the police and the community will be helpful in understanding the perspective and realities of its operations and also have a control on police activities, thereby upholding the human rights of every citizen. This kind of check and balance will make society appreciate the work of the police and also make a better society for everyone.[17]

Further, the competence of the police force can be enhanced by recruiting personnel based on merit and organizing job-oriented training at all departmental levels. This will help the police to be more efficient, effective, and professional in their conduct. There is also a need to have a structural revision and reorganization of different levels and introduce innovative methods that can include cells such as grievance redress cells and public relation cells. Decentralization of the structure and functions of the police could also be beneficial in terms of enhancing the competence level of the police personnel and efficiency, which will help minimize the violations of human rights by the police. There is also a need to revise the policies of recruitment, training, promotion, and conditions of service. This will enable the police to recruit suitable personnel for each level and department as there are instances that many police constables are not well educated and come from a poor socioeconomic background, and hence they are not able to understand the complicated problems of the police and their role in society. Such steps will help reduce or minimize the violation of human rights considerably by the police personnel and thereby increase the trust of the public on the police.

[17] James. *Human Rights and the Police.*

3

NARCO-ANALYSIS
Is It Legal or a Form of Torture?

Technology advancement in this era of globalization is fast catching up with all spheres of life. The field of law is also not untouched by it, especially the criminal justice system for investigation of crimes and punishing offenders. In this modern age, investigation is taking help of various new techniques of technology-based systems such as polygraph test, narco-analysis, brain mapping, P300, and hypnosis. The outcome or results of these techniques are used as evidence in prosecuting the accused. The objective of such scientific investigation is to prove guilt beyond reasonable doubt or innocence. But most of the time, it is seen that such techniques are used as a tool for torturing the accused even before the person is proven guilty.

Narco-analysis is one of these scientific techniques of investigation, which is widely used along with other tests such as polygraph test and brain mapping. The term 'narco-analysis' is derived from the Greek word 'narko', meaning 'anaesthesia'. It is a diagnostic and psychotherapeutic technique, which is carried out by using a psychotropic drug, which makes a person semi-conscious and thereby neutralizes his/her imagination. The person on whom the test is done is injected with sodium pentothal or sodium amytal depending on the person's age, health, sex, and physical condition. The person just responds to the questions asked and cannot speak by his volition during the test because of the effect of the drug. The term nacro-analysis was first coined by

Horseley, and in 1922, Robert House, an obstetrician based in Texas, first used this technique when he used the drug named scopolamine on two prisoners.

Narco-analysis and Its Legality in India

Though tests like narco-analysis do not have any legal validity, as the responses or confessions from a semi-conscious person are not admissible in court, these tests are still undertaken by the police during investigations. In the Arushi Talwar murder case, the Talwars as well as the three accused men (neighbourhood household staff) were put through lie-detector and narco-analysis tests. The three servants gave an entire account of their involvement in the crime and the motive to murder. Although these tests are legally inadmissible, they provide important indicators of the crime and provide a direction towards the investigation. However, after the second Central Bureau of Investigation (CBI) team took over the case, all the three accused were dropped from the murder charges.[1]

Narco-analysis is fast catching up in mainstream investigations in India, but it still does not have any legal validity in the country. Many developed and democratic countries have still not openly permitted the use of narco-analysis tests during any criminal investigation. Despite this fact and despite India being a democratic country, narco-analysis has been used in police investigations in some crucial criminal cases such as the Nithari murder case and the Mumbai train blasts case.

Many are of the view that this test violates the constitutional right of the accused or suspect with regard to the right to protection against self-incrimination. On the other hand, it is viewed as a valid test as it acts as an aid to collect information and/or evidence, thus providing assistance to the police in carrying out an investigation. In India, the test is conducted by a team that consists of an anaesthesiologist, a forensic/clinical psychologist, a psychiatrist, a nurse,

---

[1] 'Arushi Murder: The Narco-test that Cracked the Case', 11 July 2008. Available at https://www.rediff.com/news/2008/jul/11aarushi1.htm, accessed on 7 April 2019.

and an audio–video technician. The report of the test is prepared by
the forensic psychologist, which is accompanied by the audio–video
recording. In India, Narco-analysis test was first used in 2002 in the
Godhra carnage case. Nowadays, the narco-analysis test is used during
investigations and is also used as evidence in court hearings. But there
is still a very big question about its legal and ethical validity. In such
tests, there is always a life risk—a person may sink into coma, or even
die, if the dosage of the drug is more than the prescribed amount.
Thus, the validity of the test needs to be analysed before it turns into a
dangerous investigating tool at the hands of the police or investigating
officers in a country like India where there are reports of everyday
torture, custodial violence, and death at the hands of the lawmakers
or the police.

Narco-analysis, the Provisions under the Indian Constitution, and Legislations

The Indian Constitution, in its Art. 20(3), provides the accused person the privilege against self-incrimination. It is equivalent to the
Magna Carta and the laws of almost all civilized countries. As per this
provision, no person who is accused can be compelled to be a witness
against himself, and it contains the following three components:

a. It is a right of a person who is accused of an offence.
b. It is a protection against compulsion to be a witness.
c. It is a protection against such compulsion that may result in giving
   evidence against himself.

Thus, the privilege against self-incrimination under Art. 20(3)
enables the maintenance of the privacy and the observation of civilized
standards during enforcement of criminal justice. The aforementioned
three components must exist to invoke or claim Art. 20(3). But the use
of the narco-analysis test involves a fundamental question with regard
to the judicial system and human rights. From the legal point of view,
it is mostly used as an investigation tool. Yet, it definitely violates the
provisions of Art. 20(3) of the Indian Constitution and also invades the
privacy and freedom of the accused.

Right to privacy is a right which include various other rights which are inherent to one's liberty or freedom. The right of a person to be alone or to be free from unnecessary attention or publicity falls under the ambit of right to privacy. Article 21 of the CoI guarantees every citizen of the country the right to privacy under the provisions of the Right to life and personal liberty.[2] In the case of *M.P. Verma* v *Satish Chandra*,[3] the provisions under Arts 19(1)(f) and 20(3)—protection against self-incrimination were cited referring the seizure of documents as violation of fundamental right to privacy.

The landmark judgment in the case of *Smt. Selvi* v *State of Karnataka*,[4] delivered by the then Chief Justice K.G. Balakrishnan and two other judges, Justice R.V. Raveendran and Justice J.M. Panchal, declared the practice of narco-analysis, Functional magnetic resonance imaging (FMRI), brain mapping, and polygraph test as unconstitutional and void. This judgment dealt with the right to privacy and the right against self-incrimination, which is protected under Art. 20(3) of the Indian Constitution.[5]

Provision under the Code of Criminal Procedure, 1973

The CrPC, also protects the rights of the citizen against self-incrimination under the provisions of the right to silence. This right to silence, which is enshrined in sec. 161(2) of the CrPC states that every person 'is bound to answer truthfully all questions, put to him by [a police] officer, other than questions the answers to which would have a tendency to expose that person to a criminal charge, penalty or forfeiture'.[6] Thus, it has been debated that narco-analysis constitutes mental torture and violates the right to life under Art. 21 of the CoI, which deals with

---

[2] Sonakshi Verma, *The Concept of Narcoanalysis in view of Constitutional Law and Human Rights*, available at http://www.rmlnlu.ac.in/webj/sonakshi_verma.pdf.

[3] AIR 1954 SC 300: 1954 SCR 1077.

[4] AIR 2010 SC 1974.

[5] Criminal Appeal 1267 of 2004; (2010) 7 SCC 263.

[6] CrPC, sec. 161(2).

the right to privacy. Further, the law protecting the individual against encroachment in the privacy of the individual would not permit any evidence collected via brain mapping, narco-analysis, polygraph test, and so on, to be produced in court. Hence, it has been established that nobody can extract any information or statement forcefully from the accused when the individual has the right to remain silent during interrogation under the provisions of the CrPC, as pronounced in the case of *Nandini Sathpathy* v *P.L. Dani*.[7]

Provision under the Indian Evidence Act, 1872

The Indian Evidence Act, 1872, also allows some provisions to protect the right of the accused against self-incrimination in any case under the criminal justice system. Section 29 of the Indian Evidence Act states that confessions made under the influence of intoxication must be considered irrelevant. The same provision is applicable in the narco-analysis test, where the person is under the influence of a drug/medicine scientifically. While the confession made by such a person is not admissible in court, the information received from such a test leading to any incriminatory evidence can be admissible under the provisions of sec. 27 of the act. Further, it is also argued that in such tests, there is no use of coercion, force, torture or third degree by the police and that the information is received voluntarily from the person accused. This is also because a prior consent is taken from the individual before the test is made applicable. Even sec. 45 of the act permits an expert's opinion in certain cases, but it is silent on other aspects of the forensic evidence that can be admissible in criminal proceedings in court.

Criticism of the Narco-analysis Test

Although in many cases nowadays, the police is taking the help of alternative investigation methods, which are scientific and technology based, these tests too are not fully accurate. The narco-analysis

---

[7] AIR 1978 SC 1025.

test, which is fast growing to be a mainstream scientific investigation procedure in India, is not 100 per cent accurate. Social activists and human rights activists have criticized and protested against such tests. The narco-analysis test has adverse effects on the person on whom it is applied if the dosage is not proper or accurate. It is also a fact that the dosage prescribed by medical experts cannot be applied to all individuals as everyone has different health conditions, physical as well as mental. If the dosage is not proper, it may have adverse effects on the person's health and the person may also die due to wrong dosage. Hence there are risks and legal complications involved in the narco-analysis test.

Adverse Effects on Health

The drug used in narco-analysis is known as sodium pentothal, which may have harmful effects on the person on whom it is administered. It can affect the respiratory or the circulatory system of the person. Sometimes, it may even affect the nervous system of the person and cause laryngeal spasm, nausea, and headache. Since it is an anaesthetic drug, the person may even sink into a coma state or even die if proper care and treatment are not given in such cases. Thus, there is a huge risk of life to the individual while undergoing a narco-analysis test, only to provide answers or evidence in a criminal case. The right to life and liberty is provided to every citizen of the country, and hence no one can risk the life of a person by doing this test.

Accuracy of the Test

Another criticism of this test is that it is not completely accurate. A person may under the influence of this test give answers that are not true or the person may start believing what the interrogator asks him. He may not differentiate between reality and imagination or fantasy. In many cases, the responses may be contaminated with deception or fantasy in a state of such semi-consciousness as the person may be hal-lucinating. Under the influence of the drug during the narco-analysis test, a person may find it difficult to differentiate between his own thoughts and that of the interrogator. A guilty person may deny the offence, while an innocent person may admit to the crime.

Violations of Rights

The CoI under Art. 20(3) provides every individual the right against self-incrimination, which means that no person who is accused of any offence can be compelled or forced to become a witness against himself. This right was adopted from the British criminal justice system. As per this right of protection from self-incrimination, the accused person has the right to remain silent during any interrogation. But the narco-analysis test takes away this right and blatantly violates this right of the individual as guaranteed by the Indian Constitution. Many are of the view that this right might protect the actual offender or the guilty, and hence this immunity given to all individuals may be an impediment in a potential investigation procedure in a criminal case and may also hamper the greater public interest.

Mental Torture

Many consider narco-analysis to be a form of torture, a mental or psychological torture, and this is the reason why in most developed countries, it is not permitted during investigations in the criminal justice system. Torture can be not only physical but also mental, which has more adverse effects and further affects the physical health of the person. The effects of the drug, the process which the person goes through during the test, and its after-effects and medical side effects can very well be considered as a form of mental torture. It is much more harmful than the physical torture and third-degree method applied by the police during criminal investigations—mental trauma such as this may require more recovery time than physical injuries. As per the UNCAT, torture is defined as follows:

a. Any act by which severe pain or suffering, whether physical or mental, is caused.
b. It is intentionally inflicted on a person.

   c. It is used for such purposes as obtaining from him or a third person information or a confession.

   d. It is inflicted for punishing him for an act he or a third person has committed or suspected to have committed by or at the instigation of a public official or a person in an official capacity.

When the narco-analysis procedure is closely observed, it is found that all the aforementioned conditions are present in the test, and hence the test is a form of mental torture inflicted on a person. Further, in India, the narco-analysis test causes tremendous mental pressure even after the test when the police give the recording of the footage of the test to the media and the media shows it repeatedly. This causes further mental torture on the accused person through stigmatization in society.

* * *

In the criminal justice system, it is important to investigate and punish offenders and bring them to justice, but in the process, many innocent persons are punished, directly or indirectly. The police generally use force or coercion in the course of their investigation and interrogation. But nowadays, because of the knowledge and usage of narco-analysis tests, the police increasingly depend on this investigation tool as it releases them from the pressure of committing coercion or committing custodial violence and the danger of being entangled in legal and human rights issues. This test, as already discussed, uses a drug that puts a person in a semi-conscious state, whereby the person's thoughts are controlled and the person only responds to whatever is asked of him. Although this procedure is not foolproof, the police continue to use it to gather information easily. This test, however, contradicts the rights guaranteed by the Indian Constitution and various legislations in the country to protect the right to life, the right to privacy, the right to self-incrimination, and the right to remain silent. These rights are provided by the CrPC, the Indian Evidence Act, Art. 20(3) of the Indian Constitution, and the fundamental right of right to life and liberty. Everything in this world is dynamic and is always changing, and hence law must also undergo change but within the limits of ethics and the welfare of citizens. The narco-analysis test may be a useful and viable tool for investigation and to find information in a potential case rather than using third degree or custodial violence by the police, but it should also not violate the rights of the accused that are guaranteed to him by the Constitution. Hence, the narco-analysis test, while seemingly useful, must not be used in every other case. Even if it is used by the police and other officials, the findings of the test must not be made public so that the person concerned does not suffer any further mental agony.

4

POLICE IN INDIA
Its Structure and Pattern

The then British rulers enforced the Indian Police Act of 1861 to establish the British colonial state system in India and to govern the country as per their whims and fancies. It marked the ultimate transition of administration and governance from the prevalent system to that of the British, particularly in terms of law enforcement and administration in the country.[1] This period of British colonial rule can be discussed by splitting it into two parts or periods. The first period is from 1861 when the act was enforced till the year 1904, and the second period is from 1905 till the Independence of India on 15 August 1947 and the formation of Pakistan on 14 August 1947. The first period of four decades saw the strengthening of the administrative system of British rule or Raj, while the second period, which was a little more than four decades, saw the application of the divide and rule policy of the British, which proved to be successful. Present-day India is considered to be a quasi-federation,[2] comprising 29 states and seven union territories. The CoI states that 'police order' is a state subject,[3] and so the police system

---

[1] 'History of Bengal'. Available at http://sos-arsenic.net/english/intro/index.html, accessed on 30 December 2017.

[2] C. Alexandrowicz. 1954. 'Is India a Federation', *The International and Comparative Law Quarterly*, 3(3): 393–403.

[3] Constitution of India (CoI), list II; schedule VII.

in the country is based on the state police force. The IPC of 1860 originally contained 511 sections, which were divided into 23 chapters.[4] As per the Indian Police Act, 1861, the organization, structure, functions, and pattern of the police is almost uniform throughout the country in spite of having separate police forces in each and every state.

Under this act, a police officer cannot be employed in any other place or organization, unless the inspector general of police (IGP) of the respective state permits it. The act has a provision for additional police officers to be employed under the charge of the person who makes an application, and every person recruited as police officer shall be on duty in any place or any region of a state/district at any time.[5]

In India, it has been observed that any confession made before a police officer is not admissible as it is forbidden as per sec. 25 of the Indian Evidence Act. Thus any such confession cannot be used against the accused, even if the confession has the credibility to be proven and is genuine. However, a dying declaration is not bound by such regulations.[6] Furthermore, confessions made to the Directorate of Enforcement, central excise department, income tax department, railway authorities, police officials, and other such enforcement agencies are considered admissible.[7]

Organizational Structure of the Indian Police Force

The Indian Police Force has a vertical pyramid organization or administrative structure.[8] The organization structure is uniform across all states in the country. The DGP is at the top of the organization structure of the police administration in a state. He is the one who is solely

---

[4] IPC 1860 Sections. Available at https://lawrato.com/indian-kanoon/ipc, accessed on 26 September 2019.

[5] Sec. 17, Indian Police Act, 1861.

[6] Sec. 154, CrPC, 1973; Sec. 32, Indian Evidence Act, 1872.

[7] 'Indian Legislation'. Available at http://www.commonlii.org/in/legis/num_act/iea1872125/, accessed on 30 December 2017.

[8] *Police Manual*, Vol. V, Government of India.

responsible for the entire administration of the police force in every state. The DGP is the supreme authority of the police administration of a state and also has an additional duty or responsibility of advising the state government in the maintenance of law and order in the state. The administration is further sub-divided into district-level administration where the superintendent of police (SP) is the authority or the head. In case the districts are in a range, then the head is the deputy inspector general of police (Dy IGP), who reports to the additional director general of police (Addl DGP) or the DGP.[9]

The police administration is governed by the district magistrate (DM) in his/her jurisdiction. The control in a district of a state is also given to the district superintendent of police (DSP) and assistant or deputy superintendent of police as required or deemed fit by the individual state governments. The district administration is further divided into sub-divisions, which are administered or controlled by the assistant and/or deputy superintendent of police. Such sub-divisions are again divided into circles, where inspectors are in charge. These circles are then divided into police stations, which further include urban and rural outposts.[10] A police station is the fundamental and key unit of police administration and is the crime investigation centre. All crimes are recorded in police stations, and from here, the police conduct investigations and activities that are detective and preventive in nature and thus maintain the law and order of the area.[11]

As per sec. 4 of the Indian Police Act, the district police administration is controlled by the SP of that district, provided there is a control and direction of the DM. The DM is considered the head of the criminal administration of the district under his/her jurisdiction. But it is seen that there is a dual authority and control on the work and administration of the police.[12] However, the police force of each

---

[9] *Police Manual*, Vol. V.

[10] *Police Manual*, Vol. V.

[11] G. Reddy and K. Seshadri (eds). 1972. *Developing Society and Police: India.* Hyderabad: Osmania University.

[12] *Police Manual*, Vol. I, Government of India.

state has its investigation department, intelligence department, training department, and so on.

It is further observed that in the case of big cities or metropolitan cities like Delhi, Mumbai, Chennai, Kolkata, Bengaluru, Pune, Hyderabad, and Ahmedabad, the organizational structure of the police administration is different. In these cities, the commissioner of police (CP) heads the police force and directs and supervises the police force of the city. The CP is assisted by the joint commissioner of police, additional commissioner of police, deputy commissioner of police, and assistant commissioner of police (ACP), who have the authority and power to implement law and order and exercise regulatory power in the city besides having magisterial and licensing power.[13] The CP of a city is also responsible for advising the state government as well as the IGP and DGP about the administration and problems of the city besides the problems related to the police and their training and development.[14] The following is the structure and statistics of the police force of Mumbai city,[15] which will provide a better understanding (see Figures 4.1 and 4.2).

- Commissioner of police—1
- Joint commissioners of police—5
- Additional commissioners of police—12
- Deputy commissioners of police—38
- Assistant commissioners of police—124
- Police inspectors—977
- Assistant police inspectors—756
- Police sub-inspectors—2,850
- Assistant police sub-inspectors—3,329
- Head constable writers—656
- Police head constables—7,490
- Police naiks—6,010
- Police constable writers—628

[13] B. Misra. 1990. *The Bureaucracy in India*. (New Delhi: Penguin).

[14] Misra. *The Bureaucracy in India*.

[15] Mumbai Police, Official Website. Available at http://www.mumbaipolice. org/, accessed on 30 December 2017.

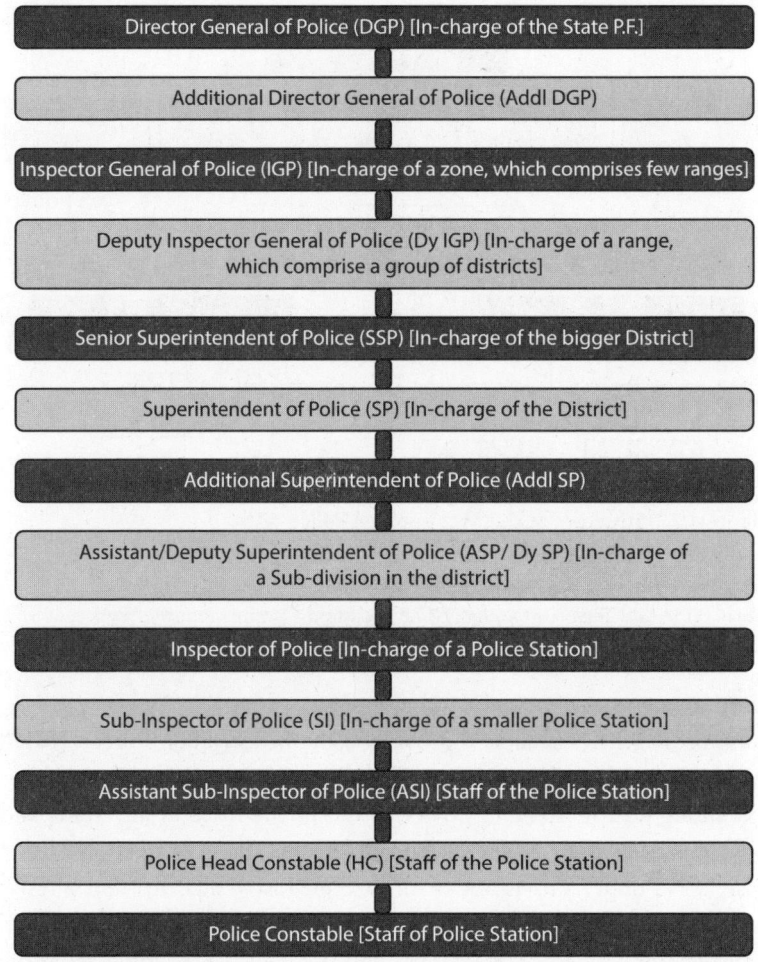

Figure 4.1 Hierarchical Organization Structure of the Indian Police Force
Source: Organization of the Police Force of India, p. 12, Commonwealth Human Rights Initiative. Available at https://www.humanrightsinitiative.org/publications/police/police_organisations.pdf, accessed on 26 September 2019.

- Police constable typists—215
- Police constables—17,823

As per Art. 246 of the Indian Constitution, the State List consists of 'police' and 'public order', whereas the Union List in its Schedule VII

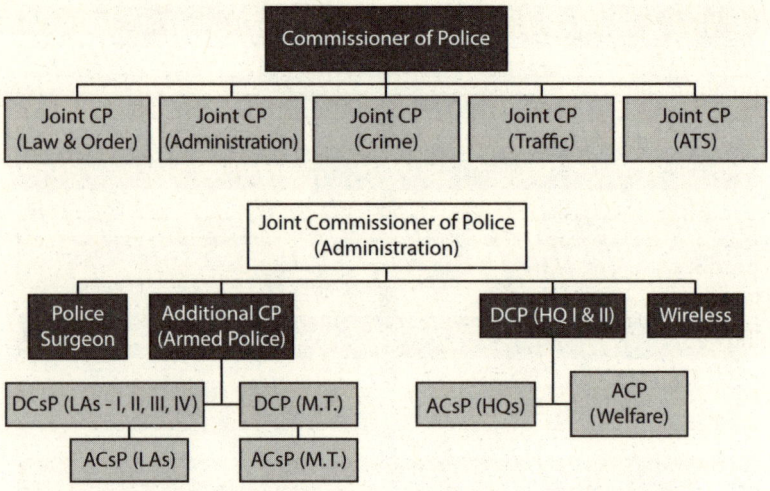

Figure 4.2   Structure of the Metropolitan Police
Source: Mumbai Police. Available at http://www.mumbaipolice.org/aboutus/
org_fun.htm, accessed on 2 January 2018.
Notes: ATS: Anti Terrorism Squad; ACsP: Assistant Commissioners of Police;
LA: Local Armed Police; M.T.: Motor Transport; and HQ: Head Quarter.

comprises agencies such as the CBI and the Investigation Bureau (IB).[16]
Apart from this, the training of police officers, functions such as
extending jurisdiction and power to the police force of any state, and
providing assistance in the technical or scientific investigation of any
case come under provisions of the Union List. Thus the central government manages and coordinates between the states by helping in
investigations by the CBI, providing intelligence gathering, scientific
investigation, training the police personnel, and so on.

The central government established an organization named Special
Police Establishment, which was created under the Delhi Special
Police Establishment Act, 1946. Later on, in the year 1963, the central
government established the CBI on 1 April 1963.[17] Following this,

[16] CoI, Art. 246.
[17] Central Bureau of Investigation. Available at http://cbi.gov.in/history.
php, accessed on 30 December 2017.

the functions of the CBI were extended, which covered the Central Forensic Science Laboratory as well as the role of the National Central Bureau for India under the International Criminal Police Organization (INTERPOL).[18]

Functions of the Police

The duties and functions of the police as per the Indian Police Act, 1861, are stated in sec. 23 of the act. These duties and functions are as follows:

- To prevent the commission of offences and public nuisances
- To obey and execute all orders and warrants lawfully issued to them by any competent authority
- To detect and bring offences to justice
- To collect and communicate intelligence affecting public peace
- To arrest and detain all persons they are legally authorized to and for which there should be sufficient ground[19]

The aforementioned functions were originally listed in the act in 1861. However, since then, the duties and functions have changed slightly and have been expanded as follows:

- Maintaining law and order
- Controlling riots
- Protecting the assets of the state
- Investigating crime
- Controlling traffic
- Protecting VIPs

Other Police Acts and Amendments

As mentioned, the Indian Police Act, 1861 governs and regulates the entire police system and administration in the country. Nevertheless,

[18] National Central Bureau (Interpol), New Delhi. Available at http://www. cbi.gov.in/interpol/interpoldelhi.php, accessed on 30 December 2017.

[19] Sec. 23, Indian Police Act, 1861.

there are quite a number of acts that have been enacted in India. To amend the existing law for the regulation of the police force, the Police Act of 1888 was enacted. This act states that any police officer could serve in any part of any state as per the central government order, and while discharging duties, the officer shall be provided with the privileges, functions, and powers of a police officer of that particular state.

In 1922, another act was enacted by the Government of India— the Police (Incitement to Disaffection) Act, 1922. It was enacted and enforced for providing penalty for spreading disaffection among the police and kindred offences.[20] This kind of provision or requirement is not included in the IPC or in the Police Act, 1861, and thus the government enacted this act to provide the authorities the mechanism to deal with such offences.

Some other acts that were enacted include the Police Act of 1949 and the Police Forces (Restriction of Rights) Act, 1966. The Police Act, 1949, provided the establishment of a general police district, which could include two or more union territories and a police force thereof. The government enacted the Police Forces (Restriction of Rights) Act, 1966, for providing restriction of certain rights that were conferred by Part III of the Constitution in their application to the members of the forces who are charged with the maintenance of public orders for ensuring proper discharge of their duties and the maintenance of discipline among themselves. Further, the central government is empowered to frame rules for regulating the restrictions provided by the act.[21]

Another act enacted by the Government of India was the State Armed Police Forces (Extension of Laws) Act, 1952, for providing extension of disciplinary laws in any state relating to the armed police force of that state. The provisions of this act are also extended to the members of the armed police force while they are serving outside that state.[22]

---

[20] The Police (Incitement to Disaffection) Act, 1922.
[21] G. Sharma. 2002. *Police and India*. Lucknow: Eastern Book Co.
[22] Sharma. *Police and India*.

Besides the aforementioned acts, there are some other laws that have been enacted by some of the states and union territories in the country. These include the Delhi Police Act, 1978; the Bombay Police Act, 1951; the Madhya Pradesh Bill, 2002; the Karnataka Police Act, 1963; and the Kerala Police Act, 1960.

* * *

Thus, we can conclude that the Police Act regulates and creates the hierarchy and organization structure as well as the functions and duties of the police force in the country. It also defines the responsibilities and the powers of the police. Further, Schedule VII of the CoI also provides limitations in the power of lawmaking of the central as well as the state governments in terms of the Union List, the State List, and the Concurrent List.[23]

Apart from the state police force, there are some special forces that operate to deal with special tasks. In case of public disturbances and problems such as caste-related or religious clashes, riots, and political rivalries, the Armed Reserve Police are given the responsibility of dealing with such cases at the district headquarters, under the control of the SP. There are also some troops of the Special Armed Police (SAP), which are utilized during critical situations. The DGP controls the SAP. Another very important force is the Criminal Investigation Department (CID), which is present in every state police department. This is a specialized agency that conducts inquiries into allegations against important public personalities and/or any police officer. It is headed by the Addl DGP or the IGP. The department is also given the responsibility of investigating significant criminal cases that the district or state police department has been unable to solve. Another organ is the Bureau of Police Research and Development, which is responsible for conducting a systematic study of the problems of the police. This department also encourages and promotes the application of science and technology in the activities of the police and organizes training

[23] *World Factbook of Criminal Justice Systems.* Available at http://www.ojp. usdoj.gov/bjs/pub/asci/wfbcjind.txt, accessed on 2 January 2018.

programmes for the development of the police personnel, both at the centre and at the state level. There are also some other armed forces that are regulated by the central government, including the Central Reserve Police Force (CRPF) and Border Security Force (BSF).[24]

---

[24] CoI, Entries 2 & 2-A in list 1 of schedule VII.

5

RESPONSE OF INDIA TOWARDS TORTURE AND CUSTODIAL VIOLENCE

International Convention on Torture and India

There are several conventions against torture across the world, which have been framed by various international organizations. One of the most important of these is the CAT. It has been 30 years since India signed the convention, but it is still not a party to it since it did not ratify it. Nevertheless, India has laid down some guidelines to prevent the crime of torture and violence, especially those occurring in police, judicial, or armed forces custody. The Supreme Court of India has regularly framed several guidelines to identify and protect the rights of victims of torture and custodial violence. It has also argued and discussed the responsibility of the government in providing appropriate legal protection with the help of reforms in the criminal justice system and especially reforms in the police system and administration.

India is not a party to the CAT but it is a party to the ICCPR and the CRC, which provide the right to protection against torture and custodial violence. Hence, it is important to find out and discuss the steps and efforts undertaken by India towards protecting victims of torture, preventing torture and custodial violence, and upholding the human rights of its citizens, thereby fulfilling the duties towards its international commitments. This chapter highlights and discusses all the legislations, enactments, and policies that have been framed by India such as the CoI; the Indian Evidence Act, 1872; the IPC; the PHRA; the AFSPA; the Chhattisgarh Special Public Safety Act (CGSPSA), 2005; the CrPC; the Gujarat Prevention of Anti-Social Activities Act, 1985; the Maharashtra Control of Organised Crime Act (MCOCA), 1999; the POTA; the Terrorist and Disruptive Activities (Prevention) Act, 1987; the Unlawful Activities (Prevention) Act, 1967 (UAPA) (amended in 2004 and 2008); and the National Investigation Agency Act, 2008 (the NIA Act). It also analyses guidelines of the NHRC on custodial death and rape, human rights of prisoners, cases of encounter deaths, polygraph tests, and measures to improve the relationship between the police and the public. The chapter also highlights reports of various commissions and committees such as the Ribeiro Committee (1998), the Soli Sorabjee Committee (2005), the Malimath Commission on Reforms of Criminal Justice System (2003), and the Padmanabhaiah Committee (2000). Besides, the chapter also discusses some important bills such as the POT Bill, 2010; the Communal Violence (Prevention and Punishment) Bill, 2005; and the Prevention of Communal and Targeted Violence (Access to Justice and Reparation) Bill, 2009. Table 5.1 presents the status of the various conventions for India.

Torture and other such related offences that are defined as crimes under CAT are not considered as offences in India. However, such related offences are defined in the IPC in its Chapter XVI in the form of murder, hurt, grievous hurt, assault, rape, and so on, which may be applicable to public servants too just like any other alleged criminal. Further, the IPC in its Chapter IX has provisions for dealing with certain offences committed by public servants, which includes disobeying direction under the law,[1] disobeying the law to cause injury,[2] punishment for non-treatment of victims,[3] and framing of incorrect documents to cause injury.[4] But any kind of prosecution against public servants can only be commenced after prior sanction is received from the government.[5]

[1] IPC, sec. 166A.
[2] IPC, sec. 166.
[3] IPC, sec. 166B.
[4] IPC, sec. 167.
[5] CrPC, sec. 197.

Table 5.1   Status of India: Conventions on Torture

International Convention	India's Status
ICCPR	Signed and ratified
OP-ICCPR-I 1966	Not signed
OP-ICCPR-II 1989	Not signed
CAT	Signed
OPCAT 2002	Not signed
CRC	Signed and ratified
OP-CRC	Signed and ratified
CED 2006	Signed
GC-I	Signed and ratified
GC-II	Signed and ratified
GC-III	Signed and ratified
GC-IV	Signed and ratified
AP-I	Not signed
AP-II	Not signed
ICC Rome Statute	Not signed

Source: NHRC. 2012. *A Handbook on International Human Rights Conventions.* Available at http://www.nhrc.nic.in/sites/default/files/A_Handbook_on_ International_HR_Conventions.pdf, accessed on 2 February 2018.
Notes: OP—Optional Protocol, CED—International Convention for the Protection of All Persons from Enforced Disappearance, GC—Geneva Convention, AP— Additional Protocol, ICC— International Criminal Court.

United Nations Special Rapporteur on Extrajudicial, Summary or Arbitrary Executions: Mission to India

The report submitted by the United Nations Special Rapporteur on Extrajudicial, Summary or Arbitrary Executions, Christof Heyns, after an analysis of the condition of human rights in India especially the right to life and liberty with respect to extrajudicial, summary, and arbitrary executions during his visit to India from 19 to 30 March 2012[6] provides important insights into assessing the performance of India in safeguarding human rights—whether these are at par with the international standards. This report gave some striking information on a number of violations of

---

[6] A/HRC/23/47/Add.1 (Human Rights Council 23rd session, 26 April 2013).

human rights cases and custodial violence. As per the report, encounter deaths by the police during the period from 1993 to 2008 were about 2,560. Among this, 1,224 cases were found to be cases of fake encounters, which were also reported by the investigation of the NHRC.[7]

During the visit, the special rapporteur also reviewed sec. 46 of the CrPC and found it to be too broad, which provided the police the power to use excess force while arresting or detaining any person. Section 46 further laid down provisions for using all required means or ways to overpower forcible resistance by the person being arrested and hence to go beyond the permissible limits, which the IHRL does not support.[8]

Some instances of fake encounters and use of force by the police and armed forces were mentioned in the report. It took a strong stand against cases of fake encounters that had been used as a means for targeting and harassing specific groups in some parts of the country. For instance, in Gujarat, encounters have been permitted and conducted against a particular minority community. These cases are still being investigated by independent SITs.[9] A judgment by the Andhra Pradesh High Court on 13 July 2007 made it mandatory to lodge a first information report (FIR) and to initiate investigation and trial in instances of death by police in crossfire. It further lay down that the police must prove the plea of self-defense during the trial. This was reported as a positive judgment by the rapporteur.[10]

Another such incident of fake encounter and use of force was reported in Jammu and Kashmir. The report noted the incident of 2010 where at least 100 lives were lost due to the use of excessive force to control protests and demonstrations. This act undermined the international standards of principles of necessity and proportionality while using force in circumstances that included manning and dispersing violent assemblies.[11] The rapporteur also included an encounter

---

[7] A/HRC/23/47/Add.1, para. 12.
[8] A/HRC/23/47/Add.1, para. 10.
[9] A/HRC/23/47/Add.1, para. 16.
[10] A/HRC/23/47/Add.1, para. 19.
[11] A/HRC/23/47/Add.1, para. 12.

conducted by the armed forces in the Machil sector of Kupwara District in Jammu and Kashmir on 30 April 2010 where three youths were branded as terrorists. After investigation, it was confirmed that these three youths were innocent civilians who were missing from Nadihal in Baramullah. After this incident, criminal proceedings were initiated against the officers of the armed forces, but these have not yet concluded.[12]

This report further highlighted the non-compliance of the Supreme Court ruling in the *Naga People's Movement of Human Rights* v *Union of India* (henceforth the *Naga* case), which made a six-monthly review of notification of disturbed areas under AFSPA mandatory.[13] The report also emphasized the rising demands of the repeal of AFSPA from every corner of the country as well as the world, including the former United Nations Special Rapporteur on Extrajudicial, Summary or Arbitrary Executions, the Special Committee of Government of India 2004, the fifth Report of the Second Administrative Reforms Commission 2007, and the NHRC.[14] However, the rules laid down by the Supreme Court and the dos and don'ts for the armed forces that were laid down in the *Naga* case were found to be inadequate by the special rapporteur to make AFSPA compliant with the international human rights standards.[15] He gave his views on the nature of the powers under AFSPA, which were found to be far wider than what is permissible even during an emergency as per international standards. This is because it suspends the right to life and that too without the safeguards. The rapporteur expressed concern that the rules and provisions under AFSPA would allow any large-scale military to set up an environment where exceptions are treated as the rule and the application of lethal force is legitimized as the prime reaction to conflict. Such an environment and rules will make it difficult in future to reconcile with India's claim that it is not been involved in an internal armed conflict. Further, he opined that such acts and rules will prove to be counterproductive to the health of

---

[12] A/HRC/23/47/Add.1, para. 15.
[13] A/HRC/23/47/Add.1, para. 24.
[14] A/HRC/23/47/Add.1, para. 25.
[15] A/HRC/23/47/Add.1, para. 26.

democracy and the status of human rights in India. Hence, to secure the human rights and the democracy of the country, AFSPA should be repealed or amended and the laws of the country should be as per international standards.[16]

The special rapporteur identified the measures taken by the Government of India for standardizing norms for the treatment of persons in custody so as to guarantee the human rights of prisoners or detainees. These included the NHRC's guidelines on custodial deaths and rapes, the D.K. Basu Guidelines, and mandatory judicial inquiries in all custodial deaths under the CrPC (Amendment) Act of 2005. Despite mentioning the norms set up by the agencies of the Government of India for upholding the human rights of prisoners, the report also mentioned issues of serious non-compliances.[17]

Further, the special rapporteur found that impunity is the major weakness of custodial justice in India.[18] Impunity is intertwined with accountability and functions in a layered manner in the country. For instance, the refusal to lodge FIRs at the entry level, even in cases of serious and grave crimes; the unapproachable manner and behaviour of the police towards persons who try to register FIRs; or not treating complaints seriously in some cases. Given such behaviour of the police, registering an FIR against police abuse or atrocity proves to be very difficult. This certainly discourages victims from taking help or assistance from the police or the criminal justice delivery system, and it thus strengthens the unaccountability and impunity of the police.[19] In other cases, where the families of the victims try to initiate civil, criminal, or writ proceedings for redress in cases involving illegal killings, the burden is borne by them always. The vulnerability of family members of the victims also obstructs their ability to demand and ensure accountability.[20] Besides such hurdles in getting justice, the lack of deterrence and prosecution, which further strengthens

---

[16] A/HRC/23/47/Add.1, para. 27.
[17] A/HRC/23/47/Add.1, para. 32.
[18] A/HRC/23/47/Add.1, para. 64.
[19] A/HRC/23/47/Add.1, para. 65.
[20] A/HRC/23/47/Add.1, para. 66.

impunity, makes prosecution or registering complaints against police and armed forces difficult and nearly impossible as there are legislations and acts in India that prevent any kind of prosecution against the police or armed forces. Hence, the rapporteur recommended the repealing of such immunities provided to the police and the armed forces.[21]

Further, the rapporteur reported that the award of monetary compensation to victims without any criminal justice recourse definitely undermines the principles of individual criminal responsibility and thus enables impunity. He also emphasized the significance of such monetary compensation, which can be considered as an important part of the justice system but not substitute the criminal justice system of the country.[22]

On the situation of Jammu and Kashmir, the rapporteur made his observations and laid emphasis on extrajudicial executions and enforced disappearances. He also specially mentioned the discovery of 2,700 unmarked graves that hid corpses of 2,943 victims of fake encounter killings and disappearances made during the period 1990–2009. He further reported that no actions have been taken so far by the government in spite of giving assurances.[23] With regard to the number of missing persons or disappeared persons, which ranged from 4,000 as estimated by the government to around 10,000 as per the estimation provided by various other agencies, he emphasized the inability of ratifying the CED and the CAT by India.[24]

In his report, the special rapporteur gave some important and valuable recommendations to the Government of India, some of which are listed here:

1. To promptly ratify the CAT, the CED,[25] the Optional Protocols (I and II) to the ICCPR, the Optional Protocol to the CEDAW,

---

[21] A/HRC/23/47/Add.1, para. 71.
[22] A/HRC/23/47/Add.1, para. 73.
[23] A/HRC/23/47/Add.1, para. 86.
[24] A/HRC/23/47/Add.1, para. 87.
[25] A/HRC/23/47/Add.1, para. 97.

the Rome Statute of the ICC, and the two Optional Protocols to the Geneva Conventions[26]

2. To set up a time-bound commission of inquiry to investigate extra-judicial executions; to offer necessary steps to deal with them; to chalk out a plan of action covering areas of legal reform, institutional reform of civil, paramilitary, and military institutions, and impunity and accountability[27]

3. To repeal or amend AFSPA (in the northeast and Jammu and Kashmir) to ensure respect to the internationally recognized principles such as proportionality and necessity and removal of immunity[28]

4. To enact an internationally compliant the POT Bill[29]

5. To amend sec. 46 of the CrPC and review other local laws that legitimize use of force and lethal force, to ensure observance of internationally accepted principles of proportionality and necessity[30]

6. To review sec. 197 of the CrPC to eliminate legal bar and necessity of prior governmental sanction for prosecution of public servants[31]

7. To ensure application of command responsibility for infringement of the right to life by security personnel[32]

8. To set up a permanent system for regular monitoring and review of the observance of guidelines of the Supreme Court and the NHRC[33]

9. To amend sec. 19 of the PHRA to enable the NHRC with the jurisdiction vis-à-vis the armed forces[34]

10. To establish an efficient programme for the protection of witnesses and victims[35]

---

[26] A/HRC/23/47/Add.1, para. 98.
[27] A/HRC/23/47/Add.1, para. 96.
[28] A/HRC/23/47/Add.1, para. 100.
[29] A/HRC/23/47/Add.1, para. 99.
[30] A/HRC/23/47/Add.1, para. 102.
[31] A/HRC/23/47/Add.1, para. 103.
[32] A/HRC/23/47/Add.1, para. 113.
[33] A/HRC/23/47/Add.1, para. 108.
[34] A/HRC/23/47/Add.1, para. 120.
[35] A/HRC/23/47/Add.1, para. 116.

Custodial Violence: Fact Sheet of India

The NHRC and the National Crimes Record Bureau (NCRB) are the two major sources for providing data and fact sheets on custodial violence and torture happening in the country. The NHRC reports are based on the statements of victims, which is not the case with the NCRB. The latest annual report of NHRC was published in the year 2016–17 and the latest *Crime in India* report released by the NCRB was for the period 2016. The most recent statistical report on custodial violence is that of the NCRB for 2013. The data given in this chapter are based on the latest five-year statistics from both the agencies. This has been presented in the form of figures given in the appendix to this chapter.

With reference to custodial deaths in India, the NHRC reported 16,836 incidents of this crime, which included 2,207 deaths in police custody and 14,629 deaths in judicial custody during the period 1994–2010. The NHRC, during 2007–8, reported a record number of custodial deaths—1,977 such incidents occurred, including 188 in police custody and 1,789 in judicial custody. The data presented in the annual reports of the NHRC for 1994–2010 showed an upward trend, barring a few years in which there was a significant drop in incidents of custodial deaths reported. The trend showed that the highest increase in the reporting of custodial deaths was between 2006–7 and 2007–8—an increase by almost 400 deaths. Likewise, the period 2002–3 showed a significant increase of around 270 custodial deaths as compared to the previous reporting year. Similarly, in 2005–6, there was a huge increase by nearly 240 deaths compared to the previous year (Figure 5A.1).

As per the reports of the NHRC for 2005–10, out of the 9,484 custodial deaths reported, 878 cases were encounter deaths (nearly 9 per cent of the total reported deaths in custody). The report of 2006–7 mentioned 301 encounter deaths. It is the highest number of encounter deaths reported in India. During this five-year period, there were 37 instances of custodial rapes, which were reported by the NHRC. Encounter deaths, however, have showed a negative trend from 2006 to 2010 (Figure 5A.2).

Besides cases of custodial deaths, illegal detention, and related violence by the police in India, the NHRC provides information on the general conditions of prisons in India. With regard to cases of violation disposed by the NHRC during 2005–10, a total of 1,685 complaints about poor conditions in prisons were disposed of, including 703 cases of harassment, 210 cases of lack of medical facilities, and 772 cases relating to poor conditions in prisons (Figure 5A.3).

Though the NHRC provides data on custodial deaths, it does not provide data with regard to actual reporting of cases of disappearance, illegal arrests and unlawful detention, custodial violence, false implications by the police, and breach of law by the police. However, it provides data on the year-wise disposal of such cases, which is used in this chapter to reflect on the trend. The reports of the NHRC mention 2,379 cases of illegal arrest, 4,217 cases of unlawful detention, and 126 cases of disappearance during 2005–10. The reports provide worrying information about an upward trend with reference to cases such as disappearance, illegal arrest, unlawful detention, and custodial violence, with 2008–9 being an exception. The trend is just the opposite in cases of false implication, unlawful omissions, and so on. Hence, this shows that the NHRC is increasingly handling more cases and more serious cases, a trend that seems to be on the rise. The reports also highlight that cases of illegal arrests and detention constitute one-fifth of the total number of cases reported (Figure 5A.4).

In 2013, 133 cases of deaths in police custody were reported, which included 21 deaths in police remand, 97 deaths while not in police remand, and 15 deaths while in transit to the court. During 2009–13, a total of 569 deaths in police custody were reported, including 138 during police remand, 347 without police remand, and 84 while in transit to court. The trend shows a decrease in custodial deaths in police remand but an upward trend in custodial deaths without being in police remand and during transit to courts. The deaths in police custody while not in police remand and during transit show that deaths occurred either in illegal custody or within 24 hours of arrest or at least within a very short span from the time of arrest. This trend is on the rise as observed from these reports and is definitely an area of concern (Figure 5A.5).

With regard to the actions taken for such incidents of custodial deaths, it was reported that out of 569 cases of death in police custody in the period 2009–13, a magisterial enquiry was conducted for only 270 cases, which accounts for less than 50 per cent of the total cases, while a judicial enquiry was conducted in just 170 cases, which is less than 30 per cent of the total cases. A formal case was registered only in 294 cases, which is more than 50 per cent of the total cases, out of which charge sheets were filed only in 65 cases, that is, in around 12 per cent of the total incidents and more than 20 per cent of the registered cases. Conviction was secured only in eight cases, which amounts to less than 1.5 per cent of the total incidents, less than 3 per cent of the registered cases, and around 12 per cent of the charge sheets filed (Figure 5A.5).

As per the reports of the NCRB, 283,559 complaints of abuse and violation of human rights by the police were registered during the period of 2009–13. Of these, departmental enquiries were initiated in around one lakh complaints, magisterial enquiries conducted in only 1,818 complaints, and judicial enquiries completed in 1,902 complaints (Figure 5A.7). Out of the total registered complaints of human rights abuse by the police during 2009–13, 145,539 complaints or more than half of the total complaints were rejected, whereas administrative action was initiated in 40,603 cases (7 per cent) and charge sheets were filed or trial initiated in only 5,030 cases (less than 2 per cent).

In all the complaints reported by the NCRB, cases against 6,012 police personnel were sent for trial. Out of this, cases against 1,793 police personnel were withdrawn, 238 persons were convicted, and 860 persons were acquitted, while the remaining cases are still pending in courts (Figure 5A.8).

Administrative actions were initiated against 131,205 police personnel involved in the aforementioned cases of human rights violation. Out of these, cases against 32,810 police personnel were withdrawn, 3,338 police personnel were dismissed from service, and 97,268 personnel were given other disciplinary punishments (Figure 5A.9).

Parliamentary Laws

Based on international conventions and treaties, India too has enacted/ amended laws for the protection of human rights at the domestic level.

India also has obligations to attend and recommend in the Universal
Periodic Review (UPR) sessions hosted by the United Nations Human
Rights Council (UNHRC) towards this objective. The UNHRC hosts
its UPR sessions, organized by the UPR working group, once in every
four years. The first UPR session was held in 2008. In 2017, India submitted its report, which included its commitment to and fulfilment of
its human rights obligations, and its responses on AFSPA, and repeated
instances of custodial violence and sexual assault. In the previous
UPR (2008–12) as well as in the latest UPR (2013–16), questions/
recommendations were put forth by the member nations to ratify CAT,
which India is yet to do. Between 2012 and 2017, there have been
more than 300 cases of custodial deaths as recorded by the NCRB.[36]
In the report of 2015, NCRB recorded 97 custodial deaths and most
deaths were a result of physical assault by the police in police remand
and without judicial custody. It is still to be seen when India ratifies
CAT and adheres to the protection of human rights and reduces such
violence and torture by the police.

The following are some acts that have been enacted in the country
towards protection of human rights and protection against any kind
of violence.

The Unlawful Activities (Prevention) Act, 1967

The UAPA was enacted by the Government of India so as to enable
efficient deterrence of unlawful activities and associations[37] and terrorist activities.[38] It has been made applicable throughout India, including
Jammu and Kashmir,[39] and came into effect on 30 December 1967, though
it became effective in Jammu and Kashmir only on 1 September 1969.[40]

---

[36] Devirupa Mitra. 2017. 'Indian Comes in the Line of Fire at UNHRC over
Rights Record, Racism'. Available at https://thewire.in/diplomacy/india-unhrc-
universal-periodic-review, accessed on 7 April 2019.

[37] UAPA (Amendment) 2008, Preamble.

[38] UAPA (Amendment) 2004, sec. 2.

[39] UAPA (Amendment) 2004, sec. 1(2).

[40] Notification No. G.S.R. 2098, 30 August 1969, Gazette of India
(Extraordinary), Part II, Section 3(i), p. 615.

The UAPA enables the exercise of extra-territorial jurisdiction in case of non-citizens or foreigners so as to include all persons/individuals who are involved in crimes that are punishable under the POTA 2002 even outside the territory of India. It further enables the criminal justice system of India to book, prosecute, try, and punish all such foreigners or alien offenders just like in case of any terrorist activity that has taken place in Indian territory.[41] The UAPA extends to all citizens of India including those who live outside the country in a foreign jurisdiction. It also includes government servants within and outside the country as well as persons on board ships and air carriers with Indian registration irrespective of their territory of operation at the time of the commission of any such crime as defined under the UAPA.[42]

'Unlawful activities' as per the UAPA are defined as any such activity which is carried out by a person or an organization, covering physical acts; oral or written expression; or expression through signage or visible representation, with an intention to or for support and promotion of a claim to cede or secede a portion of Indian territory or incites anyone for the same; or renunciation, objection, disruption of the sovereignty and territorial integrity of India.[43] Similarly, 'unlawful association' is defined as an organization, which has been set up with an objective to carry out unlawful activities or promote animosity between groups under sec. 153A of IPC or causing imputation or assertion harmful for national integration under sec. 153B of IPC or either directly or through its members or by promoting or supporting others.[44] The UAPA also provides power to the Government of India to declare and notify such organizations as unlawful association, but it is subject to confirmation by the tribunal.[45] In doing so, a reference should be made within a period of 30 days from the date of the notification and such notification must be approved or denied within six months by the

---

[41] UAPA (Amendment) 2004, sec. 1(4).

[42] UAPA (Amendment) 2004, sec. 4; UAPA 1967, secs 1(5)(a), 1(5)(b), 1(5)(c).

[43] UAPA 1967, sec. 2(o).

[44] UAPA 1967, sec. 2(p).

[45] UAPA 1967, sec. 3(3).

tribunal,[46] which is constituted as the Unlawful Activities (Prevention) Tribunal by the government.[47] The notification shall be operative up to expiry of two years (substituted by sec. 3 of Act 3 of 2013 for 'two years', with effect from 1 February 2013) unless de-notified suo moto by the central government or on the basis of an application by the aggrieved party.[48]

The UAPA also grants further powers to the central government for prohibiting utilization of funds of such associations, including payment, delivery, or transfer of funds, by a person having charge of such fund including money, securities, or credits, which is used or meant for carrying out activities of the unlawful association, subject to challenge by the aggrieved person before a district judge within a period of 15 days.[49] The central government may further declare and notify any place, including a house or building, a part of a house or building, or a tent or vessel, which is being used by such an association. The DM concerned or any authorized officer is required to prepare a list, in presence of two witnesses, of the entire movable properties found on the premise. He/she may further issue orders for (a) imposing conditions on use of such articles; (b) prohibiting use in case if he/she believes that such materials are likely to be used for the purposes of such an organization; and (c) prohibiting entry or use of the premise by persons other than a regular inhabitant of such a premise, without his/her permission. Anyone who enters, visits, or tries to enter or visit such a premise can be subjected to search and detention for searching by a sub-inspector, superior police officer, or any other authorized person or by a female officer in the case of a woman. Any unauthorized person visiting the premise is liable to be removed. The notification can be questioned before a district judge within a period of 30 days.[50] The offences and penalties as enforced by the UAPA are presented in Table 5.2.

---

[46] UAPA 1967, secs 4(1), 4(2), 4(3).
[47] UAPA 1967, sec. 5(1).
[48] UAPA 1967, sec. 6.
[49] UAPA 1967, sec. 7.
[50] UAPA 1967, sec. 8.

Table 5.2 Offences and Penalty under the UAPA

Offence	Punishment
Membership of an unlawful association Giving support to an unlawful association Participation in meetings of an unlawful association Contributing, receiving, or raising funds for an unlawful association	2-year imprisonment and fine*
Dealing in, payment, delivery, or transfer of money, securities, or credits with respect to the prohibited funds of an unlawful association	3-year imprisonment and/or fine@
Violation of prohibitory order in relation to a notified premise and its property Willful entry or attempt to enter premise subjected to prohibitory order	1-year imprisonment and fine#
Commission, participation in commission, advocating, abetment, advise, or incitement of unlawful activities	7-year imprisonment and fine$
Assistance in unlawful activities of an unlawful association	5-year imprisonment or/and fine**
Terrorist Act	
Causing death	Death or life imprisonment with fine@@
Causing injury, loss to property, etc.	5-year to life imprisonment with fine##
Conspiracy, attempt, advocating, abetment, advise, aid, or facilitate with knowledge in commission or preparation	5-year to life imprisonment with fine$$
Harbour or conceal or attempt to harbour or conceal terrorists	5-year to life imprisonment with fine***
Membership of terrorist outfit involved in terrorist activities	5-year to life term imprisonment with fine@@@
Holding or acquisition of property from the proceeds of terrorist activities	5-year to life imprisonment with fine###
Demanding of radioactive substance and device	10-year imprisonment with fine$$$
Organizing terrorist camps	5- to 10-year imprisonment with fine****

(Cont'd)

Table 5.2 (*Cont'd*)

Offence	Punishment
Giving training to terrorists	5- to 10-year imprisonment with fine[@@@@]
Enhanced punishment[####]	
Willful aid to person involved in terrorist or disruptive activities in contravention of the acts and rules made under Arms Act, 1959; the Explosives Act, 1884; the Explosive Substances Act, 1908; or the Inflammable Substances Act, 1952	5-year to life imprisonment with fine
Attempts, abets, aids, attempts to abet, or preparation to do any act in contravention of the aforementioned acts and rules	5- to 10-year imprisonment with fine[$$$$]

Source: UAPA (including the amendments of 2004 and 2008).
Notes: *UAPA, (Amendment) 2004, sec. 6.
[@]UAPA 1967, sec. 11.
[#]UAPA 1967, sec. 12.
[$]UAPA 1967, sec. 13.
[**]UAPA 1967, sec. 13.
[@@]UAPA (Amendment) 2004, sec. 7.
[##]UAPA (Amendment) 2004, sec. 7.
[$$]UAPA (Amendment) 2004, sec. 7; UAPA (Amendment), 2008, sec. 7 (for including 'incites or knowingly facilitates').
[***]UAPA (Amendment) 2004, sec. 7.
[@@@]UAPA (Amendment) 2004, sec. 7.
[###]UAPA (Amendment) 2004, sec. 7.
[$$$]UAPA (Amendment) 2008, sec. 5.
[****]UAPA (Amendment) 2008, sec. 8.
[@@@@]UAPA (Amendment) 2008, sec. 8.
[####]UAPA (Amendment) 2004, sec. 23(1).
[$$$$]UAPA (Amendment) 2004, sec. 23(2).

Bar on Exercise of Jurisdiction in Any Suit, Application, Appeal, Revision, or Injunction and Prosecution under the UAPA

Under the UAPA, the central government or the DM or any authorized officer should be subjected to any proceeding including any suit, application, appeal, or revision in any court, and any action taken in exercise of powers provided by this act is not subjected to injunction.[51] Further, only a court with prior sanction of the central government can take cognisance of any offence punishable under this act.[52]

The UAPA was amended soon after the repeal of POTA and most of the provisions of POTA were incorporated in this act in its original form or with slight modifications. These included, for example, addition of a completely new chapter on definitions, covering definitions such as 'proceeds of terrorism',[53] 'designated authority',[54] 'property',[55] and 'terrorist gang'.[56] In the amendment, the most controversial provisions, which were related to admissibility of confessions before a police officer, presumption of guilt, guidelines for arrest, crime of abuse or malicious use of power by police, bar on bail and anticipatory bail, compensation to victim of abuse of power, and the chapter on interception, were removed from the act.

The definition and punishment for the crime of 'terrorist act' as defined under the Terrorist and Disruptive Activities (Prevention) Act (TADA) and POTA were adopted in the UAPA (Amendment) 2004, according to which, any member of an unlawful organization who willfully aids or promotes the goals of such an association; possesses any unlicensed firearms, ammunition, explosives, device, or substance capable of causing mass destruction; and commits any act causing death, serious injury, or massive property loss or damage is liable for death penalty or life term with fine when such an act causes death or shall be punished with five years imprisonment, which can extend up to life imprisonment in all other circumstances.[57] The UAPA further incorporated POTA's definition of 'terrorist act'[58] and prescribed the

---

[51] UAPA 1967, sec. 47.

[52] UAPA (Amendment) 2008, sec. 45(1). (Originally sec. 45 of UAPA 1967).

[53] UAPA (Amendment) 2004, Sec. 4(2)(g).

[54] UAPA (Amendment) 2004, sec. 4(2)(e).

[55] UAPA (Amendment) 2004, sec. 4(2)(h).

[56] UAPA (Amendment) 2004, sec. 4(2)(l).

[57] UAPA (Amendment) 2004, sec. 6; UAPA 1967, sec. 10(b).

[58] UAPA (Amendment) 2004, sec. 7.

same punishment,[59] and the provisions related to punishment for membership of a terrorist organization;[60] raising funds;[61] conspiracy, attempts, advocate, abetment, advising or incitement;[62] harbouring;[63] holding the proceeds of terrorism;[64] threat to witness;[65] enhanced penalty;[66] the chapters on procedure for forfeiture and attachment of proceeds of terrorism;[67] and on terrorist organization including notification and de-notification,[68] and so on.

In 2008, the UAPA was once again amended, during which a new offence was added, viz., making demands of radioactive substances, nuclear devices, and so on, which is punishable with a maximum of 10 years imprisonment along with fine, and accordingly, any willful use of force or threat to require any explosive including bombs, dynamites, flammable materials, arms and weapons, or deadly substances such as fire arms, lethal weapons, and chemical, biological, radiological, or nuclear material or devices in order to aid, abet, or commit a terrorist act.[69] Further, two more new offences were added, which are, 'organizing terrorist camps' and 'recruiting terrorists'. Therefore, anyone organizing training camp(s) for giving training to terrorists shall attract criminal liability with an imprisonment of 5–10 years with fine.[70] Moreover, any person recruiting or facilitating recruitment of terrorists shall be held criminally liable and punished with imprisonment of 5–10 years and fine.[71] This also expanded the scope of offences of

---

[59] UAPA (Amendment) 2004, sec. 7.
[60] UAPA (Amendment) 2004, sec. 7.
[61] UAPA (Amendment) 2004, sec. 7.
[62] UAPA (Amendment) 2004, sec. 7.
[63] UAPA (Amendment) 2004, sec. 7.
[64] UAPA (Amendment) 2004, sec. 7.
[65] UAPA (Amendment) 2004, sec. 7.
[66] UAPA (Amendment) 2004, sec. 7.
[67] UAPA (Amendment) 2004, chapter V.
[68] UAPA (Amendment) 2004, chapter VI.
[69] UAPA (Amendment) 2008, sec. 5.
[70] UAPA (Amendment) 2008, sec. 8.
[71] UAPA (Amendment) 2008, sec. 8.

fundraising for terrorist organizations by covering fundraising within and outside India.[72]

Further, the provisions related to bar on bail, anticipatory bail, and presumption of guilt were incorporated in the UAPA (Amendment) 2008.[73] However, POTA provisions related to admissibility of confession before a police officer, guidelines of arrest and crime, penalty for abuse or malicious use of power, and compensation to victims of abuse of power were not included.

In 2011, the Ministry of Home Affairs, Government of India, proposed some more changes to the UAPA and introduced the Unlawful Activities (Prevention) Bill, 2011 (the UAP Bill), but the bill has not yet been passed. The most striking features of the proposed UAP Bill are as follows:

a. To increase the period of operation of notification of an unlawful association from two to five years[74]
b. To treat threat to economic security as a terrorist act and hence a punishable offence[75]
c. To make societies or trusts criminally liable[76] through some unique provisions and to prescribe the most severe punishment under the UAPA with prison term of seven years, which can be extended to life and a fine of INR 5–10 crore[77]

It is worth highlighting that the third provision makes for the severest criminal responsibility under the UAPA since the current provisions do not prescribe any fine limits in all other offences and the minimum

---

[72] UAPA (Amendment) 2008, sec. 6.

[73] UAPA (Amendment) 2008, sec. 12.

[74] UAP Bill (Bill No. 38 of 2011) (Amendment introduced to sec. 6 of UAPA), sec. 3.

[75] UAP Bill (Bill No. 38 of 2011) (Amendment introduced to sec. 15 of UAPA), sec. 4.

[76] UAP Bill (Bill No. 38 of 2011) (Amendment inserted a new sec. 22B in UAPA), sec. 7.

[77] UAP Bill (Bill No. 38 of 2011) (Amendment inserted a new sec. 22C in UAPA), sec. 7.

punishment prescribed is five years even for the offence of causing
death due to a terrorist act.

In July 2019, the Ministry of Home Affairs, Government of India,
introduced the Unlawful Activities (Prevention) Bill, 2019 which was
passed by both the Houses of Parliament and recently received the
assent of the President. It amended and inserted the following in the
original act:

a. Section 25 of the principal act was amended and the new
   amendment included the National Investigation Agency (the
   NIA) Officers the power to investigate cases related to terrorist
   activities and organizations and also to search and/or seize the
   properties which may be connected with terrorist or terrorist
   activities.[78]
b. Section 43 of the principal act was amended by insertion of a new
   clause (ba) after sec. 43B stating that the NIA investigating officer
   should not be below the rank of Inspector.[79]

The Protection of Human Rights Act

The PHRA is a parliamentary law which came into force on
28 September 1993 and is applicable to whole of India including the
state of Jammu and Kashmir, relating to matters in the Lists I and III of
the Seventh Schedule of the CoI, that is, except matters enumerated
in the State List.[80] This act was enacted to constitute the NHRC, State
Human Rights Commissions (SHRCs), and Human Rights Courts.[81]

The PHRA was one of the first laws in India that recognized the
human rights guaranteed under international covenants. It defined
'human rights' as the individual right to life, liberty, equality, and dignity as protected by the CoI and included in Part III of the Constitution.
These rights have been made enforceable as per the rights guaranteed

---

[78] UAPA (Amendment) 2019, sec. 3.
[79] UAPA (Amendment) 2019, sec. 8.
[80] PHRA 1993, sec. 1.
[81] PHRA 1993, Preamble.

by international covenants,[82] but it restricted the territory of its application by further defining 'international covenants'. Thus for the efficiency and success of the PHRA, it included international covenants such as the ICCPR the International Covenant on Social, Economic and Cultural Rights (ICSECR), and other UN covenants and conventions notified by the central government.[83] This further helped the PHRA in securing the human rights of all individuals of the country by including the rights guaranteed by the aforementioned international covenants as human rights, including the right to protection against torture and other inhuman and degrading punishments guaranteed by the ICCPR besides the fundamental rights that are already guaranteed by the CoI.[84]

The PHRA is the statute under which the NHRC[85] and SHRCs[86] were set up for acting as the grievance redress quasi-judicial bodies and promoters of human rights, and for conducting human rights literacy programmes and research in the field of human rights and national and international policy. The NHRC and SHRCs are bound to perform functions specifically with regard to conducting enquiry into complaints of violation of human rights and failure or negligence of public officers to protect human rights; interventions in the proceedings of courts in cases involving violation of human rights; visiting and reviewing the condition of inmates in institutions like jails and other detention facilities and recommending steps for improvement; reviewing constitutional safeguards and recommending measures for their proper implementation; and reviewing factors such as terrorism and responsible curtailment of enjoyment of human rights and recommending suitable remedial steps.[87] However, the NHRC also has some limitations as prescribed by the PHRA in terms of its jurisdiction in cases that involve acts of violation of human rights by the armed

---

[82] PHRA 1993, sec. 2(d).
[83] PHRA 1993, sec. 2(f).
[84] PHRA 1993, sec. 2(f).
[85] PHRA 1993, sec. 3.
[86] PHRA 1993, sec. 21.
[87] PHRA 1993, secs 12 and 29.

forces.[88] Nevertheless, the NHRC and SHRCs have powers of a civil court under the CPC with reference to the enquiry of complaints for the purposes of summoning witnesses, discovery and production of documents, receipt of evidence on affidavit, requisition of public records, and examination of witnesses.[89] The NHRC and SHRCs are also empowered to investigate,[90] and as per the provisions of the PHRA, they can constitute special courts at the district-level special courts[91] and appoint special public prosecutors (PP)[92] for speedy and efficient trial of offences related to the violation of human rights.

The Terrorist and Disruptive Activities (Prevention) Act, 1987

The 1987 act superseded the Terrorist and Disruptive Activities (Prevention) Ordinance 1987,[93] and it was in force for eight years for the abetment of terrorist and disruptive activities and to provide for separate means for prosecution and criminal administration. It was extended to the whole of India including the state of Jammu and Kashmir, and it covered every citizen of India including those who lived outside India in foreign jurisdiction, government servants within and outside India, and persons on board ships and air carriers with an Indian registration, irrespective of their territory of operation at the time of the commission of any crime under TADA.[94] The act had set an automatic timeline for its expiry, that is, eight years from its date of implementation, thus covering the period from 24 May 1987 to 24 May 1995. However, any investigation, legal proceeding, or remedy would remain effective even after its expiry.[95] TADA included many

---

[88] PHRA 1993, sec. 19.

[89] PHRA 1993, secs 13 and 29.

[90] PHRA 1993, secs 14 and 29.

[91] PHRA 1993, sec. 30.

[92] PHRA 1993, sec. 31.

[93] TADA 1987, sec. 30.

[94] TADA 1987, sec. 2.

[95] TADA 1987, sec. 1(4).

new offences with stringent punishments and also constituted designated courts[96] called TADA courts for trying the cases registered
under the act. It had a provision for the transfer of cases to any other
competent TADA court within or outside the state[97] and it entrusted
TADA courts with the power to try matters involving offences in
addition to those under TADA.[98] The act included provisions in the
form of stricter procedures and lower standards of evidence and
proof. The TADA courts were equivalent to sessions courts and were
authorized to take direct cognisance of cases without committal and
to hold summary trial where offences were punishable with imprisonment only up to three years.[99] Public prosecutors and additional
public prosecutors (APPs) were appointed especially for prosecuting
TADA cases.[100]

Definition of Terrorist Act and Disruptive Activities   The definition of
a 'terrorist act'[101] and 'disruptive activities'[102] under this act prescribes
punishment for commission, attempt, abetment, and conspiracy to
commit such activities. An act would be considered as a terrorist act or
an act of terrorism when

1. the act is done with an intention to overawe the Government of
   India or to strike terror on the population or a section of the population or to alienate the population or a section of the population
   or to badly affect the existing harmony amongst diverse groups;
2. the act is accomplished by the use of explosives such as bombs and
   dynamite, inflammable matter, deadly weapons, poison, noxious
   gases, and chemicals or hazardous matter including biological
   substances;

---

[96] TADA 1987, sec. 9.
[97] TADA 1987, sec. 11(2).
[98] TADA 1987, sec. 12.
[99] TADA 1987, sec. 14.
[100] TADA 1987, sec. 13.
[101] TADA 1987, sec. 2(h).
[102] TADA 1987, sec. 2(d).

3. the act is committed in a manner that it results or is likely to result in loss of human life or injury; loss, damage, or destruction of property; disruption of supplies or essential services; or

4. the act involves taking hostages and threatening to kill or harm such hostages for compelling the government or anyone to fulfil a demand.[103]

Likewise, any activity would be considered as a 'disruptive activity' when any conduct such as an act, speech, use of media or any other means is done

1. to question or disrupt or with an intention to disrupt the sovereignty or territorial integrity of India;

2. with an intention to claim or support cession (that is, admittance of any foreign territory or part of territory in India) or secession (that is, claim of withdrawal of a territory from India); or

3. to advocate, advise, suggest, incite, predict prophesy, pronounce, or express in order to incite, advise, suggest, or prompt murder or assassination of persons bound by oath to protect the sovereignty or integrity of India or any public servant.[104]

Offences and Punishment   The provisions of TADA included various offences as defined under the heads of terrorist act and disruptive activities and also prescribed different punishments according to the nature of offence mentioned in the act. The details of offences along with their punishment are provided in Table 5.3.

Powers of Investigating Officers to Seize or Attach Certain Property   The TADA provides certain extraordinary powers to investigating officers (IOs) that empower them to order seizure or attachment of such property that, based on reasonable belief, is possessed or acquired from the proceeds of the terrorist or disruptive activities being investigated. This has to be done with prior approval of the SP concerned. The

---

[103] TADA 1987, sec. 3(1).
[104] TADA 1987, sec. 4, clauses (2) and (3).

Table 5.3 Offences and Punishment under TADA

Offence	Punishment
Terrorist Act*	
Causing death	Death or life term with fine
Causing injury, loss to property, etc.	Five years to life term with fine
Conspiracy, attempt, advocating, abetment, advise, aid, or facilitate with knowledge in commission or preparation	Five years to life term with fine
Harbour or conceal or attempt to harbour or conceal terrorists	Five years to life term with fine
Membership of terrorist outfit involved in terrorist activities	Five years to life term with fine
Holding or acquisition of property from the proceeds of terrorist activities	Five years to life term with fine
Disruptive Activities@	
Conspiracy, attempt, advocating, abetment, advise, aid, or facilitate with knowledge in commission or preparation	Five years to life term with fine
Harbour or conceal or attempt to harbour or conceal persons involved in disruptive activities	Five years to life term with fine
Other Offences	
Possession of unauthorized arms and ammunition listed in Columns 2 & 3, Categories I & III (a), Schedule I of the Arms Rules, 1962, or explosives, e.g., bombs and dynamite in specified areas$	Five years to life term with fine
Violation of TADA court's direction to protect witnesses**	One year to life term and/or fine
Enhanced Punishment@@	
Willful aid to a person involved in terrorist or disruptive activities in contravention of the acts and rules made under the Arms Act, 1959; the Explosives Act, 1884; the Explosive Substances Act, 1908; or the Inflammable Substances Act, 1952	Five years to life term with fine
Attempt, abets, aid, attempt to abet, or preparation to do any act in contravention of aforementioned acts and rules	5–10 years' term with fine

Source: TADA 1987. Available at https://www.satp.org/satporgtp/countries/india/document/actandordinances/Tada.htm#12 (accessed on 3 August 2019).
Notes: *TADA 1987, sec. 3, clauses (2), (3), (4), (5), and (6).
@TADA 1987, sec. 4, clauses (1) and (4).
$TADA 1987, sec. 5.
**TADA 1987, sec. 16.
@@TADA 1987, sec. 6.

IO should then inform the TADA court about such seizure or attachment within 48 hours for its confirmation or cancellation.[105]

Forfeiture of Property by the TADA Court   Under the provisions of TADA, the TADA court can order forfeiture of property of the accused on conviction or can order during trial attachment of property. On the written request of the police, the TADA court can also issue and publish a proclamation demanding a suspect hiding or absconding from police to avoid his/her arrest or apprehension to appear before the TADA court within a specified time, from a minimum of 15 days and up to 30 days, and at a specified place. The TADA court can further order attachment of the accused's property.[106]

Admissibility of Confessions Made before a Police Officer   The inadmissibility of confession clause of the Indian Evidence Act is superseded by TADA in its provision of admissibility of confession made before the police in the court of law. As per this provision, a confession made before a SP or a senior police officer, and recorded in writing, audio or audio-visual form, is admissible in the trial of the accused or in the trial of the co-accused, abettor, or conspirator. It is the duty of the police officer concerned to ensure that the confession is made voluntarily and to explain to the accused that he/she is not bound to make such incriminatory confessions and its effect on his/her case.[107]

Presumption of Guilt   Under the provisions of TADA, there is a non-rebuttable presumption for the commission of a terrorist act, according to which such persons will be considered guilty of committing an act of terrorism under TADA, provided the following conditions are fulfilled:

1. Arms, explosives, or any other substance is recovered from the possession of the person(s) accused of an offence under TADA and there is a reason to believe that these things are meant to be used for terrorist activities.

[105] TADA 1987, sec. 7A.
[106] TADA 1987, sec. 8.
[107] TADA 1987, sec. 15.

2. Expert evidence confirms recovery of fingerprint(s) of the accused from the crime scene or from the objects used in the crime such as vehicle, ammunition, and arms.[108]

Relevance of Photo Identification and Preclusion of Identification Parade in Certain Circumstances   According to the provisions of TADA, there is an extraordinary and different treatment for the identification of a declared proclaimed offender and the procedure for the identification of such an accused person is further relaxed. Accordingly, TADA treats photo identification at par with the procedure of identification parade.[109]

Bar on Anticipatory Bail and Condition for Grant of Regular Bail   Under TADA, the grant of anticipatory bail as provided under sec. 438 of the CrPC is completely barred.[110] The act has very stringent provisions to discourage bail by making it subject to the fulfillment of mandatory conditions such as affording the PP an opportunity to oppose the bail and TADA court's objective of satisfaction about innocence of the accused or possible apprehension about commission of any offence whilst on bail.[111] The bail cannot be granted unless these conditions are fully adhered to.

Witness Protection and Non-disclosure of Identity of Witnesses   There is a detailed mechanism for ensuring the witness protection under TADA. Hence, a TADA court is empowered to order a camera trial; it can take steps, on its own motion or on the request of witnesses or the PP to protect the identity of the witnesses and addresses including the place of proceedings and exclude names and addresses of the witnesses in the TADA court order or other records; it can issue suitable directives to the persons or authority concerned for protecting and not disclosing the identity and addresses of the witnesses; and

---

[108] TADA 1987, sec. 21.
[109] TADA 1987, sec. 22.
[110] TADA 1987, sec. 20(7).
[111] TADA 1987, sec. 20(8).

it can even bar the media from reporting on the case. Further, anyone violating these directions would attract criminal liability of maximum imprisonment of one year and fine up to Rs 1,000.[112]

The Prevention of Terrorism Act, 2002

Although POTA was repealed by a presidential ordinance[113] and later by the Prevention of Terrorism (Repeal) Act, 2004 (POTA 2004)[114] on 21 September 2004[115] by replacing and superseding the ordinance,[116] this does not affect any investigation, legal proceedings, or remedy, and all of these would remain effective even afterwards.[117] Further, it did not repeal the provision related to the POTA Review Committee under Section 60 of the POTA and rather amended it by incorporating a mandatory duty for the POTA Review Committee to review all the cases that are registered under POTA and to assess the maintainability of POTA charges within a period of one year. During review, if the POTA Review Committee finds the POTA charges untenable or weak, the cases stand withdrawn from the POTA courts or any such investigation stands closed.[118] The POTA courts cannot take cognisance of any POTA matter after the expiry of one year.[119]

Just like TADA, POTA too identified and listed offences related to 'terrorist act' with stringent punishments; constituted special courts[120] called POTA courts, specifically for trying cases under POTA; and provided the provision for transfer of cases to any other competent POTA court within or outside the state.[121] It has also given powers to the POTA courts to try matters involving other offences in addition

---

[112] TADA 1987, sec. 16.
[113] The Prevention of Terrorism (Repeal) Ordinance, 2004.
[114] POTA 2004, sec. 2(1).
[115] POTA 2004, sec. 1(2).
[116] POTA 2004, sec. 3(1).
[117] POTA 2004, sec. 2(2).
[118] POTA 2004, sec. 2(3).
[119] POTA 2004, Proviso to sec. 2(2)(d).
[120] POTA, sec. 23.
[121] POTA, sec. 25.

to those under POTA.[122] But unlike TADA, new provisions have been incorporated related to the notification and ban of terrorist groups, and the interception of and punishment to public officers for abuse or malicious use of powers.

Like TADA, POTA is also applicable throughout India including the state of Jammu and Kashmir and covers all citizens of India including those who live outside India in foreign jurisdictions, government servants within and outside India, and persons on board ships and air carriers with Indian registration irrespective of their territory of operation at the time of the commission of any crime under POTA. It also set an automatic timeline for its expiry, which is three years from the day of its implementation (thus being effective from 24 October 2001 to 24 October 2004). However, any investigation, legal proceeding, or remedy would remain effective even after the completion of its term.[123] Unlike TADA, POTA was enacted for enabling extra-territorial jurisdiction in the case of non-citizens so as to include all persons who are involved in the commission of crimes that are punishable under the act. POTA also enabled the criminal justice system of the country to book, prosecute, try, and punish all such foreign offenders in the same way as in acts of terrorism that took place within Indian territory.[124]

A POTA court constituted under the act is considered equivalent to a sessions court and is authorized to take direct cognisance of cases without committal and can also hold summary trials where offences are punishable with imprisonment of only up to three years.[125] PPs and APP are appointed especially for prosecuting POTA cases.[126]

The POTA combined both the definitions and crimes of terrorist and disruptive activities as defined under the TADA and provided a single comprehensive and broad definition of terrorist acts.[127] As per the POTA, the definition of terrorist act is to a large extent similar to

---

[122] POTA, sec. 26.
[123] POTA, sec. 1.
[124] POTA, sec. 1(4).
[125] POTA, sec. 29.
[126] POTA, sec. 28.
[127] POTA, sec. 2(g) and 3(1).

the definitions given under TADA except the addition of a few new expressions and the inclusion of new offences. For example, the POTA includes destruction of any property or equipment used or intended to be used for defence of India or any other purpose of the union, state, and government agency of India.[128] Further, membership of any terrorist group declared unlawful under the UAPA, 1967, or involved in performing activities, aiding, or promoting activities or the vision and mission of such an organization; and possessing any unlicensed firearms, ammunition, explosives, device, or substance capable of causing mass destruction and commission of any act causing death, serious injury, or massive property loss or damage is considered to be a terrorist act under POTA. Raising funds for the purpose of terrorist activities is also covered by this definition.[129]

Like the TADA, the POTA also deals with the offence of 'terrorist acts' and, accordingly, prescribes same punishment for terrorist acts causing death, injury, loss to property, and so on, and conspiracy, attempt, advocating, abetment, advise, aid, or facilitate with knowledge in commission or preparation. However, it provides different punishments for rest of the offences. Further, the POTA creates a new offence, which is, 'threat to witnesses', which means that if any person threatens witness(es) or any person interested in such witness(es) by using violence, wrongful restraint, or illegal confinement, he/she shall be liable for a maximum punishment of three years imprisonment and a fine.[130] Table 5.4 lists all the offences and the corresponding punishment as prescribed under POTA.

Prohibition on Holding Proceeds of Terrorism and Its Forfeiture   The POTA prohibits the holding or possession of any proceeds of terrorism,[131] which includes properties derived or acquired from any terrorist act or through funds related to terrorist acts including

---

[128] POTA, sec. 3(1)(a).
[129] POTA, sec. 3(1)(b).
[130] POTA, sec. 3(7).
[131] POTA, sec. 6(1).

Table 5.4   Offences and Punishment under POTA

Offence	Punishment
Terrorist Act*	
Causing death	Same as TADA
Causing injury, loss to property, etc.	Same as TADA
Conspiracy, attempt, advocating, abetment, advise, aid, or facilitate with knowledge in commission or preparation	Same as TADA
Harbour or conceal or attempt to harbour or conceal terrorists (except wife/husband)	Three years to life term in prison with fine
Membership to terrorist outfit involved in terrorist activities	Life term imprisonment and/or fine up to Rs 100,000
Holding or acquisition of property from the proceeds of terrorist activities	Life term imprisonment and/or fine up to Rs 100,000
Threat to witnesses by use of violence, wrongful restraint, or illegal confinement	Three years' prison term and fine
Other Offences	
Possession of unauthorized arms and ammunition listed in Columns 2 & 3, Categories I & III (a), Schedule I of the Arms Rules, 1962, or explosives, e.g., bombs and dynamite in specified areas@	Life term imprisonment and/or fine up to Rs 100,000
Violation of POTA court's direction to protect witnesses	Same as POTA
Failure to provide or denial of information to IO#	Three years' prison term and/or fine
Membership of a terrorist organization$	10 years' prison term and/or fine
Giving support to a terrorist organization**	10 years' prison term and/or fine
Raising funds for a terrorist organization@@	10 years' prison term and/or fine
Malicious use of power by police officer##	Two years' prison term and/or fine
Enhanced Punishment$$	
Willful aid to a person involved in terrorist or disruptive activities in contravention of the acts and rules made under the Arms Act, 1959; the Explosives Act 1884; the Explosive Substances Act, 1908; or the Inflammable Substances Act, 1952	Life term imprisonment and fine

(Cont'd)

Table 5.4   (*Cont'd*)

Offence	Punishment
Attempt, abetment, aid, attempt to abet, or preparation to do any act in contravention of the aforementioned acts and rules	10 years' prison term and fine

Source: POTA. Available at https://mha.gov.in/sites/default/files/A1967-37_0.pdf (accessed on 3 August 2019).
Notes: *POTA, sec. 3, clauses (2), (3), (4), (5), (6), and (7).
@POTA, sec. 4.
#POTA, sec. 14.
$POTA, sec. 20.
**POTA, sec. 21.
@@POTA, sec. 22.
##POTA, sec. 58.
$$POTA, sec. 5.

cash.[132] Such property includes title deeds or any instrument of interest involving assets and bank accounts,[133] and the government is authorized to forfeit such proceeds of terrorism.[134]

Powers to Seize, Attach, or Forfeit Certain Property   POTA also provides some extraordinary powers to any SP who is investigating any case under POTA to issue an order of seizure or attachment of any property with prior approval of the DGP of the state concerned, based on his/her rational belief that such property is possessed or acquired from the proceeds of a terrorist act. The SP should inform the designated authority about such seizure or attachment within 48 hours for its confirmation or cancellation. Further, the IO is authorized to seize and detain cash including any coin or currency, postal orders, traveller's cheque; banker's notes, or any other monetary instrument on reasonable suspicion that such cash is meant for accomplishing any act of terrorism or is the fund or resource of any banned terrorist outfit. The POTA also has a provision for any aggrieved person to appeal to the POTA

[132] POTA, sec. 2(c).
[133] POTA, sec. 2(d).
[134] POTA, sec. 6(2).

court by an order of the designated authority.[135] Any transfer of such property subjected to seizure, attachment, or forfeiture shall be treated null and void.[136] The POTA court can order forfeiture of property after being thoroughly satisfied about the existence of sufficient grounds to hold such property as the proceeds of a terrorist act[137] and after serving a show-cause notice on the property holder and affording him/her representation.[138] The order of forfeiture can be challenged in the high court by submitting an appeal, and in the event of annulment of forfeiture, the property holder is entitled to the restitution or return of such property.[139] The POTA court should also order attachment of property of an undertrial and order its forfeiture on conviction.[140]

Power of the IO to Require Information from Certain Authorities   The IO, with a prior approval of the SP or any other superior or senior officer is authorized to require and call for information relevant to the proceedings under POTA from government authorities, local authorities, banks, companies, firms, institutions, establishments, organizations or individuals. Such authorities or institutions are compulsorily required to furnish such information, failing which attracts criminal liability.[141]

Terrorist Organizations   Any organization listed or with an identical name as an organization listed in the schedule is considered to be a terrorist organization. The names of organizations can be added to or removed from the schedule by the central government. The names of organizations can be added in the schedule only when the organization in question is involved in

1. the commission of or participation in acts of terrorism,
2. the preparation of terrorism,

[135] POTA, sec. 7.
[136] POTA, sec. 15.
[137] POTA, sec. 8.
[138] POTA, sec. 9.
[139] POTA, sec. 10.
[140] POTA, sec. 16.
[141] POTA, sec. 14.

3. the promotion or encouragement of terrorism, or
4. any other manner of terrorism.[142]

Procedure of Denotification of a Terrorist Organization　The central government has the power of to order the denotification of a terrorist organization from the schedule after receiving an application by the organization or by the person(s) affected by such inclusion and naming. If the relief is not granted by the central government, a review petition can be filed before the POTA Review Committee within one month, which may be allowed and reviewed accordingly. The central government should delist such an organization if the POTA Review Committee rules so.[143]

Punishment for Membership of a Terrorist Organization　Anyone who is a member or claims to be a member of a terrorist organization listed in the schedule is criminally liable to a maximum imprisonment of 10 years and/or fine. The members are not liable if it is proved that the organization was not a banned outfit listed under the schedule of POTA at the time of his/her membership and he/she has never ever participated in any of the activities of the organization during the period of such ban or listing.[144]

Punishment for Giving Support to a Terrorist Organization　Anyone who calls for support by organizing, managing, or assisting in organizing or managing a meeting to gather support for, to promote and expand the activities of, to be addressed by a member of, or to address the meeting to solicit and encourage support to a terrorist organization listed in the schedule but not just to seek monetary support or property is criminally liable to a maximum imprisonment of 10 years and/or fine.[145]

---

[142] POTA, sec. 18.
[143] POTA, sec. 19.
[144] POTA, sec. 20.
[145] POTA, sec. 21.

Punishment for Raising Funds for a Terrorist Organization   Anyone who calls for giving monetary help or property, receives such money or property, or provides such money or property, intentionally or willfully or has reasonable grounds to belief that such money or property is meant to be used for the purposes of terrorism, is criminally liable to a maximum imprisonment of 10 years and/or fine, irrespective of the money or property being given, lent, or made available in any manner, with or without consideration.[146]

Power to Order Collection of Certain Samples from the Suspect/ Accused   The chief judicial magistrate or chief metropolitan magistrate, after receiving a written request from the IO, is authorized to direct or order the accused or suspect to give such samples, as and when required, including handwriting, finger and foot prints, photographs, blood, saliva, semen, hair, and/or voice to the IO or police officer concerned. The court shall draw adverse inference on refusal by the accused so directed or ordered.[147]

Power to Intercept   An SP can make an application before the competent authority appointed under sec. 37 of the POTA for seeking to authorize an IO to intercept wire, electronic, or oral communication on the basis of the existence of firm grounds and evidence about the involvement of such persons in the commission of any crime under the POTA.[148] The competent authority may authorize interception[149] for a period not more than 60 days at once, subject to further extension after the expiry of the said period.[150] The order of such permission should immediately and not later than seven days be placed before the POTA Review Committee for its approval.[151] In case there is any

146 POTA, sec. 22.
147 POTA, sec. 27.
148 POTA, sec. 38.
149 POTA, sec. 39.
150 POTA, sec. 41.
151 POTA, sec. 40.

unusual situation, the Addl DGP or any higher police officer may allow interception, subject to subsequent approval of the competent authority within 48 hours of the commencement of such interception, failing which or in the event of denial of approval, such interception shall be considered illegal.[152]

Power to Impound Passport and Arms Licence   The POTA court is also authorized to impound the passport and arms licence of a person charge-sheeted under the POTA.[153]

Punishment and Compensation for Malicious Use of Power   Any police officer when found exercising his/her power with malicious or corrupt intentions against an innocent person, knowing that there are no reasonable grounds for proceedings under the POTA, shall be held criminally liable, with a maximum imprisonment of two years and /or fine. Further, the POTA court may order the police officer concerned, the person concerned, authority, or government to pay suitable compensation to such accused person(s) who are prosecuted maliciously under the POTA by the said police officer.[154]

Mandatory Guidelines for Arrest   The POTA also provides some guidelines and steps that must be followed and undertaken by the police officer concerned while making an arrest under the POTA. The following are the steps to be followed:

1. Prepare a memo of arrest or custody at the time of arrest.
2. Inform the arrestee about the right to consult an advocate when brought to the police station.
3. Inform his family or relatives about the arrest and record details of such communication countersigned by the accused.
4. Allow the accused to meet an advocate during interrogation; however, the lawyer is not entitled to remain present during the entire interrogation.[155]

---

[152] POTA, sec. 43.

[153] POTA, sec. 59.

[154] POTA, sec. 58.

[155] POTA, sec. 52.

Witness Protection and Non-disclosure of Identity of Witnesses   As in the case of the TADA, the POTA also provides a detailed mechanism for ensuring witness protection. Under this provision, a POTA court is empowered to order an in camera trial; to take steps, on its own motion or on the request from witnesses or the public prosecutor, to protect the identity of the witnesses and addresses including the place of proceedings and exclude the names and addresses of witnesses in the POTA court order or other records; to issue suitable directives to the persons concerned or authority for protecting and not disclosing the identity and addresses of the witnesses; and to impose a bar on media reporting. Further, anyone found violating these directions would attract criminal liability with a maximum imprisonment of one year and fine up to Rs 1,000.[156]

Admissibility of Confessions Made before a Police Officer   Like the TADA, the POTA also overrides the general rule under the Indian Evidence Act on the inadmissibility of confession made before a police in the court of law. Thus, under the provision of the POTA, a confession made before a police and recorded in writing, audio, or audio-visual form by an SP or a superior police officer is admissible in a court of law during the trial of the accused, co-accused, abettor, or conspirator. However, it is the duty of the police officer concerned to ensure that such a confession is made voluntarily by the accused and he/she should also explain to the accused that he/she is not bound to make such incriminatory confessions and its effect on his/her case.[157]

Admissibility of Evidence Collected through Interception   Any evidence collected through the interception of wire, electronic, or oral communication is admissible as evidence against the accused in the POTA court but is subject to supply of the authorization order of the competent authority and the application to the accused, at least 10 days prior to the hearing by the IO.[158]

---

156 POTA, sec. 30.
157 POTA, sec. 32.
158 POTA, sec. 45.

Presumption of Guilt   Just as in the TADA, the POTA also provides for a non-rebuttable presumption as to the commission of a terrorist act, where such persons will be considered guilty of committing an act of terrorism under it if they fulfil any of the following conditions:

1. There is a recovery of arms, explosives, or any other substance from the possession of the person(s) accused of any offence under POTA and there is a reason to believe that these things are meant to be used for terrorist activities.
2. Expert evidence confirms recovery of fingerprint(s) of the accused from the crime scene or from objects such as vehicle, ammunition, and arms used in the crime.
3. It is established that the accused has given financial aid knowingly for commission of any offence under POTA.[159]

Bar on Anticipatory Bail and Condition for Grant of Regular Bail
Similar to the TADA, the POTA also imposes an absolute bar on granting anticipatory bail as provided under sec. 438 of the CrPC,[160] and it has further laid down stringent provisions to discourage bail by making bail subject to the fulfillment of mandatory conditions such as affording the PP the opportunity to oppose the bail[161] and the POTA court's objective satisfaction about the innocence of the accused or possible apprehension about commission of any offence while on bail.[162] Further, the bail can be granted only after expiration of one year from the time of detention[163] and after strictly adhering to the conditions as laid down by the act.

The National Investigation Agency Act, 2008

The NIA Act was enacted to set up an investigation agency at the national level for investigating and prosecuting offences that affect

---

[159] POTA, sec. 53.
[160] POTA, sec. 49(5).
[161] POTA, sec. 49(6).
[162] POTA, sec. 49(7).
[163] POTA, sec. 49(7).

the sovereignty, security, and integrity of the country; security of the state; friendly relations with foreign states; and offences under acts[164] having jurisdiction across the whole of India including the state of Jammu and Kashmir. The act has certain features that are similar to the UAPA and the MCOCA, 1999. It covers all Indian citizens including those living outside the country in foreign jurisdictions, persons in the service of the government wherever they may be, and persons on ships and aircrafts registered in India wherever they may be.[165] The NIA was set up by[166] and under the supervision and order of the central government[167] for investigating offences committed under the UAPA, 1967 (37 of 1967); the Suppression of Unlawful Acts against Safety of Civil Aviation Act, 1982 (66 of 1982); the Atomic Energy Act, 1962 (33 of 1962); the Anti-Hijacking Act, 1982 (65 of 1982); the South Asian Association for Regional Cooperation (SAARC) Convention (Suppression of Terrorism) Act, 1993 (36 of 1993); the Suppression of Unlawful Acts Against Safety of Maritime Navigation and Fixed Platforms on Continental Shelf Act, 2002 (69 of 2002); and the Weapons of Mass Destruction and their Delivery Systems (Prohibition of Unlawful Activities) Act, 2005 (21 of 2005).[168]

Under the provisions of the act, the NIA is empowered to investigate offences in the following three ways:

1. On its own motion in concurrence with the approval of a state government and the subsequent order and approval of the central government
2. On the order of the central government when requested by a state government
3. On the order of the central government (suo moto)[169]

---

[164] NIA Act, Preamble.
[165] NIA Act, sec. 1(2).
[166] NIA Act, sec. 3.
[167] NIA Act, sec. 4.
[168] NIA Act, sch.
[169] NIA Act, sec. 6.

The NIA can also investigate other offences connected with the offences under the aforementioned laws.[170] As in the UAPA, the NIA Act also provides for the Constitution of special courts[171] and the appointment of special public prosecutors.[172] The court can decide certain matters summarily, when the offence is punished with imprisonment of up to three years.[173] Further, as provided in the UAPA, the NIA Act also provides for the protection of witnesses including in-camera proceedings, maintenance of confidentiality, non-disclosure of names in public and court records, and prohibition on publication by the media.[174] It also makes it mandatory to obtain prior governmental sanction for prosecuting public servants.[175]

Armed Conflict and Insurgency: The Armed Forces (Special Powers) Act, 1958

Initially, AFSPA was named as the Armed Forces (Assam and Manipur) Special Powers Act, 1958 (AFSPA [A&M]), and it was enacted to confer extraordinary powers to the armed forces in the states of Assam and Manipur.[176] In 1972, the states of Meghalaya, Nagaland, Tripura, Arunachal Pradesh, and Mizoram were also included,[177] and accordingly, it was renamed as the AFSPA.[178]

Disturbed Areas and Application of AFSPA   Under this act, the governor of a state or the administrator of a union territory is empowered to declare and notify a part or whole of a state or union territory as a disturbed area in situations when the state or union territory is in a

---

[170] NIA Act, sec. 8.

[171] NIA Act, sec. 11.

[172] NIA Act, sec. 15.

[173] NIA Act, sec. 16.

[174] NIA Act, sec. 17.

[175] NIA Act, sec. 18.

[176] AFSPA, sec. 1 and Preamble.

[177] AFSPA (A&M), sec. 2.

[178] AFSPA (A&M), sec. 1.

disturbed or dangerous situation and deploy armed forces to the aid of civil powers.[179]

Special Powers to the Armed Forces   The AFSPA provides extraordinary powers to commissioned officers, warrant officers, non-commissioned officers, or other members of the armed forces who are deployed in disturbed areas, and such officers are authorized for the following actions:

1. If the officer of the armed force thinks necessary to open fire or use force, for maintaining public order that may even result in death of a person or group of persons, who is believed to have contravened any law or order in the disturbed area such as prohibitory orders against assembly of five or more persons or carrying weapons, objects usable as weapon, firearms, ammunition, or explosives

2. If the officer thinks it fit and necessary to demolish the deposits or storages of arms; prepared or fortified positions, posts, or shelters used or likely or attempted to be used to carry out armed attacks; any structure serving the purpose of raising a training setup or facility for the armed groups or a hiding place for armed groups or wanted absconders

3. If the officer thinks fit to arrest and use necessary force to arrest a person without warrant on grounds of suspicion that s/he is involved in commission or is going to commit a cognisable offence

4. If the officer thinks fit to enter and search without warrant, even by use of necessary force, any premise to arrest or to gain custody of any person considered and believed to have been subjected to wrongful restraint and confinement; to seize any stolen property or any property believed to have been stolen; or to seize illegal arms, ammunition, or explosive substances believed to have been kept illegitimately[180]

Duty of Armed Forces to Handover Arrestees or Persons in Custody to the Police   Under the AFSPA, the armed forces are duty-bound

---

[179] AFSPA, sec. 3.
[180] AFSPA, sec. 4.

to handover the custody of such arrestees or detainees to the nearest police station without any undue delay. Further, they are also required to submit a report about the arrest and the reasons thereof.[181]

Bar on Prosecution, Suit, or Other Legal Proceedings   The act states that for initiating any prosecution, suit, or legal proceedings against such officers or personnel of the armed forces for doing anything in line with the powers and authority given under AFSPA, a prior sanction from the central government is required.[182]

In line with AFSPA, 1958, the Parliament of India legislated the Armed Forces (Punjab and Chandigarh) Special Powers Act, 1983 (AFSPA [P&C]) and the Armed Forces (Jammu and Kashmir) Special Powers Act, 1990 (AFSPA [J&K]). To provide special powers to the armed forces in the state of Punjab and the union territory of Chandigarh, and the state of Jammu and Kashmir, these two separate acts were enacted and enforced on 15 October 1983[183] and 5 July 1990,[184] respectively. Both these acts are identical to the original AFSPA of 1958 except for some new additions that were incorporated by the lawmakers. The AFSPA (P&C) came into force by repealing the Armed Forces (Punjab and Chandigarh) Special Powers Ordinance, 1983,[185] while the AFSPA (J&K) came into force by superseding Presidential Ordinance 3 of 1990.[186] But these two acts operate directly under the union government's command and are applicable to the central forces, which include both the military and air force.[187]

The AFSPA (P&C) is applicable to the disturbed regions of the states as identified and thus retains all the provisions of power given to the armed forces in these disturbed areas, which is just as mentioned in

---

181 AFSPA, sec. 5.
182 AFSPA, sec. 6.
183 AFSPA (P&C), sec. 1.
184 AFSPA (J&K), sec. 1.
185 AFSPA (P&C), sec. 8.
186 AFSPA (J&K), sec. 8.
187 AFSPA (P&C) and AFSPA (J&K), sec. 2(a).

the original AFSPA of 1958.[188] On the other hand, the AFSPA (J&K) extends the scope of its operation in situations or conditions that are dangerous and calls for the use of the armed forces as a support to the civil power, specifically for preventing the activities of terrorists to intimidate the Government of India, to strike terror on the population or a section of the population, to estrange the population or a section of population, or to badly affect the harmony that exists amongst diverse groups; or actions aiming to renounce, question, or tarnish the sovereignty and integrity of India or to claim or support cession (that is, admittance of any foreign territory or part of territory in India) or secession (that is claim of withdrawal of a territory from India).[189] Under the provisions and power of AFSPA (J&K), the Governor of Jammu and Kashmir had already issued a notification in which some of the areas and districts in the state were declared as disturbed areas. These areas included Anantnag, Baramulla, Badgam, Pulwama, Kupwara, Srinagar, and all areas that were located within a 20 km radius from the line of control in the districts of Rajouri and Poonch.[190] In 2001, the list made some more additions as disturbed areas and included the districts of Jammu, Kathu, Udhampur, Poonch, Rajouri, and Doda.[191]

Furthermore, just as in the original act, both these acts provided special powers to the armed forces and also incorporated another sub-clause under which the armed forces personnel had an additional power to stop, search, and seize and use force to stop, search, and seize any vehicle or vessel on suspicion of carrying any wanted proclaimed offender, any accused, or anyone who is suspected to have committed or is going to commit a crime or carrying illegal arms, ammunition, or explosives.[192] The acts also empowered and authorized the armed forces to break open any lock in order to exercise their power to search

---

[188] AFSPA (P&C), sec. 3.

[189] AFSPA (J&K), sec. 3.

[190] SRO No. SW 4 of 06/07/1990 (Civil Secretariat, Home Department, Government of Jammu and Kashmir).

[191] SRO No. 351 of 10/07/2001 (Civil Secretariat, Home Department, Government of Jammu and Kashmir).

[192] AFSPA (P&C) and AFSPA (J&K), sec. 4(e).

and seize.[193] Retaining the provision of the original act of 1958, they further stated that the armed forces had the duty to hand over the arrested persons and all the seized property to the police[194] and also stated that there cannot be any prosecution and legal proceedings against the armed forces personnel that can be carried out without prior sanction/permission from the government.[195]

Law Applicable to the Armed Forces at the Time of an Armed Conflict
The Government of India ratifying the Geneva Conventions has enacted the Geneva Conventions Act, 1960 (GCA), taking into consideration all four Geneva Conventions, to which India is a party. The GCA is applicable and extends to the whole of India and also includes the state of Jammu and Kashmir.[196] This act punishes anyone who is found to be responsible for the commission of certain acts that breach the Geneva Convention for the Amelioration of the Condition of the Wounded and Sick in Armed Forces in the Field 1949 (GC-I), Geneva Convention for the Amelioration of the Condition of Wounded, Sick and Shipwrecked Members of Armed Forces at Sea 1949 (GC-II), Geneva Convention Relative to the Treatment of Prisoners of War 1949 (GC-III), and Geneva Convention Relative to the Protection of Civilian Persons in Time of War 1949 (GC-IV).[197] The act also includes provisions for the punishment of any person who has committed any breach of the four Geneva Conventions on foreign territory and he/she shall be subjected to the GCA when found in India and should be held criminally liable.[198]

The provisions of punishment under this act is irrespective of the accused's nationality or citizenship, for committing, attempting, or abetting the commission of grave breach of GC-I, GC-II, GC-III, and GC-IV or procuring any person on his/her behalf for committing, attempting, or abetting the commission of grave breaches, as defined

---

[193] AFSPA (P&C) and AFSPA (J&K), sec. 5.
[194] AFSPA (P&C) and AFSPA (J&K), sec. 6.
[195] AFSPA (P&C) and AFSPA (J&K), sec. 7.
[196] GCA, sec. 1(2).
[197] GCA, sec. 2(a) and Preamble.
[198] GCA, sec. 4.

under Art. 50 of GC-I, Art. 51 of GC-II, Art. 130 of GC-III, and Art. 147 of GC-IV. The punishment includes death penalty or life imprisonment for willfully killing any protected persons under the Geneva Conventions or with a maximum imprisonment of 14 years for any other offence.[199] Grave breaches have been discussed in great detail in Chapter 1.

Other Legislations

Section 197 of the Criminal Procedure Code

Section 197 of the CrPC deals with the prosecution of judges and public servants. It states that if any judge, magistrate, or public servant is accused of any offence alleged to have been committed by him while discharging his duty, no court shall take cognisance of any such offence unless there is a previous sanction of the government. Under this provision, the police and the armed forces personnel are immune from prosecution.

The Maharashtra Control of Organised Crime Act, 1999

The MCOCA was enacted in the year 1999 by repealing the Maharashtra Control of Organised Crime Ordinance 1999 (Ord. III of 1999)[200] and came into force on 24 February 1999. It was enacted by Chhagan Bhujbal, the then home minister of the state of Maharashtra.[201] This law was circulated and publicized with the hope that the spread of unlawful elements and terrorism would be controlled and worries of the society could be minimized.[202] This act acknowledges that the present system has been proved to be insufficient for combating organized crime.[203] The act also aims to make special provisions to curb the crime.[204] It is quite similar to the TADA, the POTA, and the UAPA in most aspects

---

[199] GCA, sec. 3.
[200] MCOCA, sec. 30.
[201] MCOCA, sec. 1.
[202] MCOCA, Preface.
[203] MCOCA, Preamble.
[204] MCOCA, Preamble.

except for some changes in the nomenclature, expressions, and punishment. For the purpose of a better understanding of this law, definitions of the terms 'organized crime' and 'continuing unlawful activities' are very important. Organized crime is defined as any legally prohibited act that constitutes a cognisable offence and is liable for a minimum imprisonment of three years carried out either alone or together as an organized crime syndicate or its behalf, provided that such a syndicate has been charge-sheeted and taken cognisance of by a court, for more than once in the past 10 years.[205] The term 'continuing unlawful activities' is defined as commission of any continuing unlawful activities by unlawful means such as violence and threat, intimidation, and coercion for making monetary gains or unjustified financial or added advantage to oneself or anyone promoting insurgency.[206] Just like the offence of terrorist acts as defined under the TADA, the MCOCA had also formed similar offences under the category of 'organized crime', while the punishment under this act varies from those of the TADA slightly. Table 5.5 provides all the offences and corresponding punishment under MCOCA.

Like the TADA, the POTA, and the UAPA, the MCOCA also sets up special courts for the purpose of specialized trial of cases registered under this act,[207] including the offences under other general, special, and local laws.[208] It also gives provisions to appoint advocates as special public prosecutors with at least 10 years of experience.[209] Such special courts are empowered and authorized to take direct cognisance without committal and also conduct summary trials in offences liable to be punished with three years or fewer of imprisonment.[210]

The MCOCA provides for the following exceptional provisions relating to rebuttable presumptions of certain facts:

1. The special court should consider the previous history of the accused in certain circumstances where he/she has previously

---

[205] MCOCA, sec. 2(d).
[206] MCOCA, sec. 2(e).
[207] MCOCA, sec. 5.
[208] MCOCA, sec. 7.
[209] MCOCA, sec. 8.
[210] MCOCA, sec. 9.

Table 5.5 Offences and Punishment under MCOCA

Offence	Punishment
Organized Crime*	
Causing death	Death or life term in prison with fine of not less than Rs 1 lakh
Causing injury, loss to property, etc.	Five years to life term in prison with fine of not less than Rs 5 lakh
Conspiracy, attempt, advocating, abetment, advise, aid, or facilitate with knowledge in commission or preparation of organized crime	Five years to life term in prison with fine of not less than Rs 5 lakh
Harbour or conceal or attempt to harbour or conceal members of an organized crime syndicate	Five years to life term in prison with fine of not less than Rs 5 lakh
Membership of an organized crime syndicate	Five years to life term in prison with fine of not less than Rs 5 lakh
Holding or acquisition of property from the proceeds of organized crime	Three years to life term in prison with fine of not less than Rs 2 lakh
Other Offences	
Possessing unaccounted wealth or property on behalf of a member of an organized crime syndicate	3–10 years' prison term with fine of not less than Rs 1 lakh
Intentional omission or failure to discharge duties in preventing commission or aid in the commission of organized crime by a public officer@	Maximum three years to life term in prison with fine

Source: MCOCA, secs 3(1) to 3(5). Available at https://www.nia.gov.in/writereaddata/Portal/LawReference/25_1_Maharashtra_Control_of_Organised_Crime_Act__1999__MCOCA__-_Maharashtra_Act_no_30__of_1999.pdf (accessed on 3 August 2019).
Notes: *MCOCA, sec. 3.
@MCOCA, sec. 24.

been bound under sec. 107 or sec. 110 of the CrPC, or on an earlier occasion subjected to detention under preventive detention law, or previously prosecuted under MCOCA.

2. The special court should presume that the accused has acquired property or monetary possessions through illegal activities in

circumstances where it is established that s/he is engaged in the commission of organized crimes or anyone on his behalf is or has possessed any unaccounted property.

3. The special court should presume that kidnapping or abduction is done for demanding ransom if kidnapping or abduction is established.[211]

Similar to the TADA and the POTA, the MCOCA also provides for admissibility of confession made before a police officer;[212] witness protection,[213] forfeiture of property on conviction and attachment during trial;[214] bar on anticipatory bail under sec. 438 of the CrPC;[215] bar on regular bail in certain circumstances;[216] non-rebuttable presumption to commission of organized crime under sec. 3 of the MCOCA;[217] interception of wire, electronic, or oral communications;[218] and constitution of competent authority[219] and review committee.[220]

After the enactment of the MCOCA, T. Devendra Gaud, the then home minister of the state of Andhra Pradesh, followed the suit of Maharashtra and enacted the Andhra Pradesh Control of Organised Crime Act, 2001 (APCOCA) almost identical to the MCOCA with minor modifications. The APCOCA was enacted as a temporary legislation for a period of three years.[221] The entire scheme of this act, including expression, nomenclature, and arrangement of clauses, is copied from MCOCA, except punishment for the offence of possessing unaccounted wealth or property on behalf of a member of an organized crime syndicate, which is punishable with a maximum term of five years imprisonment and a fine.

[211] MCOCA, sec. 17.
[212] MCOCA, sec. 18.
[213] MCOCA, sec. 19.
[214] MCOCA, sec. 20.
[215] MCOCA, sec. 21(3).
[216] MCOCA, sec. 21(4).
[217] MCOCA, sec. 22.
[218] MCOCA, sec. 14.
[219] MCOCA, sec. 13.
[220] MCOCA, sec. 15.
[221] APCOCA, sec. 1(4).

In 2010, the then deputy chief minister of Maharashtra, Chhagan Bhujbal, in an interview to *Tehelka*[222] shared his concerns and worries with respect to the misuse of MCOCA and suggested amendments. He further acknowledged that due to restrictive provisions of the law, people have been made to be behind bars for many years without the remedy of bail. Due to such misuse and many lacunae and shortcomings of the act, many innocent persons have suffered. Hence, there is a need to have some safeguards that should be maintained, and therefore amendments to this law are necessary to prevent false implication of innocent people.[223]

The Chhattisgarh Special Public Safety Act, 2005

The CGSPSA, also known as the Chhattisgarh Vishesh Jan Suraksha Adhiniyam 2005, was enacted for the safety of the public from the hands of unlawful organizations and their activities. However, this act was challenged on the basis of violating the CoI. This challenge was registered in the Chhattisgarh High Court, but the court upheld its constitutionality.[224]

The CGSPSA includes some of the features of the UAPA and further provides for notification of unlawful organizations,[225] punishment for unlawful activities,[226] forfeiture of property,[227] notification and seizure of property of unlawful organizations,[228] bar on prosecution without prior governmental sanction,[229] and bar on legal proceeding on the grounds of good faith.[230]

---

[222] Rana Ayyub. 2010. 'MCOCA Needs Amendment to Check Its Misuse', *Tehelka* 7, no. 5 (6 February).

[223] Ayyub, 'MCOCA Needs Amendment to Check Its Misuse'.

[224] *PUCL v Union of India and Another*, Writ Petition (C) No. 2163 of 2009.

[225] CGSPSA, sec. 3.

[226] CGSPSA, sec. 8.

[227] CGSPSA, sec. 11.

[228] CGSPSA, sec. 9.

[229] CGSPSA, sec. 12.

[230] CGSPSA, sec. 15.

The act further gives a very broad definition and includes action in the form of any act or oral or written words and signs and visible representation of individuals as well as organizations causing danger or threat to public order, peace, and tranquility; interference or having tendency to cause interference with maintenance of public order; interference with the administration of law, institution of law, and personnel; design to overawe any public servant, state force, and central force; propagation of violence, terrorism, vandalism, or any other act causing fear in public by use of arms, explosives, or any device; disrupting services, railways, or roads; encouraging and preaching disobedience to the established law and institution; or forcible collection of money or goods for carrying out unlawful activities.[231] Unlawful organizations for the purpose of CGSPSA refers to such organizations that engage in or work with an objective to aid, abet, assist, support, or encourage unlawful activities.[232] The government can notify such organizations for one year continuously, and the notification can be renewed only once in sequence.[233]

Supreme Court of India on the Right to Protection against Torture

The Supreme Court of India has laid down various principles vis-à-vis torture and criminal justice administration. It has also ruled out the use of third degree torture methods and observed that third degree should be prohibited since torture is prohibited under law. It is the primary duty of the criminal justice administration to secure justice by establishing the truth with the help of evidence. Such methods for establishing the truth should be as good as the ends, and further a person's self-respect, dignity, and liberty cannot be forfeited by applying improper means. With reference to 'compelled testimony', the Supreme Court described the methods of obtaining information and testimony in which evidences are secured by various ways that include not only

---

[231] CGSPSA, sec. 2(e).
[232] CGSPSA, sec. 2(f).
[233] CGSPSA, sec. 3.

threats and physical violence but also mental torture. Such measures create an environment that is full of force or coercion and pressure, exhausting interrogations, and arrogant and intimidating methods, which ultimately violate Art. 20(3) of the Constitution.[234] Late Justice Krishna Iyer referred to torture and prison justice as a 'virgin area of jurisprudence' in India, which is painfully turning into an important act to extract information. He further observed that in India, the area of prison justice, the communication of what freedom is inside the prison or any detention centre, and the rights conferred to every individual are significant, and it is the responsibility of the judiciary to provide protection inside the prison as per the constitutional provisions, given that there is an increasing number of torture cases and custodial violence by the lawmakers and the security forces in the present time. The Supreme Court further apprehended that the court has all the power and jurisdiction to interfere in cases where a prisoner or a detained person received cruel, inhuman, and degrading treatment. Furthermore, it informed that para. 399(3) of the Jail Manual and sec. 56 of the Prison Act impose inhuman and brutal restrictions on inmates of prisons and subject them to torture. Hence, these should not be considered as laws since they work against the humanity, decorum, civility, and values of people and society.[235]

Justice Chinnappa Reddy and late Justice Krishna Iyer gave their views on the matter and said that the court has the power and the responsibility to interfere and protect any prisoner who is subjected to torture and inhuman treatment since each and every individual in the country has fundamental rights that cannot be deprived. Thus, every individual, inside or outside prison, is protected by the principle of fair and just behaviour and fundamental rights, and has the right to protection as per the provisions of Art. 32 of the CoI. Further, the justices held the prison superintendent responsible for crimes of torture and custodial violence since it is his duty to maintain vigilance and ensure that no corporal punishment or personal violence is inflicted on prisoners. Following this, the Supreme Court gave its directives for protecting

---

[234] *Nandini Satpathy v Dani (PL) and Another*, 1978 SCC (2) 42.
[235] *Sunil Batra v Delhi Administration*, AIR 1978 SC 1675.

and ensuring that each prisoner is given rights. These directives are as follows:

1. Lawyers should be nominated by the DM or a judge of the sessions court, high court, or the Supreme Court, and prison authorities should facilitate such a lawyer in interviewing, visiting, and maintaining confidential communication with prisoners without compromising security and discipline.
2. Such designated lawyers have an obligation to visit, record, and report periodically to respective courts.
3. A complaint box should be managed under DM's and sessions judge's orders, which must be accessible to prisoners and scrutinized regularly for proper action.
4. The DM and judge of the sessions court should make personal visits or authorize someone to visit on their behalf in order to give sufficient and meaningful chance to prisoners to voice their grievances and should make speedy investigation to take appropriate corrective action.
5. The DM and judge of the sessions court should, in suitable cases, report to the high court to initiate habeas action if warranted.
6. Solitary or punitive cell, hard labour, or dietary change such as painful additives, other punishment or denial of privileges and amenities, and transfer to other prisons with penal consequences should not be imposed on prisoners without judicial scrutiny by the judge of a sessions court, and when information is not transmitted to the judge of a sessions court due to an emergency, he/she should be intimated within two days.[236]

In another instance, Justices Ranganath Misra and M.M. Dutt voiced that 'when human rights are hashed behind bars, constitutional justice impeaches such law', which means that constitutional justice warrants the protection of human rights even inside the prison or lock-ups. Therefore, the courts, which send citizens to prisons, have an important obligation to ensure that the detainee's right to freedom

---

[236] *Sunil Batra* v *Delhi Administration*, 1980 SCC (3) 488.

from torture is respected and protected at all the times during his/her detention.[237]

In another case, the bench of Justice E.S. Venkataramiah and late Justice V.R. Krishna Iyer of the Supreme Court of India held that any form of torture or cruel, inhuman, or degrading treatment is contrary to human dignity, and thus such acts prevent the right to live. Hence such acts are prohibited under Art. 21 of the CoI, subject to the procedure established by law. They also stated that there is no law or procedure established by law that supports and legitimizes torture, cruelty, or inhuman or degrading treatment and such acts cannot stand the test of reasonableness and non-arbitrariness. Such acts are completely unconstitutional and void since they violate the provisions of Arts 14 and 21 of the CoI, which fully guarantee the right to protection against torture or cruel, inhuman, or degrading treatment, in line with Art. 5 of the UDHR and Art. 7 of the ICCPR.[238]

In a case of torture and compensation being tried at the Supreme Court, the bench of Justice Kuldip Singh and Justice A.S. Anand observed that monetary or financial compensation is the only appropriate remedy in such cases where there is a confirmed violation of the fundamental right to life of a citizen at the hands of public servants on the grounds of vicarious liability of state for the actions of its servants or agents, taking into account the legality and appropriateness of monetary compensation in such cases of proven breach of provisions and rights guaranteed under Arts 21 and 22 of the Constitution.

It is still noticed that there is an extraordinary increase in the number of torture and custodial violence cases despite the enactment and enforcement of several international conventions and declarations preventing and aspiring to absolutely ban any kind of torture. Article 21 of the CoI too prohibits all forms of torture and cruel, inhuman, or degrading treatment, which is irrespective of whether it is caused during interrogation, investigation, or extracting any information by public servants and security forces. While the government might regard state

---

[237] *Sheela Barse* v *State of Maharastra*, AIR 1983 SC 378.

[238] *Francis Coralie Mullin* v *Administrator, Union Territory of Delhi*, 1981 SCC (1) 608.

action as always right, just, and fair and thus defend torture as justified, the Supreme Court has stated this as an insult to Article 21 of the Constitution and upheld that torture cannot be considered as right, just, and fair. Further, the Supreme Court has developed a unique principle for the application of international law in the courts in India, in spite of reservations towards the right to compensation in cases of illegal detention under Art. 9(5) of the ICCPR. This principle states the ordering of compensation for the breach of the right to life of a citizen by holding the state vicariously liable for the acts of public servants.[239]

The Supreme Court, during the early 1980s, over a period of time, evolved the concept of constitutional torts according to which any person who has been subjected to torture and deprived of his/her fundamental rights and the right to life and personal liberty by means of violence is entitled to the right to compensation for violation of life and liberty at the hands of agents of the state. For the first time, in a case of illegal detention of a prisoner named Rudul Shah, the Supreme Court awarded monetary compensation under the writ jurisdiction under Art. 32 of the CoI. The person was kept in illegal detention for over 14 years even after he was acquitted. Thus, the Supreme Court has recognized and upheld the right to compensation in cases of such grave violations of the right to personal liberty.[240] In another case, where a person was subject to enforced disappearance at the time of his police custody, the Supreme Court considered this act of enforced disappearance similar to custodial death and held the state responsible and made it liable to pay compensation to the victim and his family.[241] The Supreme Court, in one more case of custodial death, which occurred in the state of Orissa (now Odisha), awarded compensation to the victim's family and further laid down the rule for award of compensation by extending the jurisdiction of the Supreme Court under Art. 32 of the Constitution and to the high courts under Art. 226 of the Constitution.[242]

---

[239] *Shri D.K. Basu* v *State of West Bengal,* AIR 1997 SC 610.

[240] *Rudul Shah* v *State of Bihar,* AIR 1983 SC 1086.

[241] *Sebastian M. Hongray* v *Union of India,* AIR 1984 SC 1026.

[242] *Smt. Nilabati Behera alias Lalit Behera* v *State of Orissa & Others,* (1993) 2 SCC 746.

While deciding on the constitutional validity of AFSPA and abuse of power and authority by the armed forces under this act, the Supreme Court of India consolidated its guidelines in the form of a list of dos and don'ts, which must be followed by the armed forces while acting under AFSPA. For example, the armed forces should not use third-degree methods for extracting information or confession. Besides, the Supreme Court has also made a similar list where the armed forces provide aid to any civil authority, for example, the armed forces should not ill-treat anyone, especially women and children, and they should not harass civilians and should not commit acts of torture in any form and in any circumstance. Further, the ruling of the Supreme Court of India stated that any breach of these guidelines would be subject to punishment as per secs 41, 42(e), 63, and 64(f) of the Army Act, 1950. This case also ruled out the commission of torture even on the grounds of necessity.[243]

Role of Statutory and Other Commissions in Preventing Torture and Custodial Violence

The Law Commission of India

The Law Commission of India has played an important role in law reform activities in the country. It has repeatedly made several recommendations with reference to bringing in reforms in custodial justice and administration of the criminal justice system. With regard to custodial violence, the following three reports have been very important:

1. *113th Report on Injuries in Police Custody*, 1985, submitted by the 10th Law Commission of India, chaired by Justice K.K. Mathew
2. *135th Report on Women in Custody*, 1989, submitted by the 12th Law Commission of India, chaired by Justice M.P. Thakkar, 1988–91
3. *152nd Report on Custodial Crimes*, 1994, submitted by the 13th Law Commission of India, chaired by Justice K.N. Singh

[243] *Naga People's Movement of Human Rights* v *Union of India*, AIR 1998 SC 431.

The *113th Report* of the 10th Law Commission of India was prepared in view of the Supreme Court's findings in the *State of UP* v *Ram Sagar Yadav*[244] case on the need to make appropriate amendments to the law so that fair and meaningful prosecution and adjudication of cases of custodial crimes could be facilitated and ensured. The Law Commission of India emphasized the unusual circumstances of cases that involved custodial offences, and with reference to such crimes, it recommended some important changes in the laws relating to the burden of proof and suggested the incorporation of a new section—sec. 114B—in the Indian Evidence Act.[245]

The *135th Report* of the Law Commission of India emphasized the need for special protection to women in custody and recommended the incorporation of a new and separate chapter—Chapter XXXIIIA titled 'Specific Provision as to Arrest, Interrogation and Custody of Women and Children'[246] (secs 450A to 450N)—in the CrPC and further amendments to various provisions of the IPC, the Probation of Offenders Act, 1968, and the Mental Health Act, 1987.[247] The key findings and recommendations of this report are listed in Table 5.6.

While the *152nd Report* of the Law Commission of India acknowledged the necessity of the police for the maintenance of law and order and respect of law, it emphasized that the use of torture and third-degree methods during investigation and interrogation can never be allowed by a civilized country.[248] Thus, freedom from torture is a civilizational qualifier, and the report further recommended the separation of the investigation and the law and order functions of the police by segregating it into two independent wings of the police force.[249]

[244] *State of UP* v *Ram Sagar Yadav*, AIR 1985 SC 416.

[245] *113th Report on Injuries in Police Custody* (10th Law Commission of India, 1985), para. 5.2.

[246] *135th Report on Women in Custody* (12th Law Commission of India, 1989), app. 1.

[247] *135th Report on Women in Custody*, p. 72.

[248] *152nd Report on Custodial Crimes* (13th Law Commission of India, 1994), para. 1.6.

[249] *152nd Report on Custodial* Crimes, para. 13.6, p. 56.

Table 5.6 Key Recommendations of the 135th Report of the Law Commission of India

Recommendation	Key Features of the Provision
Incorporation of a new provision in the CrPC— Section 450B	Arrest of women The police have to consider the following guidelines while arresting a woman: — Presume her submission to custody on oral intimation of the arrest — Not actually touch the person of the woman for making the arrest — Not make arrest of a woman between sunset and sunrise, except in an unavoidable situation — Seek prior written permission of a superior police officer before making arrest of a woman after sunset or before sunrise
Incorporation of a new provision in the CrPC— Section 450C	Medical examination of women — The magistrate should explain to the woman arrestee about the right to medical examination — Medical examination must be conducted by or under the supervision of a female registered medical practitioner — Medical examination report must be provided to the woman
Incorporation of a new provision in the CrPC— Section 450D	Examination of women and children under Section 160 of the CrPC — Women and children shall not be required to attend such examination at any place except their dwelling place — If the investigation is conducted by a male police officer, the relative or friend of such children or women or an NGO representative should be allowed to remain present throughout the interrogation
Incorporation of a new provision in the CrPC— Section 450G	Pregnant women and suspension of imprisonment: — A pregnant female life convict should be released from prison after executing a personal bond or surety — The imprisonment of a pregnant female life convict should be suspended till the period of delivery

(Cont'd)

Table 5.6   (*Cont'd*)

Recommendation	Key Features of the Provision
Incorporation of a new provision in the CrPC—Section 450H	Monitoring by a sessions judge The high court may issue direction to the sessions judge to monitor the safeguards and protections to women in custody
Incorporation of a new provision in the CrPC—Section 450I	Medical examination of a woman prisoner in prison — Medical examination of a woman prisoner shall be conducted at the time of her admission or readmission to the prison — Medical examination of a pregnant prisoner shall be conducted at the district hospital
Incorporation of a new provision in the CrPC—Section 450J	Women prisoner during transit — A woman prisoner should not to be handcuffed or chained during transit — A woman prisoner should be escorted by a female warden or matron during transit — A female relative should be allowed to accompany a woman prisoner while in transit
Incorporation of a new provision in the CrPC—Section 450K	Place of detention of women prisoners — A woman prisoner should be detained in a separate and suitable place — In the absence of any suitable place, a woman prisoner should be detained in an institution set up and managed for the reception, care, protection, and welfare of women and children
Incorporation of a new provision in the IPC—Section 166A	Penalty for willful disobedience to the directions of law by a public servant who — knowingly disobeys any direction of law prohibiting from requiring the attendance at any place for the purpose of investigation or — knowingly disobeys any direction of law prohibiting the manner of investigation. Such a public servant shall be punished with imprisonment, which may extend to one year or fine or both.

Source: *135th Report on Women in Custody*, Ch. II, pp. 4–6 (1989). Available at http://lawcommissionofindia.nic.in/101-169/Report135.pdf, accessed on 3 August 2019.

Further, the commission recommended the addition of a series of new provisions and amendments to the existing provisions of the IPC, the CrPC, and the Indian Evidence Act. The key findings and recommendations are mentioned in Table 5.7.

Table 5.7   Key Findings and Recommendations of the 152nd Report of the Law Commission of India

Recommendation	Key Features of the Provision
Incorporation of a new provision in the IPC— Section 166A	Same as *135th Report on Women in Custody*, 1989, 12th Law Commission of India (Provision related to penalty for willful disobedience to the direction of law by a public servant).
Incorporation of a new provision in the CrPC— Section 50A	It is the police's duty to — intimate about arrest to a relative or friend, failing which to the local legal aid committee, — prepare the custody memo or body receipt immediately at the time and place of arrest in the presence of two independent witnesses present at the scene of arrest, — duly sign the memo/receipt along with the signatures of two witnesses, and — promptly hand over the memo/receipt to the arrestee's relative.
Incorporation of a new provision to the CrPC— Section 57A	It is the duty of the magistrate to verify certain facts to — enquire about the compliance of procedures related to the safeguards, arrest, and rights on arrest by the police; and — verify police records and registers of arrest and put it on record.
Incorporation of a new provision in the CrPC— Section 154A	Petition by any person, relative, friend, legal aid committee, or NGO about custodial violence, its maintainability and jurisdiction can be filed — before the chief judicial magistrate if the alleged custodial violence does not result in death or — before the sessions judge if the alleged custodial violence results in death The court can initiate judicial enquiry in the alleged custodial violence.

(Cont'd)

Table 5.7   (*Cont'd*)

Recommendation	Key Features of the Provision
Incorporation of a new provision in the CrPC— Section 357A	Compensation to the victim of custodial violence If a public servant is found guilty and convicted of custodial offences — the court shall order the government and the convicted public servant to pay compensation to the victim or victim's family, — the liability to pay compensation shall be joint and several, and — the compensation order can also be made by an appellate court or a court of revision (sessions court or high court as the case may be). Limit of compensation: In the case of death, a minimum compensation of Rs 1 lakh or in the case of bodily injury, a minimum compensation of Rs 25,000 must be ordered
Amendment to Section 25 of the Indian Evidence Act	The existing provision covers confessions made before police officers. The amended provision shall cover all confessions made before: — a public officer who is not a police officer but with the power or authority to arrest and — a police officer, whether or not he/she has power or authority to arrest.
Amendment to Section 26 of the Indian Evidence Act	The existing provision covers confessions made in police custody. The amended provision shall cover confessions made in custody of public officers.
Incorporation of a new section as 114B in the Indian Evidence Act, 1872	Same as *113th Report on Injuries in Police Custody*, 1985, 10th Law Commission of India (Presumption as to injury in police custody).

Source: 152nd Report of the Law Commission of India on Crime in Custody (1994). Available at http://lawcommissionofindia.nic.in/101-169/Report152.pdf, accessed on 3 August 2019.

The National Police Commission, 1977–81

The NPC was constituted in 1977 under the chairmanship of Dharam Vira[250] for reviewing the Indian police system in an exhaustive manner. The NPC prepared as many as eight reports in a period of four years. These eight reports suggested 291 recommendations, which were all related to police reforms, but till date most of the recommendations have not been implemented.[251] The commission completed and submitted its first two reports during the rule of the Janata Party at the centre, but after the return to power of Indira Gandhi in January 1980, the very existence of the NPC came under threat. The reason for this was primarily because it was constituted despite her opposing its formation. In its reports, the commission also made a reference to the report of the Shah Commission, which had criticized the use and misuse of the police during the ruling of Indira Gandhi.

The following are some of the important recommendations from the eight reports prepared by the NPC:

1. The first report was concerned with the constabulary and administrative issues such as pay structure, housing, redress of grievances, and career planning for the constabulary. It made 28 recommendations, but the most significant recommendations have still not been implemented in the states.[252]
2. The second report dealt with welfare measures for the families of the police and how political and executive pressure can be avoided. The report made 33 recommendations for both the central government and the state governments to take action.[253]
3. The third report focused on the police force and weaker sections of the society, village police, corruption in the police force, economic

---

[250] Dharam Vira is the former governor of West Bengal.

[251] J. Liddle and J. Rama. 1989. *Daughters of Independence: Gender, Caste and Class in India*. New Jersey: Rutgers University Press.

[252] Commonwealth Human Rights Initiative (CHRI). 'Police Reforms in India'. Available at http://www.humanrightsinitiative.org/programs/aj/police/india/initiatives/npc_recommendations.htm, accessed on 11 February 2018.

[253] CHRI. 'Police Reforms in India'.

offences, and modernization. Some of the 54 recommendations were related to the postings of station house officers/superintendents of police, combating corrupt police officers, and guidelines for making arrests. Most of the recommendations have not been implemented.[254]

4. The fourth report concentrated on issues of investigation, trial and prosecution, industrial/agrarian issues, social legislation, and prohibition. The suggestions dealt with registration of FIRs, recording of statements of witnesses, arrest, remand, confession, and so on. Though 59 recommendations were suggested, none of them have been implemented so far.[255]

5. The fifth report attended to the recruitment of constables and sub-inspectors, training of police personnel, district police and magistracy, women police, and police–public relations. The report made 27 recommendations. The commission had once again raised the demand for a new police act in this report.[256]

6. The sixth report took up issues of the Indian Police Service (IPS), police and students, communal riots, and urban policing. It made 23 recommendations, some of them dealing with the creation of IPS cadres for central police organizations and compulsory training for promotions for IPS officers.[257]

7. The seventh report focused on the organization and structure of the police, state armed police battalions and district armed reserves, delegation of financial powers to police officers, traffic regulation, performance appraisal of police personnel, disciplinary control, role of the centre in planning, evaluation and coordination, and policing in the northeast of India. It made 60 recommendations, some of them related to the restructuring of police stations and separating crime investigation from law and order.[258]

8. The eighth report addressed the subject of accountability for police performance. The report suggested that the complaint against the

[254] CHRI. 'Police Reforms in India'.
[255] CHRI. 'Police Reforms in India'.
[256] CHRI. 'Police Reforms in India'.
[257] CHRI. 'Police Reforms in India'.
[258] CHRI. 'Police Reforms in India'.

police should be defended at the cost of the government. It also contained a draft bill for a new police act.[259]

9. The most important recommendations of the NPC centred on the problem of insulating the police from illegitimate political and bureaucratic interference.

* * *

Despite the fact that India has enacted a few legislations, constituted bodies and organizations for preventing the offences of torture and custodial violence, and ratified the UDHR and the ICCPR, the crime is still taking place in the country, especially at the hands of the security forces, such as the police force of the country and the armed forces. This chapter has references to several laws of the country and the CoI and its provisions. It also cites some cases and Supreme Court rulings for preventing torture and custodial violence, which lay down India's response towards the prevention of torture and custodial violence and protecting victims and citizens from such crimes.

Appendix 5A

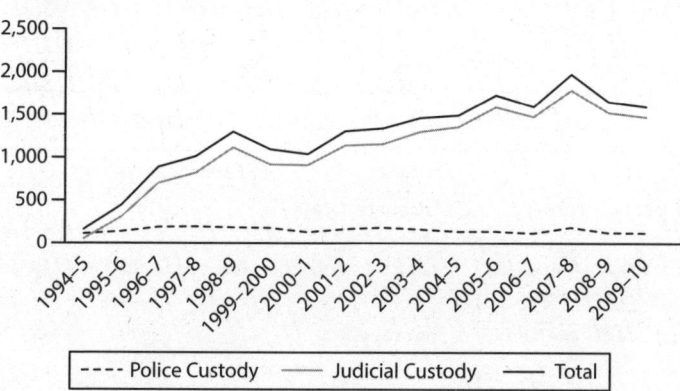

Figure 5A.1   Custodial Deaths in India: Cases Reported to the NHRC (1994–2010)
Source: NHRC annual report (various years).

[259] CHRI. 'Police Reforms in India'.

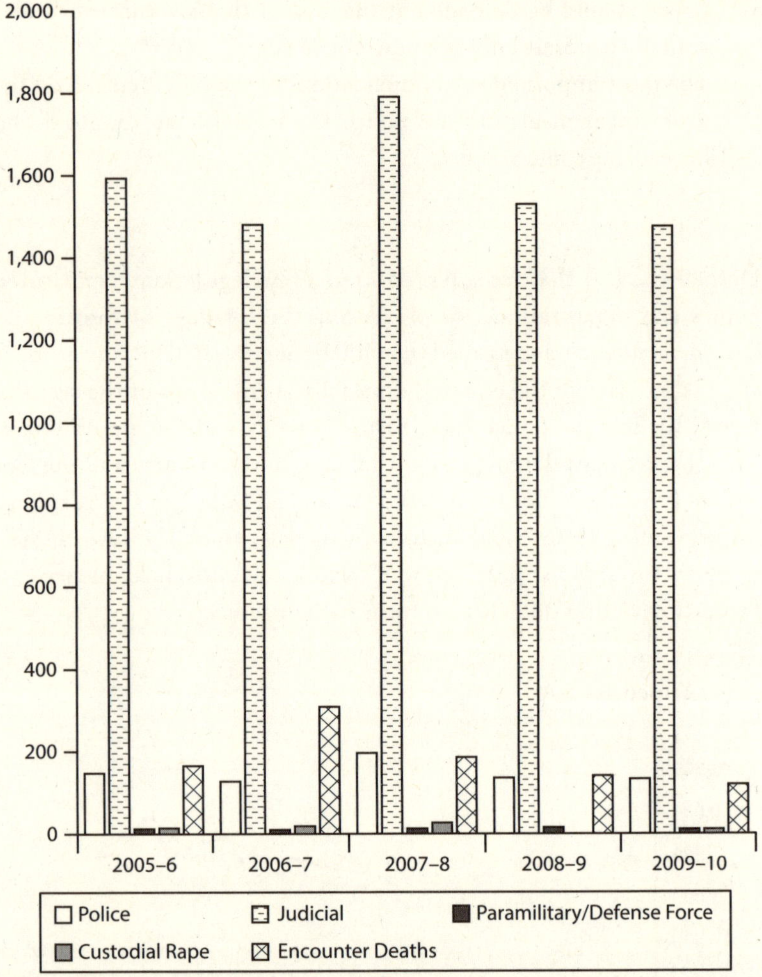

Figure 5A.2   Custodial Death, Rape, and Encounter in India: Cases Reported to the NHRC (2005–10)
Source: NHRC annual report (various years).

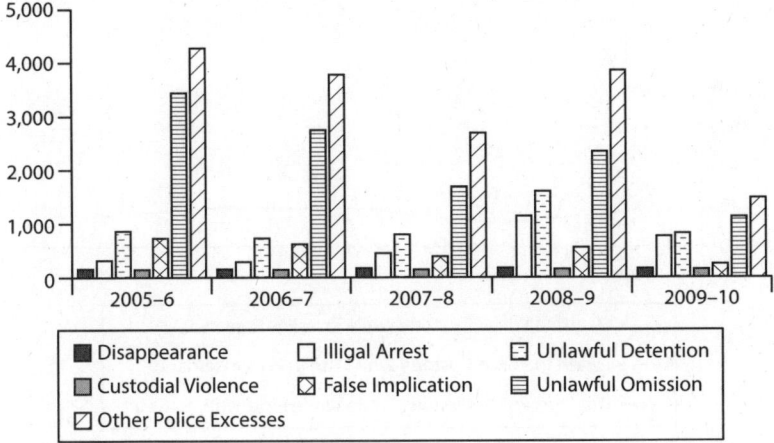

Figure 5A.3   Violence and Atrocity in Police Custody: Cases Disposed of by the NHRC (2005–10)
Source: NHRC annual report (various years).

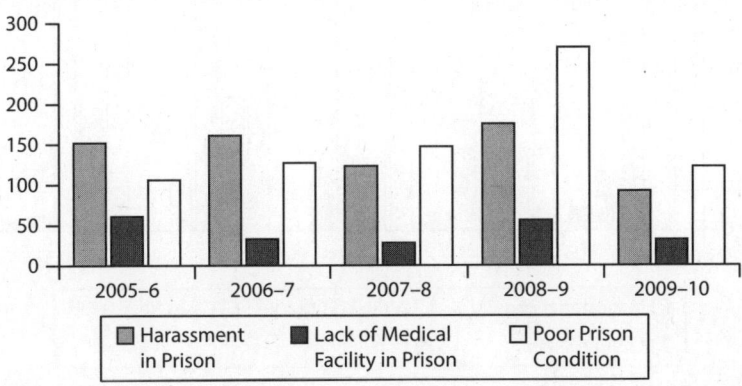

Figure 5A.4   Prison Conditions: Cases Disposed of by the NHRC (2005–10)
Source: NHRC annual report (various years).

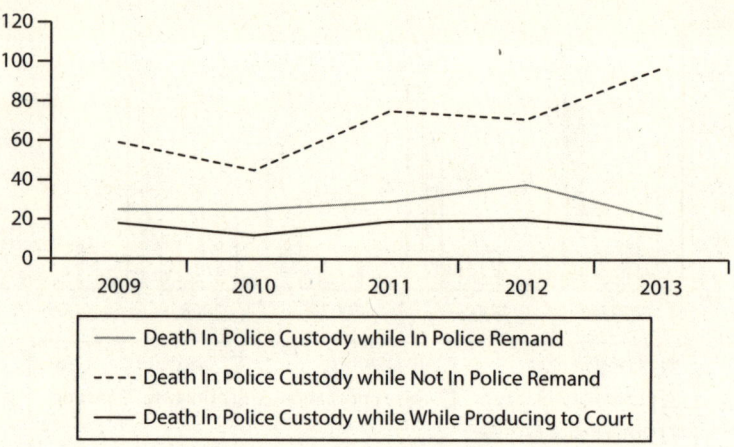

Figure 5A.5 Incidents of Death in Police Custody: NCRB (2009–13)
Source: *Crime in India* (various years), NCRB.

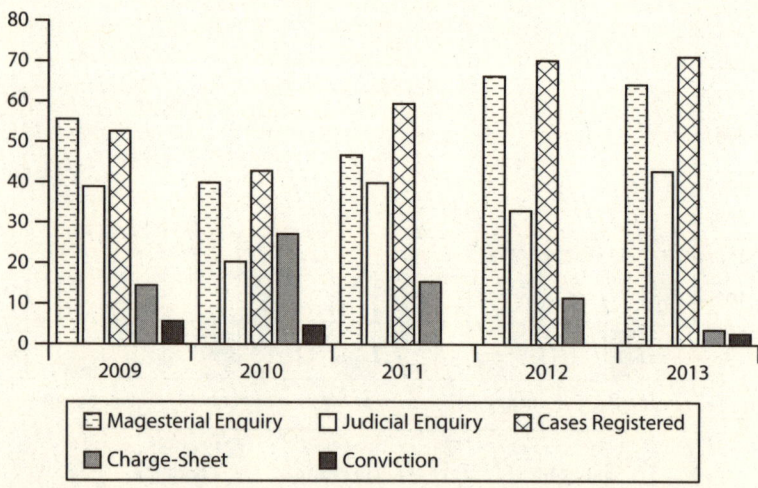

Figure 5A.6 Action Taken in Cases of Death in Police Custody: NCRB
(2009–13)
Source: *Crime in India* (various years), NCRB.

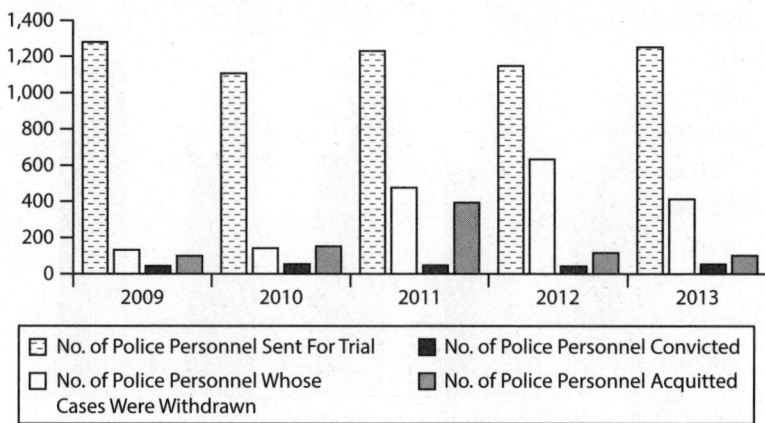

Figure 5A.7   Action Taken against Police Personnel in Cases of Human Rights Abuse: NCRB (2009–13)

Source: *Crime in India* (various years), NCRB.

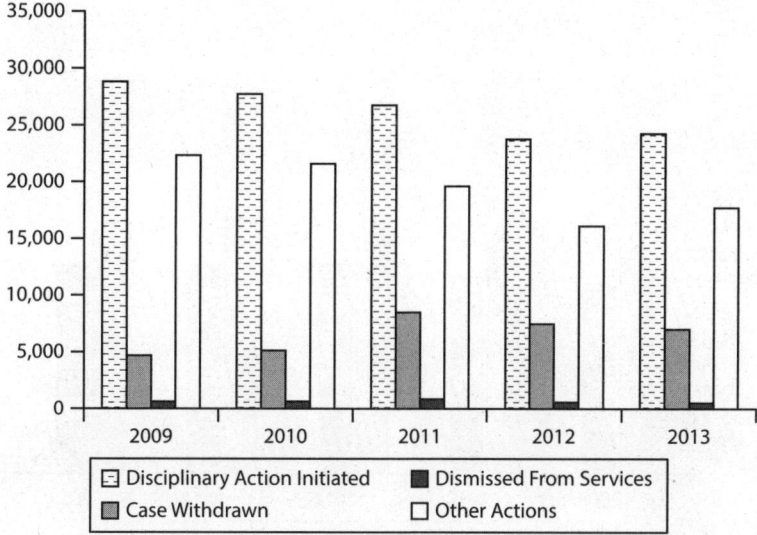

Figure 5A.8   Disciplinary Action Taken against Police Personnel in Cases of Human Rights Abuse: NCRB (2009–13)

Source: *Crime in India* (various years), NCRB.

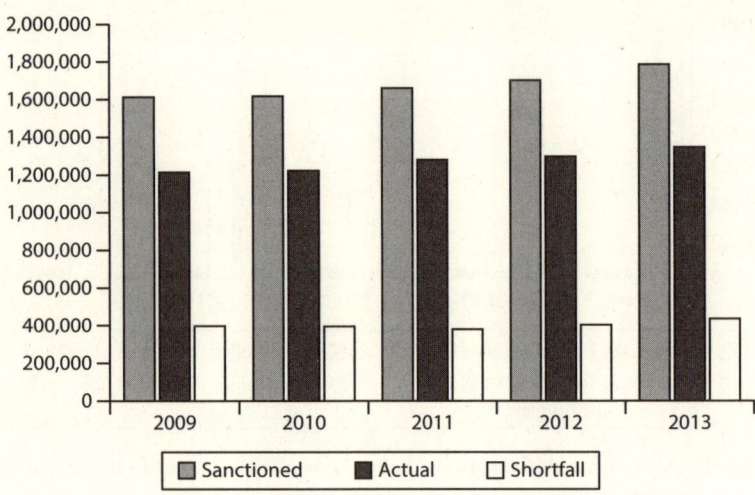

Figure 5A.9   Strength of Police Force (Civil and Armed)—Sanctioned,
Actual, and Shortfall: NCRB (2009–13)
Source: *Crime in India* (various years), NCRB.

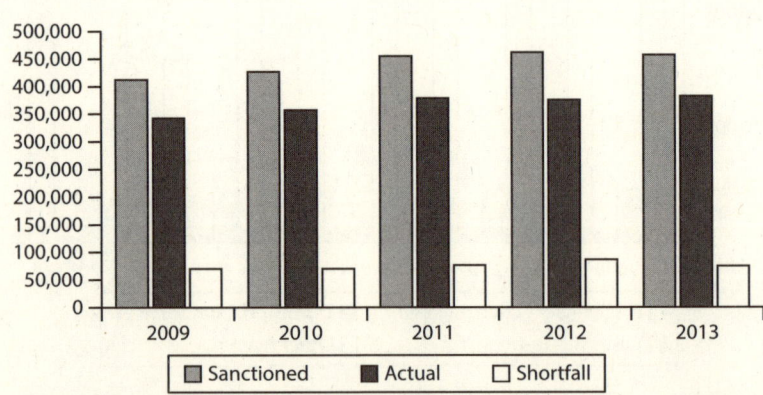

Figure 5A.10   Strength of Armed Police Force—Sanctioned, Actual, and
Shortfall: NCRB (2009–13)
Source: *Crime in India* (various years), NCRB.

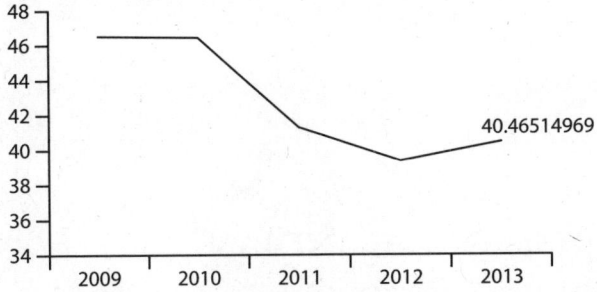

Figure 5A.11   Annual Case Load Per Investigating Officer: NCRB (2009–13)
Source: *Crime in India* (various years), NCRB.

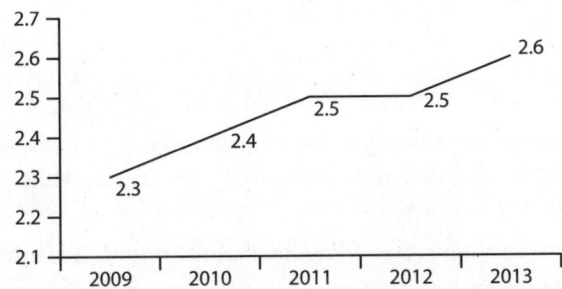

Figure 5A.12   Annual Case Load Per Capita Police Force: NCRB (2009–13)
Source: *Crime in India* (various years), NCRB.

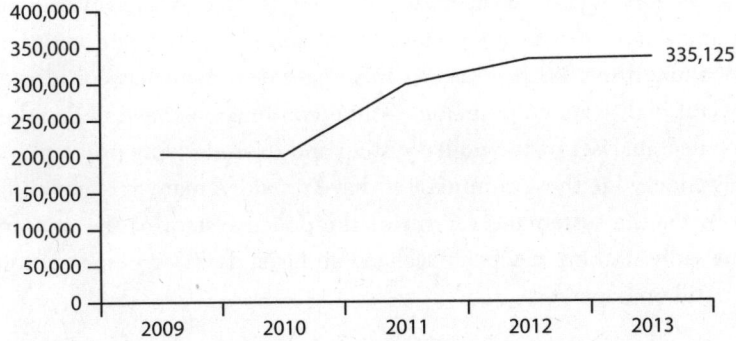

Figure 5A.13   Average Annual Per Capita Cost of Police Force: NCRB (2009–13)
Source: *Crime in India* (various years), NCRB.
Note: The values are in INR.

6

CRISIS IN THE INDIAN POLICE SYSTEM

The general public rarely helps the police or trusts them. The role and participation of the public in assisting the police in maintaining law and order in the country has diminished considerably, which has been quite noticeable in the past few years. Taking into account the huge role of the police in the biggest democracy of the world, it is quite strange to understand that the citizens of this country have little or no faith in its police system. It is very important for the development of any nation to have complete cooperation from its citizens for the effective and efficient performance of its police force. Considering this situation and the loss of faith in the police force by its citizens, the government of India has been giving assurances of reforming the police system for a long time. With regard to this, the government has constituted several high level commissions. These commissions have undertaken detailed analyses of the police system and its underlying problems. In this endeavour, these commissions have provided many recommendations for the systematic reform of the police system of the country. But sadly nothing has been realized so far and all recommendations are still on paper.[1]

[1] 'A Democratic Police Act of India'. Available at http://www. humanrightsinitiative.org/new/2006/democratic_police_act_for_india.pdf, accessed on 11 February 2018.

The citizens of India are reluctant to contact the police and are afraid of them. They are more afraid to be eyewitnesses in many cases of crime since they know the ways or methods used by the police during crucial interrogation and the suffering they will have to go through. This lost of trust and faith on police among the citizens and the way the police force functions play a major role in affecting the readiness of eye witnesses in substantiating or for giving statements in most criminal cases. Eyewitnesses also have the fear of stalking by a criminal's aids/partners/assistants. Further, there have been many incidents where the associates of criminals or offenders have killed witnesses even after many years of their testimony. These incidents discourage the public to go to the police.[2]

It is a fact that the police system in India is not citizen friendly and is especially known for its hostile, aggressive, and unfriendly manner with minority groups.[3] Even after more than seven decades of independence from British rule, the Government of India still follows the old police act and has neither made a single amendment nor implemented any recommendation given by the police commission.[4] The motive behind the government turning a deaf ear to the public is very clear—it is because politicians and other powerful people do not want to lose their control over the police and want to use them for their personal and political gains. Such scenarios date back to the colonial rule in the country when the police force was always a supporter of the ruling government and the powerful. This has given birth to many organized crimes in the country, as it has been the police that helps criminals or perpetrators of organized crimes to carry on with their tasks.[5]

[2] Human Rights Watch. Available at http://www.hrw.org/reports/1999/india/India994-02.htm, accessed on 12 February 2018.

[3] B. Jan. 1999. 'Silencing the Voice of Agricultural Labourers in South Gujarat', *Modern Asian Studies* 33, no. 1: 1–22.

[4] Human Rights Watch Report. 2002. 'State and Police Participation and Complicity in Communal Violence in Gujarat', Human Rights Watch 14, no. 3(C). Available at https://www.hrw.org/reports/2002/india/index.htm#TopOfPage, accessed on 24 August 2019.

[5] P. Reichel. 2005. *Handbook of Transnational Crime & Justice*. London: Sage Publishing.

The general public has always criticized the police for being cruel and overzealous as well as ineffective and inefficient in combating crime and punishing offenders.

Many examples of the status of the police in various Indian states have proved the reality of the situation in the country. In a study conducted by Transparency International India (TII) and the Centre for Media Studies (CMS), the state of Bihar has been declared and rated as the most corrupt state in the country. This can further be observed in the role of the police in the state and the rising crime rates.[6] That the police are an easy and a flexible instrument at the hands of dishonest and corrupt politicians instead of being an instrument for enforcing the rule of law has become normalized in the country. The police in India have an image of being corrupt and being incapable of upholding the law and protecting citizens, and thus they are condemned of being the judge, jury, and executioner.

Police and Its Politicization

As per the CoI, the doctrine of 'separation of powers' has been acknowledged as an integral and a vital part of its basic features.[7] Thus, based on this doctrine, it is already established that all the three organs of the state, that is, the legislature, the judiciary, and the executive are bound by and subject to the provisions of the Constitution. The Constitution, hence, demarcates their respective powers, jurisdictions, responsibilities, and relationship with each another. Thus, it is believed that no organ of the state would exceed its powers as laid down in the Constitution, which is also applicable to the judiciary. In the greater interest of the country and the society and for the public good, all the three organs of the state will work in tandem and in harmony, despite their separate and demarcated jurisdictions.[8] Conversely, the doctrine

---

[6] *The Hindu.* Available at http://www.hindu.com/2005/07/01/stories/2005070103931500.htm, accessed on 12 February 2018.

[7] B. Shiva Rao. 1972. 'The Framing of India's Constitution', *Modern Asian Studies* 6, no. 3: 357–60.

[8] G. Austin. 1966. *The Indian Constitution: The Cornerstone of a Nation.* London: Oxford University Press.

of separation of power is just a myth and the actual situation is entirely different.

As per the provisions of the CoI, every state in the country shall have its own police force. Apart from this, the Government of India has also established some police organizations for some specialized functions at the centre and directly under the control of the union government. As per the statistics for 2003, the total strength of the police force in India was more than two million personnel, which included both the central and the state police forces. Out of this, 1.47 million belonged to the states and union territories, while the rest belonged to the centre.[9]

State governments in the country have been provided with many powers under the Police Act of 1861, and thus as per the provisions of this act, the executive under this authority tries to control the legislature and hence abuses the doctrine of separation of powers. The Indian Police Act, 1861 in its sec. 3 states that, 'The superintendence of the police throughout the general police district shall vest in and shall be exercised by the state government to which such district is subordinate and except as authorized as under the provisions of this Act, no person, officer or Court shall be empowered by the state government to supersede or control any police functionary.'[10] Thus, this provision very clearly reduces the powers of the courts. In the state police force, the head of the state police, that is, DGP or IGP, enjoys his tenure at the pleasure of the chief minister of the respective state. Such a state of affairs has given rise to widespread politicization of the police force, which has been observed to be more committed, supportive, and loyal to the ruling political party and other powerful people of the state.

There have been various instances of unfavorable interference from politicians in the investigation of the police, which terribly obstructs the applicability of the rule of law. It is seen that police officers are

---

[9] 'Police Accountability in India: Policing Contaminated by Politics'. Available at http://www.hrsolidarity.net/mainfile.php/2005vol15no05/2448/, accessed on 12 February 2018.

[10] Sec. 3, Indian Police Act, 1861.

often found to be under pressure for using their powers to shield those who enjoy the support of politicians belonging to the ruling party.[11] On the other hand, officers who refuse to bow down before these politicians or act as per their whims and fancies have to face frequent transfers and, in some extreme cases, departmental inquiries in false legal proceedings. This has resulted in a weak and paralytic criminal justice system in the country.

Accountability of the Police

As per Lord Acton's dictum, 'Power tends to corrupt and absolute power corrupts absolutely.'[12] This is the reality of the Indian police system. The police system is being considerably used with the increased criminalization of police and politicization of criminals increased in the country. Due to this, the effectiveness, reliability, and integrity of the police have taken a back seat.[13] The rule of law is said to be the foundation of democracy and thus entails the right to equality before law and the right to equal protection of law.[14] These rights are protected under the CoI in Art. 14, which mentions the fundamental rights. But the existence of this rule of law is doubtful, given the condition of the politics and administration of the country. We all know that responsibility comes with accountability, and hence the police must be answerable to the public as they are the ones to maintain law and order in the country and thereby protect the citizens of this country. Usually, the police are accountable to their departments and the judiciary for any kind of abuse of power. Despite this, many countries have realized that there is a need to enhance and enlarge the internal systems to ensure that police misconduct or abuse is investigated without any bias. With

[11] 'Need for Thoroughgoing Reforms'. Available at http://www.boloji.com/opinion/0014.htm, accessed on 21 February 2018.

[12] 'Strike the Roots'. Available at http://www.strike-the-root.com/4/bylund/bylund3.html, accessed on 21 February 2018.

[13] 'Policing the Wind Rush Generation'. Available at http://www.historyandpolicy.org/archive/policy-paper-45.html, accessed on 21 February 2018.

[14] CoI, Part III.

regard to the importance of accountability of the police, Y.K. Sabarwal, former CJI, pointed out that 'public accountability' is an important aspect of administrative efficiency.[15]

There have been a number of instances where senior and daring police officers have been denied promotion as they did not bend down before corrupt politicians and did not follow their instructions. The *Times of India*, Pune edition of 27 July 2007, reported that there is a dire need for reforms in the Indian Police Act. Considering the present situation and changes in the society and its mindset, the law seems to be outdated and irrelevant. Another example of the use of the police by corrupt politicians is when India's first woman IPS officer and super cop Kiran Bedi was denied the topmost post of Delhi Police despite her credentials being very strong and having adequate qualifications to be the CP of New Delhi for the reason that 'She did not indulge in "networking" and did not have "booze buddies".'[16] Her junior was appointed as the CP. This was said to be the gravest injustice done in the police administration. Hence, there is an obvious and immediate need for reforms in the Indian Police Act. In India, the Indian Police Act, 1861, and the Prison's Act, 1894 are still followed. Comparing the corporate sector and the government sector, Kiran Bedi said that 'the latter lacked transparency and accountability and there were no performance appraisals. Once someone enters the government sector, he is never questioned and his performance doesn't matter. It is the other way around because if someone raises his voice against the system, he is pulled up for trying to bring about reform.'[17]

[15] Human Rights Watch. Available at http://www.sifyblogs.com/blogs_preview.php?blogid=1430, accessed on 21 February 2018.

[16] Sujata Dutta Sachdeva. 2007. 'Does All Work and No Play Make Women Lose Out?'. *The Times of India* (New Delhi edition), 27 July. Available at https://www.pressreader.com/india/the-times-of-india-new-delhi-edition/20070727/281590941163886, accessed on 24 August 2019.

[17] Times News Network. 2007. 'Kiran Bedi Heads to Shirdi'. Indiatimes, 29 July. Available at https://timesofindia.indiatimes.com/city/pune/Kiran-Bedi-heads-to-Shirdi/articleshow/2241480.cms, accessed on 24 August 2019.

The accountability of the Indian police can be in the following two forms:[18]

1. Internal accountability
2. External accountability

The method of internal accountability would deal with the hierarchical setup, in a system where a police officer should be answerable to his senior officer. This accountability is provided by the Indian Police Act of 1861, which authorizes senior police officers of the rank of SP and above to dismiss, suspend, or reduce in rank any police officer below the rank of inspector of police who they think is negligent in the discharge of his duties or is unfit for the same. The senior police officer also has the power to impose punishments for any misconduct by any junior officer, which could be in the form of a fine not exceeding one month's pay, confinement to quarters not exceeding 15 days, deprivation of good conduct pay, and removal from any office of distinction or special emolument.[19] However, this method of internal accountability is found to be biased and weak most of the time.

In case of external accountability, the method would include organizations such as courts, human rights organizations, and the NGO. In doing this, writ petitions and public interest litigations (PILs) can be filed in higher courts, while criminal prosecutions may be initiated in lower courts. In many instances, quite a few significant judgments have been delivered by the higher courts, which have laid down guidelines and safeguards for controlling the manner and conduct of the police in the course of arresting, interrogating, and various other stages of investigation and also recommended compensation from the government in cases of custodial violence.[20] But the actual situation in the

---

[18] Association of Police Authorities. 1999. *Pounding the Beat: A Guide to Police Finance in England and Wales*. London: Association of Police Authorities.

[19] Sec. 7, Indian Police Act, 1861.

[20] G.P. Joshi. 2005. 'Police Accountability in India: Policing Contaminated by Politics', Commonwealth Human Rights Initiative, pp. 12–13. Available at https://www.humanrightsinitiative.org/programs/aj/police/papers/gpj/police_accountability_in_india.pdf, accessed on 24 August 2019.

country is very grave as there have always been severe delays in the court procedure, and the lack of accountability of the police department further adds to it. This situation has literally distanced the poor and the needy, who actually require justice, and thus a loss of trust has built up. These deprived people bear the brunt of the system and the lack of accountability of the police.

At the international level and worldwide, various human rights organizations such as the Red Cross and Amnesty International play a significant role in holding the police accountable in various cases of gross misconduct and violation of human rights. They play same role in the country by their active presence and by fighting for justice, upholding the human rights and dignity of people, as well as holding the police accountable for crimes committed by them. At the national level too, one organization that is actively working towards human rights protection is the NHRC. It was established on 12 October 1993.[21] The NHRC, like its international counterparts, has worked towards the protection of people from any kind of violence by the police, including custodial violence and violations of human rights. A number of achievements have been attributed to its credit in terms of its efforts to make the police accountable for their actions. But the NHRC has also experienced difficulties and problems because of certain deficiencies and infirmities in the law that governs its activities and operations. Hence, the right to information[22] in India has been a greater achievement since it has ensured more accountability and transparency of the activities of the government as well as the police.

* * *

In recent times, many cases of torture and custodial violence have been reported from many parts of India, and this has been possible because of the procedure of external accountability such as reporting by the media. The Right to Information Act too has helped in such matters of violence by the police, thereby making them accountable.

[21] NHRC, 'About the Organisation', Available at http://nhrc.nic.in/about-us/about-the-Organisation, accessed on 24 August 2019.
[22] The Right to Information Act, 2005.

The reports pointed out that crimes of custodial deaths have occurred more in areas of the country where normally these kinds of violence are not observed, such as in Kerala.[23] It has been further observed that the number of crimes have increased considerably since independence. The Asian Human Rights Commission (AHRC) too has reported many cases where torture was the major means during criminal investigation by the police. Thus, the rising number of such crimes, torture, and custodial violence by the police has put a big question mark on the steps taken by the government to combat and prevent it and secure its citizens from such acts of violence. The AHRC has been doubtful about any procedure being followed or implemented as per the provisions of the UNCAT,[24] to which India has been a party, but has not ratified it yet. Further, it is also seen that the victims of custodial violence have nowhere to go to seeking redress and justice for the violence and torture they have been subjected to. Taking the legal route puts a lot of financial burden, which the general public cannot afford.[25]

Towards providing justice to the common people and preventing corruption among the police, the Supreme Court of India delivered a landmark judgment on 18 December 1997, which made the CBI and the Directorate of Enforcement autonomous, thereby protecting and shielding them from any kind of influence from the external world so that they would function efficiently and effectively without being biased and serve the rule of law. Further, this landmark judgment made the Single Directive null and void, according to which the CBI needed prior permission from the government to enquire, investigate and take action against senior executives and civil servants of the rank of joint secretary and above.

---

[23] 'India: Government of Kerala Must Criminalise Torture to Prevent Custodial Deaths', available at http://www.ahrchk.net/statements/mainfile. php/2006statements/688/, accessed on 28 February 2018.

[24] UNCAT. Available at http://www.austlii.edu.au/au/other/HRLRes/2002/5/, accessed on 28 February 2018.

[25] Asian Human Rights Commission—Statement. Available at http://www.ahrchk.net/statements/mainfile.php/2006statements/855/, accessed on 28 February 2018.

Furthermore, the enactment and enforcement of the Right to Information Act, 2005, was another landmark achievement towards seeking transparency, accountability, and justice in the country. This right enabled and ensured every citizen the right to get information from the government, the police, or any other organization about their activities and operations, which made government departments including the police more accountable for their own actions.

7

REFORMS IN THE POLICE FORCES
The Need of the Hour

The Indian police system is embodied in an organization that is absolute in its institution. There have been many initiatives and recommendations for reforming the Indian police system as a result of the growing concern of the public and the government about the insufficiencies of certain practices and procedures of the police. Towards this initiative, many high-level committees, headed by eminent jurists, reformers, bureaucrats, and so on, have been established. These include the Gore Committee on Police Training 1971, the NPC 1977, the Riberio Committee on Police Reforms 1998, the Padmanabhaiah Committee on Police Reforms 2000, and the Malimath Committee on Reforms of Criminal Justice System 2001.[1] These committees made a number of recommendations and proposals, which were accepted, but some of the significant proposals have not been introduced so far.

The following sections present some of the reports and recommendations of these committees, which are discussed here so as to recognize the efforts of the members who extensively worked for restructuring and reforming the Indian police system.

---

[1] Human Rights Blog. Available at http://www.humanrightsblog.org/archives/cat_india.html, accessed on 4 March 2018.

Committee on Police Training, 1971–73 (the Gore Committee)

On 10 November 1971, the Government of India set up the Gore Committee, under the chairmanship of M.S. Gore.[2] The committee was set up to review the training process of the state police from constabulary level to IPS level,[3] identify gaps, and suggest suitable measures to achieve the set standards. The Gore Committee recommended areas covering development of necessary knowledge and skills, right attitudes, effective decision-making and leadership abilities, and critical and innovative thinking.[4] The basic premise recommended by the committee was to shift the focus from law and order and crime mitigation towards sensitizing and soft skills such as humane behaviour, sensible communication skills, and attitude.[5] The committee made 186 recommendations out of which 45 were related to police reforms.[6] The recommendation that relates to the police training has mostly been implemented. However, the reforms relating to the structure of the police system have been overlooked.

Ribeiro Committee on Police Reforms, 1998[7]

The Ribeiro Committee was constituted in view of the SC's directions[8] following a PIL on police reforms. The committee was headed by

[2] M.S. Gore was Indian social scientist and a former director of the Tata Institute of Social Sciences, Mumbai.

[3] *The Gore Committee Report on Police Training*, Ministry of Home Affairs, Government of India. Available at http://bprd.nic.in/writereaddata/mainlinkfile/File692.pdf, accessed on 4 March 2018.

[4] 'Indian Police System: A Reform Proposal'. Available at http://www.loksatta.org/indianpolicesystem.pdf, accessed on 4 March 2018.

[5] Commonwealth Human Rights Initiative (CHRI). Available at http://www.humanrightsinitiative.org/index.php?option=com_content&view=article&id=683%3Apolice-india-gore-committee&catid=91%3Apolicereformsindia&Itemid=98, accessed on 4 March 2018.

[6] CHRI.

[7] Ministry of Home Affairs. 1998. Memorandum No. 11018/1/98-PM, 25 May. New Delhi: Government of India.

[8] Writ Petition (Civil) No. 310 of 1996.

J.F. Riberio,[9] and it proposed five major recommendations related to state security, selection of the DGP, and complaints against the police. The committee was set up to review implementation of the guidelines of the NPC, the NHRC, and the Vohra Committee and to recommend suitable measures and modalities for their implementation. The Supreme Court directed the Ribeiro Committee to evaluate the feasibility of constituting security commissions or police authorities at various levels; the steps for a transparent and efficient procedure for appointment of the police chief; and the separation of the investigative wing from the law and order wing of the police force.[10] It recommended the establishment of a statutory state security commission; a district police complaint authority to hear, address, and redress public complaints about police excesses, arbitrary arrests and detentions, false implication in criminal cases, and custodial violence;[11] and establishment of a police establishment board to monitor transfers, promotions, rewards, and so on.[12]

Committee on Police Reforms, 2000 (Padmanabhaiah Committee)

The Government of India constituted a five-member committee headed by K. Padmanabhaiah in January 2000 to inspect the recruitment of the police force, training, duties and responsibilities, the behaviour of police officers, and police investigation and prosecution. The committee suggested 99 actionable recommendations, out of which 54 needed to be implemented by the central government and 69 by state governments.[13]

---

[9] J.F. Ribeiro is a retired IPS officer and former ambassador of India to Bulgaria.

[10] *Report of the Ribeiro Committee on Police Reforms: A Critical Analysis.* Available at http://www.humanrightsinitiative.org/programs/aj/police/india/initiatives/analysis_ribeiro.pdf, accessed on 5 March 2018.

[11] *Report of the Ribeiro Committee*, p. 12.

[12] *Report of the Ribeiro Committee*, p. 14.

[13] Commonwealth Human Rights Initiative (CHRI). 'Police Reforms: India'. Available at http://www.humanrightsinitiative.org/programs/aj/police/india/initiatives/padmanabhaiah.htm, accessed on 5 March 2018.

The summary recommendations of the Padmanabhaiah Committee are as follows:[14]

1. To examine and specify the challenges that the police in India would face during the next millennium
2. To adopt a philosophy of community policing
3. To support community policing activities, with the Government of India funding pilot programmes, initiating training, developing training material, and so on
4. To separate investigation from law and order work
5. To evaluate the strengths and weaknesses of the police force, as it is organized and structured today, to assess if it would be able to meet those challenges in future
6. To understand and appreciate the gap between the expectations of the public and police performance, and whether this gap can be filled without making any basic changes in the structure, organization, and the attitudes of the police
7. To envision a modern, cultured, people-friendly, and fighting-fit police force, which is able to win the confidence and trust of the people and at the same time effectively tackle the problems of organized crime, militancy, and terrorism
8. To bring about the changes in the police force and its functions in order to transform them into the most professional and competent force
9. To suggest measures to equip the police to adequately meet the challenges of fighting modern, hi-tech criminals and cybercrime
10. To recommend changes in the weaponry, communication, and mobility of the police force
11. To examine how the intelligence gathering machinery can be revamped, both at the centre and within the states, and how their mutual interaction for intelligence sharing can be made faster and more reliable
12. To have an addl SP to exclusively handle crime and investigation works

[14] CHRI. 'Police Reforms'.

13. To delete secs 25 and 26 of the Indian Evidence Act in order to make confessions before an SP or superior officer admissible before a court of law

14. To make judicial inquiry compulsory in cases involving rape or death in police custody

15. To devise methods of insulating the police from politicization and criminalization[15]

16. To devise ways of securing public trust and cooperation in preventing and solving crime

17. To examine the need to clarify some crimes as 'federal crimes' and to create a federal law enforcement agency under the Ministry of Home Affairs

18. To introduce structural changes so that the police function more efficiently and professionally

19. To establish a permanent national commission for police standards to adopt standards and monitor their enforcement

20. To initiate public–police partnership or confidence-building measures at various levels

21. To replace the Police Act of 1861 with a new act

Committee on Reforms of Criminal Justice System, 2001–3 (Malimath Committee)

The Malimath Committee addressed the principles of the criminal justice system, investigation, prosecution, judiciary, crime, and punishment. Its report has been heavily criticized by human rights organizations for its suggestion of changing the burden of proof. The committee made 158 observations and recommendations. There are 55 major recommendations of which 42 have to be implemented by the central government and 26 by the state governments.[16]

---

[15] CHRI. 'Police Reforms'.

[16] Amnesty International. Available at http://web.amnesty.org/library/index/engasa200252003, accessed on 12 March 2018.

The Malimath Committee[17] recognizes that the accused has certain legal and constitutional rights, which also includes the state's obligation to respect and follow in letter and spirit the due process of law; speedy, independent, and impartial trial; restraint on torture and forced testimony; and legal aid.[18] It recommends changes in the criminal justice system to improve the competence and credibility of the investigating agency. It is the duty of every investigating agency and its officers to ensure that statements are recorded authentically, with full integrity and the informed consent of the accused or suspect and witnesses and without them being subject to any form of torture, threats, or inducements for extracting information.[19]

In case of torture, violence, or rape of a person in custody, the person should be free to inform the competent magistrate about such violence. In such instances, a detailed enquiry must take place to ascertain the truth and initiate appropriate action, and the magistrate has further authority to send the person on judicial remand.[20] The chief metropolitan/judicial magistrate should diligently record the statement of the person complaining about torture, violence, or rape in custody and take his signature on the statement. The person subjected to torture, violence, or rape in custody must be sent for medical examination by an assistant civil surgeon or a more senior medical officer.[21]

Police Act Drafting Committee, 2005
(Soli Sorabjee Committee)

The Government of India constituted the Soli Sorabjee Committee in October 2005 for the purpose of preparing a new model police act

---

[17] *Report of the Committee on Reforms of Criminal Justice System*, Ministry of Home Affairs, Government of India, March 2003.

[18] Malimath Committee, para. 4.2.

[19] Malimath Committee, para. 3.12.

[20] Malimath Committee, para. 4.9.

[21] Malimath Committee, para. 19.6.4.

keeping in mind the ever changing roles, responsibilities, and challenges of the police. This act would provide a guiding framework for states to adopt with modifications suiting their contexts. The Soli Sorabjee Committee submitted a draft Model Police Act, 2006, on 30 October 2006, which included provisions related to recruitment, qualification, and public–police partnership.[22]

Second Administrative Reforms Commission or ARC (Veerappa Moily Committee), 2005

The Second Administrative Reforms Commission or ARC (Veerappa Moily Committee) was formed by the Government of India on 31 August 2005. It was formed so as to prepare a detailed blueprint for revamping the public administration system and suggest measures to achieve a proactive, responsive, accountable, sustainable and efficient administration for the country at all levels of the government. It was headed by Veerappa Moily who was the Chairman of the Commission.[23] Apart from a number of mandates about which reports of recommendation were prepared, there was also one of those reports which dealt with the police reforms in the country.

The Report of the Commission on Public Order, the Commission dealt with the crucial reform of police system and the criminal justice system, the need for reform of prisons, the future of some special laws, and the role of political parties, civil society and the media.

Some of the significant recommendations of the Report were related to the separation of investigation of crimes and police functions. It included the protection of the police force from political interferences, formation of a separate machinery for prosecution under a district attorney, formation of police establishment

---

[22] CHRI. Available at http://www.humanrightsinitiative.org/index.php?option=com_content&view=article&catid=35%3Apolicereforms&id=600%3Athe-police-act-drafting-committee&Itemid=98, accessed on 12 March 2018.

[23] About ARC, Department of Administrative Reforms & Public Grievances. Available at https://web.archive.org/web/20110206020059/http://darpg.nic.in/ArticleContent.aspx?category=106, accessed on 2 November 2019.

committees for ensuring fixed tenures for senior police functionaries, reinforcement of the intelligence mechanism, formation of a transparent complaint system by appointing independent complaint authorities at the state as well as the district level. Apart from these, the Commission also recommended significant reforms in the criminal justice system which included citizen-friendly FIR registration system, setting up of local courts, laying down the rules for investigation, recommending amendment to secs 161 and 162 of the CrPC, making confessions before the police admissible as evidence, suggesting amendments to sec. 311 of the CrPC, and modernization and reforms of the prison system. The Report also included recommendations related to local policing, metropolitan policing and traffic management.[24]

Role of the NHRC

The NHRC has issued several guidelines that are important for the purpose of this chapter, and which are detailed in the next few paragraphs:

1. Guidelines on Human Rights in Prisons[25]
2. Guidelines on Custodial Death and Rape[26]
3. Guidelines on Cases of Encounter Deaths[27]
4. Guidelines on Polygraph Tests and Arrests[28]

[24] Government of India. 2009. *State Administration: Public Order*, Fifteenth Report of Second Administrative Reforms Commission, April, pp. 13–14. Available at https://darpg.gov.in/sites/default/files/sdadmin15.pdf, accessed on 02 November 2019.

[25] NHRC. 1996. 'Guidelines on Human Rights in Prisons' (as revised on 25 September 1996, 11 February 1999, and 8 November 1999).

[26] NHRC. 1993. 'Guidelines on Custodial Death and Rape' (as revised on 21 June 1995, 10 August 1995, and 27 March 1997).

[27] NHRC. 1996. 'Guidelines on Cases of Encounter Deaths' (as revised on 29 March 1997 and 2 December 2003).

[28] NHRC. 1997. 'Guidelines on Polygraph Tests and Arrests' (as modified on 22 November 1999 and 11 January 2000).

5. Guidelines Relating to Administration of Lie Detector Test[29]
6. Guidelines on Measures to Improve Police and Public Relationship[30]

Guidelines on Human Rights in Prison

1. Compensation should be awarded to the family of mentally ill persons when imprisoned in jails, recoverable from the erring officer.
2. Proper healthcare facility and periodic medical examination should be provided for undertrials or convicts.
3. Health screening of a prisoner should be mandatory at the time of admission.
4. NHRC's pro forma for health screening of prisoners on admission to jail should be mandatorily complied with.

Guidelines on Custodial Death and Rape

1. It is mandatory to video film all post-mortem in cases of custodial death and to submit the report and video record to the NHRC.
2. Every custodial death and rape must be reported to the NHRC within 24 hours by the DM and SP.
3. It is also compulsory to follow the NHRC's Model Autopsy pro forma, which is based on the United Nations Model Autopsy Protocol.

Guidelines on Cases of Encounter Deaths

1. Details of encounter must be entered in the register maintained for the purpose by the police.
2. An encounter should be investigated circumstances where prima facie it appears as the commission of a staged encounter.
3. Investigation should not be done by the police station concerned if the suspected police officer belongs to the same.

[29] NHRC. 1999. 'Guidelines on Administration of Lie Detector Test'.
[30] NHRC. 1999. 'Guidelines on Measures to Improve Police and Public Relationship' (as modified on 22 December 1999 and 24 December 1999).

4. Investigation should be handled by an independent investigation agency, such as the CID.
5. A magisterial inquiry must be held and relative(s) of the victim must be involved.
6. Prompt prosecution and disciplinary action must be initiated when a person is found guilty in the enquiry or investigation
7. Compensation should be awarded to victim in case of conviction of the police officer(s) involved.
8. Out-of-turn promotion or instant gallantry rewards should not be bestowed on officers involved in such an encounter immediately after the incident.
9. Chief ministers and the DGP must submit bi-annual reports on encounter cases.

Guidelines on Polygraph Tests and Arrests

1. Force should not be used as a general rule while and during arrest unless the suspect resists arrest but only to the minimum extent required to overcome him/her.
2. Utmost care should be taken to ensure that injuries do not take place during arrest.
3. Dignity of the arrestee must be ensured and protected.
4. Public exhibition or parading of arrestees is forbidden in all circumstances.
5. Body search of arrestees should be done with care to his/her privacy and women's decency and in dignified and respectful manner, without using force or aggression.
6. Handcuffs or chains should not be used as a general rule but can be used only in strict compliance of the Supreme Court's guidelines.
7. Arrest of a woman should not be done after sunset and before sunrise and only by or in the presence of women police officers.
8. Use of force or violence is forbidden while arresting children or juveniles, and coercion can be used to a minimal level in special circumstances.

9. Concerned citizens should be involved while arresting children and juveniles to make sure that the latter are not intimidated.
10. Grounds for arrest must be communicated immediately in the arrestee's language.
11. These grounds must have already been recorded in writing in police records and should be shown and provided on the request to the arrestee.
12. Arrestee can demand intimation of place of his/her arrest to family, relative(s), or friend(s), which should be duly recorded in a register by the police.
13. In case of a bailable offence, the arrestee should be informed about the right to be released on bail by the police to enable him/her suitable arrangement for sureties.
14. Arrestee should also be informed about his/her entitlement to consul and seek advice and be defended in court by a lawyer of his/her choice.
15. Arrestee should be informed about the right to free legal aid.
16. Arrestee should be informed about the right to medical aid and accordingly necessary medical aid should be provided on request to such arrestee or in certain exceptional circumstances where he/she is incapable to request, medical aid should be arranged by the police; in case of a woman arrestee, the female requesting for medical help should be examined only by a female registered medical professional.
17. The details of such medical arrangements should be duly recorded by the police in a register.
18. The police should promptly transmit information about the arrest and place of custody to the control room and district/state headquarters.
19. There should be a 24×7 monitoring system in place.
20. Injuries at the time of arrest must be immediately noted in detail, including its nature and reasons, in the register of arrest by the police officer concerned.
21. A duly-signed injury certificate must be issued at the time arrestee's release by the police.

22. Periodic medical examination of the arrestee in police remand should be done every 48 hours by a trained medical officer or by a medical officer on the panel.

23. A duly-signed medical certificate must be issued at the time of the arrestee's release by the police.

24. The arrestee should be produced before a competent court within a period of 24 hours.

25. The arrestee must be allowed to meet his lawyer at any time while undergoing interrogation.

26. Interrogation must take place at a notified place, which should be informed to the family, relatives, or friends, who should be allowed to access.

27. Rights to life, dignity and liberty, and protection against torture and degrading treatment should be respected during interrogation and in the means of interrogation.

28. The arrest guidelines must be translated in vernacular languages and circulated to all police stations.

29. The arrest guidelines should be incorporated in a handbook meant for the police.

30. The arrest guidelines must be fully publicized in the media.

31. The arrest guidelines must be conspicuously exhibited in all police stations.

32. A complaint redress mechanism must be established by the police.

33. Complaints against police officers must be addressed, investigated, and remedied in a timely manner.

34. The location, address, and procedure of the complaint redress mechanism should also be prominently displayed in the police station.

35. Non-governmental organizations and institutions such as courts, health centres, hospitals, and educational institution should also be engaged to sensitize masses about the aforementioned guidelines.

36. The complaint redress mechanism must function transparently.

37. Reports of the complaint redress mechanism should be accessible.

38. Timely action on complaints should be carried out, including departmental and criminal action.

39. The police should be trained and sensitized.

Guidelines Relating to Administration of Lie Detector Test

1. Lie detector tests must be conducted only with the consent of the accused.
2. The investigating agency must give an option to the accused to express his willingness or non-willingness for the test.
3. If the accused volunteers for undergoing such tests, s/he should be allowed to consult a lawyer, and the physical, emotional, and legal consequences must be described by the police and the lawyer.
4. A competent judicial magistrate should hear and record the consent of the accused.
5. A consenting accused must be appropriately represented by a legal practitioner at the hearings.
6. During such hearings, the consenting accused should be informed in an unequivocal and clear manner about the non-confessional status of the statements or disclosures and that they will be treated as statements given to the police.
7. The detention, interrogation, and its length should also be considered during such hearings.
8. An independent agency should conduct and record such tests in the presence of a lawyer.
9. The record of such tests should include a detailed medical and factual commentary of the information obtained and not its interpretation.

Guidelines on Police–Public Relationship

1. The Human Rights Cell (henceforth HRC) will serve as a bridge between the police and the NHRC.
2. Complaints referred by the NHRC to HRC should be investigated by an officer of appropriate level.
3. The NHRC's recommendations must be followed up diligently to ensure suitable actions and subsequent compliance.
4. The HRC can recommend investigation by independent agencies such as the CID or CBI in situations where a fair investigation is unlikely.

5. The HRC should remain watchful of human rights violations by police personnel through the media and other sources.

6. The HRC should monitor all matters concerning police atrocities, harassment, or abuse of power that are sent by the NHRC to the SP.

7. The HRC should be in direct interaction with the SP on a regular basis and give appropriate instructions or guidelines for the abatement of human rights abuse by the police.

8. The HRC should undertake surprise visits to monitor and prevent illegal detention and abuse of power in police stations.

9. The HRC should make sure to display the D.K. Basu Guidelines in all police stations.

10. The HRC should coordinate with state police academies and training centres in order to ensure the incorporation of human rights in the training curriculum.

11. The HRC should organize sessions or short-term courses in all the training centres with the help of the expertise of outstanding personalities, advocates, and NGO functionaries.

12. The HRC should identify areas of human rights violations and chalk out schemes for its prevention and rehabilitation.

13. The HRC should directly monitor investigation, remedial measures, and follow-up of departmental action in deaths, rape, torture, and illegal detentions in police custody.

14. The HRC should be active in the promotion of human rights awareness and literacy by using media programmes and publications.

15. The HRC's quarterly newsletter on human rights in law enforcement should be circulated to the police.

16. The police should launch a toll free phone number for the public to share crime intelligence or information with the police.

17. This public number should be set up in the police control rooms, police stations, or sub-divisional offices.

18. The police cannot compel callers to disclose their identity and address.

19. The police should recognize distinguished contributions of the public and reward such contributions.

20. Police stations should organize meetings to share individual and public grievances.

Bills on Custodial Violence: Prevention of Torture Bill, 2010

The Union Ministry of Home Affairs introduced the Prevention of Torture (POT) Bill in the Lok Sabha on 26 April 2010. The bill was introduced with a twofold objective: (a) as a precursor to ratification of the CAT by India and (b) to punish public servants for commission of torture.[31] The bill was meant to fill gaps in the IPC.[32] It was a very short bill consisting of only six sections. It defined torture as an intentional act of public servants or anyone instigated or authorized by a public servant or with the consent and knowledge of a public servant that inflicts grievous hurt or danger to life, limb, and health for extracting confessions or information.[33] If a public officer tortures any person for obtaining confessions and information and on the grounds of caste, race, religion, place of birth, residence, language, or community, he/she shall be punished with a maximum of 10 years imprisonment and fine,[34] subject to a mandatory government sanction for his prosecution.[35]

The bill was passed by the Lok Sabha in 2010, but it did not pass the Rajya Sabha, which referred the bill to a select committee. The select committee requested amending the bill to make it more compliant with CAT. But nothing was done and the bill lapsed. Besides, the AFSPA, the provisions of which had led to a number of torture and human rights violation incidents, was not repealed. Again in May 2017, the POT Bill was tabled in the Parliament as per the recommendation of the Law Commission of India in its 273rd report. But since then it has not been passed by the Lok Sabha. On 21 January 2019, the Supreme Court allowed three weeks' time to all states and union territories to send their inputs on the bill.

---

[31] The POT Bill, 2010, Preamble.
[32] The POT Bill, 2010, Object and Reasons.
[33] The POT Bill, 2010, sec. 3.
[34] The POT Bill, 2010, sec. 4.
[35] The POT Bill, 2010, sec. 6.

The Law Commission also suggested that the Government of India ratify CAT.[36]

The main features of the POT Bill include the following:[37]

- Punishment, including life term to officials for any kind of act of torture and inhuman treatment against any person
- Provisions for compensation to victims of torture; the courts to have the authority to decide a justiciable compensation after taking various aspects of the case into account
- The courts to take into account the socioeconomic background of the victim to ensure that the compensation is helpful to the victim to bear the expenses on medical treatment and rehabilitation

The Law Commission of India recommended the amendment of the CrPC, 1973, and the Indian Evidence Act, 1872, and the enforcement of this standalone legislation on torture. The commission also recommended that the state needs to own the responsibility for any kind of injuries or acts of torture caused by its agents such as officers, police, and security personnel on citizens and that the 'principle of sovereign immunity cannot override the rights assured by the Constitution'.[38]

* * *

Besides the aforementioned recommendations of various high-level committees and organizations to bring reforms in the Indian police system, several other NPC as well as state police commissions have regularly suggested structural reforms in the police department and

---

[36] The POT Bill, 2017. Available at https://www.gktoday.in/gk/law-commission-273rd-report-and-prevention-of-torture-bill-2017, accessed on 11 February 2019.

[37] The POT Bill, 2017.

[38] Press Trust of India (PTI). 'Law Panel: Life Term for Government Officials Indulging in Torture'. Available at https://economictimes.indiatimes.com/news/politics-and-nation/law-panel-life-term-for-government-officials-indulging-in-torture/articleshow/61354978.cms, accessed on 13 February 2019.

emphasized the need to insulate and shield the police from external pressures (political), but their core recommendations have never been implemented by the executive. The Supreme Court of India recommended seven directives on reforms of the police for both the central and state governments in the judgment for the case of *Prakash Singh and Ors v Union of India*[39] in 2006.[40] Following this judgment and the Supreme Court directive, the Indian Police Foundation was formed in 2015 to exert pressure on state governments for implementing the directives of the Supreme Court on police reforms. But most states have failed to follow and implement the Supreme Court directives on police reforms.[41]

As per the Kerala Police Reorganization Committee (1959)[42] 'the greatest obstacle to efficient police administration flows from the domination of party politics under the state administration ... the result of partisan interference is often reflected in lawless enforcement of laws, inferior service and in general decline of police prestige followed by irresponsible criticism and consequent widening of the cleavage between the police and the public.' The Punjab Police Commission (1961–2)[43] criticized that 'members of political parties, particularly of the ruling party, whether in the legislature or outside interfere considerably in the working of the police for unlawful ends'. The West Bengal Police Commission (1960–1)[44] found that influential persons who

---

[39] (2006) 8 SCC 1.

[40] Gaurav Vivek Bhatnagar. 'No State Fully Complied with SC Directives on Police Reforms, Finds Study'. Available at https://thewire.in/government/sc-police-reforms-directives, accessed on 21 February 2019.

[41] 'Insights into Editorial: Awaiting Police Reforms'. Available at https://www.insightsonindia.com/2017/10/05/insights-editorial-awaiting-police-reforms/, accessed on 21 February 2019.

[42] Manithan. 'Life's Right for Human Rights'. Available at http://www.tamilinfoservice.com/manitham/article/2004/1.htm, accessed on 16 March 2019.

[43] Manithan. 'Life's Right for Human Rights'.

[44] 'Police Reform in India—A Distant Dream'. Available at http://www.milligazette.com/Archives/15042002/1504200253.htm, accessed on 16 March 2019.

were highly placed in society interfered in the investigation of offences. The Tamil Nadu Police Commission (1971) stated that the problem of political interference had grown over the years in spite of the most explicit public declarations made by successive chief ministers.[45] The Delhi Police Commission (1968) observed that political interference was the main source of corruption.

Thus, it is clear that the recommendations of various committees and commissions disturbed the entrenched and well-established elite at the prospect that they will lose control over an organization that they had been misusing for such a long time. This has resulted in undermining the rule of law and obstructed the growth and development of society and the formation of a healthy and professional system of policing.

[45] *Dialogue* 6, no. 1. Available at http://www.asthabharati.org/Dia_July04/Prakash.htm, accessed on 16 March 2018.

8

COMMUNITY POLICING
A Reform and the Indian Scenario

Community policing is often referred to as neighbourhood policing.[1] It is one of the most dynamic steps that has been taken towards the democratization of policing, and thus, such an approach requires the police to be unbiased, open minded, and sensitive towards the problems of society. The police cannot function efficiently and effectively unless and until it has good support from society or the community.[2] Hence, a team including police personnel, members of the community, the common public, and members of different organizations needs to be formed, which may further include police community support officers, special constables, community wardens, volunteers, and partners who would work together in a partnership so as to build a secure environment in society. For preventing crime and maintaining law and order in any society, the support of the community is a *sine qua non*.[3] Community policing or more so

---

[1] G.P. Alpert and R.G. Dunham. 1986. 'Community Policing', *Journal of Police Science and Administration* 14: 212–22.

[2] Hazelwood Police Department Organization. Available at http://www.ci.hazelwood.mo.us/department/police/organizn.cfm, accessed on 18 March 2018.

[3] 'Training for Transformation'. Available at http://www.india-seminar.com/1999/483/483%20sankar%20sen.htm, accessed on 18 March 2018.

democratic policing can only be possible when there is an involvement of the public. Information, assistance, and inputs received from the public strengthen the collaboration between the police and the community and help solve community problems and reduce crimes. A successful community policing programme needs a change in the decision-making process whereby street-level police officers are involved in decision-making and entrusted with responsibility, furthering their interaction with the community and thereby fulfilling the goals of community policing. Such an approach and programme requires inputs from the public in all dimensions of the processes that the police undertake, and this will help in the preparation of budgets, planning, gathering information about various crimes, and so on. To do this, further, the community and the police should have shared values, responsibilities, and duties. In places where society consists of people from diverse backgrounds and where there are unequal power relations, the responsibility of the community policing programme and its representatives increases so as to ensure that the unequal groups of people are balanced and that the marginalized are not left out because of the dominant groups.[4]

This approach is actually one kind of reform in the police system. Besides this, intelligence-led policing and problem-oriented policing are other possible reforms in police functioning (see Table 8.1). While the community policing model aims to improve the quality of service and customer satisfaction, intelligence-led policing explains the way of doing police business and problem-oriented policing, as a part of community policing, closely identifies problems and provides solutions to these.[5] Of these three types of policing, there is a need for intelligence-led policing in India.

---

[4] Commonwealth Human Rights Initiative (CHRI). Available from, http://www.humanrightsinitiative.org/publications/nl/newsletter_spring_2006/article9.htm, accessed on 18 March 2018.

[5] Nick Tilley. 2003. 'Modern Approaches to Policing: Community, Problem-Oriented and Intelligence-Led' in *Handbook of* Policing, edited by T. Newburn, second edition, pp. 373–403. Milton, UK: Willan Publishing.

Table 8.1 Dimensions of Intelligence-Led Policing, Community Policing, and Problem-Oriented Policing

Dimension	Intelligence-Led Policing	Community Policing	Problem-Oriented Policing
Background and raison d'être			
1. Problem addressed	Poor detection rates	Lack of legitimacy	Demand exceeding capacity
2. Critique of traditional policing	Ineffective at clearing crime, inadequate at providing protection	Detached from community which funds policing and on whom policing depends; issue of consent	Ineffective in dealing with spiralling demand, not oriented to core problems
3. Inspiration	David Phillips	John Alderson, Robert Trojanowicz	Herman Goldstein
Conception of policing and police officers			
4. Police mission	Law enforcement	Community governance	Deal with police-relevant problems
5. Who defines policing needs	Police	Community	Constitution/law/rights
6. Scope of policing	Narrowed to law enforcement	Broadened to all community concerns/demands	Mid-range, police function defined
7. Dominant discourse	Law	Politics/ideology	Science
8. Core personnel	Intelligence units/Tasking and Co-ordinating groups	Community beat officers	Analysis
Characteristic forms of thinking and action			
9. Openness to others	Enforcement contingent	Value in itself	Problem contingent
10. Source of legitimacy	Government/authority	Local community	Core police functions
11. Appeal	To the police	To the community	To government
12. Problem diagnosis	Bad people	Communities in need	Unintentional crime opportunities
13. Intervention focus	Person	Place	Event pattern
14. Analytic inputs	Evidence/intelligence	Community concerns	Data

Source: Tilley. 'Modern Approaches to Policing'.

Community Policing in India and Its Success Rate

Community policing has made its presence in the Indian police system as it is a very important area for building trust and confidence among the public. There are a number of instances where some states have taken initiatives to reduce the huge gap of communication that exists between the police and the public, but more states need to adopt community policing. States such as Bihar and Uttar Pradesh in particular need to build such an approach and overhaul the dilapidating state of their police system. The following are some of the initiatives taken by the state government police towards the community policing approach.

The Tuticorin Experiment

In the Tuticorin experiment in Tamil Nadu, several police camps were organized in some communally sensitive villages. The main objectives of these camps were to reinstate the confidence of the people on the police force, to improve the police–public relationship, and to maintain the law and order situation in the villages. During this experiment, nobody was permitted to play the role of a mediator between the public and the police. Police officers interacted with the villagers personally and discussed petty matters on the spot and provided immediate solutions, which were welcomed and accepted by both the parties.[6]

Trichy Community Policing

The city of Trichy in Tamil Nadu is known for its religious and racial conflicts, murders, riots, and various other anti-social activities. Trichy is infamous for its high crime rate.[7] Thus there was an immediate need for the police to take the matter seriously and win the confidence and trust of the people. Hence, the initiative of community policing was

---

[6] Tilley. 'Modern Approaches to Policing'.

[7] 'Crime Prevention'. Available at http://www.tn.gov.in/police/crimeprev. htm, accessed on 18 March 2018.

undertaken. J. Tripathy, the then joint CP of Trichy introduced the following strategies for the city:

- *Wide Area Network*: In July 2000, a new initiative was undertaken that linked all the police stations and offices with Internet facility, including email services. This network was known as the Wide Area Network, which helped in bringing the public and the police closer. This, in turn, made the police more transparent, responsive, and interactive.[8]

- *Beat Officers' System*: The city of Trichy was divided into 57 beat zones, and each beat zone was manned by four constables who were called beat officers, which inculcated a sense of pride in them and provided them with powers to make independent decisions and be more responsible towards the needs of the public.[9]

- *Complaint Box System*: Several complaint boxes were provided for the public at various places across the city for helping the public to participate in assisting the police force in reducing crimes. This proved to be a good solution for those who did not want their identity to be known or those who were hesitant to come forth earlier to provide information. It helped the police considerably in receiving information from the public. The letters received from the public were collected every day and were quickly addressed, which further encouraged the public informants.[10]

- *Helpline for Women in Distress*: A helpline was launched on 15 August 2000 for helping the women of the city to provide them assistance, reach them, and receive calls from those who were in distress or faced any kind of problem. This service was available 24×7 and was manned by a team that comprised police, activists

---

[8] 'Crime Prevention'.

[9] Navaz Kotwal and Sanjay Patil. 2011. 'Building Bridges: Experiments with Community Policing in South Asia'. Commonwealth Human Rights Initiative Available at https://humanrightsinitiative.org/publications/police/Building-Bridges-2012-CHRI.pdf, accessed on 22 March 2018.

[10] Alpert and Dunham. 'Community Policing Experiments'.

and students. Under this scheme, the authorities provided victims with legal help, counseling, medical facilities, and so on.[11]

- *Slum Adoption Scheme*: The police department also started a scheme called the Slum Adoption Scheme in which they identified a number of slums and provided the inhabitants various facilities by conducting awareness programmes on the evils of drug addiction, alcoholism, hygiene, AIDS, and so on. Due to the poverty in these slums and other socioeconomic factors, these areas had become a breeding ground for criminals. The police had a tough time in entering these slums to nab criminals and stop crimes from being committed. Thus this initiative was a good attempt by the police. The initiative also included programmes such as vocational training, education, formation of women self-help groups, and providing assistance to people to manufacture and market their products.[12]

Samarth Yojna Community Policing Experiment, Coimbatore City

K. Radhakrishnan, the then CP of Coimbatore City, thus introduced community policing in the city of Coimbatore as a response to its increasing crime rate. As this city had already faced many inhuman activities and crime such as communal riots, and ethnic riots, a community policing scheme was a dire need of the city.[13] The major objective of this scheme was to understand and provide a solution for the communal problems and intolerance among the public and to restore the trust and faith of the public on the police.[14]

Friends of Police Organization, Tamil Nadu

In the state of Tamil Nadu, a perfect example of community policing is the establishment of an organization called Friends of Police (FOP). This organization has strengthened the relationship between the police

---

[11] Alpert and Dunham. 'Community Policing Experiments'.

[12] Alpert and Dunham. 'Community Policing Experiments'.

[13] 'Crimes Against Humanity'. Available at http://genocidehomicide.blogspot.com/2006/09/crimes-against-humanity.html, accessed on 22 March 2018.

[14] Kotwal and Patil. 'Building Bridges'.

and the public, which is really commendable. The successful functioning of FOP for the last 13 years, which has further spread across all
the districts of Tamil Nadu, proves this strengthened relation. This
organization is pro-active and works with a psychological approach
towards policing in the state. In this partnership, citizens are provided
with some powers, rights, and duties towards the objective of reducing
crimes and restoring justice, law, and order in the state. Hence, this
organization helps ordinary citizens in contributing towards preventing
crime and also helps to detect crime in the state effectively. To be a
member of this organization, citizens have to have a clean background.
This means that any citizen who does not have a criminal record or is
not involved in any civil or criminal case is eligible to be a member of
this organization. This organization also prevents the abuse of power by
the police and corruption in the department besides providing useful
information for solving crimes. Such a unique initiative by the state
of Tamil Nadu has helped considerably in enhancing the relationship
between the police and the public, building trust between them, and
ensuring the flow of correct information at the right time to reduce
crimes and corruption.[15]

Prahari: The Community Policing Initiative in Assam

Assam introduced a community policing programme called Project
Prahari on 3 July 1996. It was started by the then SP Kuladhar Saikia
to discuss the idea and model of a 'neighbourhood watch scheme' and
launch it and further to promote policing with the help of community
participation. The objective of this scheme was to change the attitude
of the police towards the public, to make them people friendly, and to
improve their living and working conditions. The aim was also was to
tackle social problems and match the wavelengths of the police and the
community.[16]

---

[15] Kotwal and Patil. 'Building Bridges'.
[16] M. Sanjeev Singh, Deepak Sharma, and Anil Monga. 2014. 'Community
Policing: Initiatives and Challenges'. *Public Affairs and Governance* 2, no. 1, pp.
10–31.

Maithri: Community Policing in Andhra Pradesh

'Maithri' means friendship. This is the name of the community policing initiative in the state of Andhra Pradesh, which was introduced by
the government in 2000. The mission of this scheme was to 'render
courteous, compassionate and caring responsive police personnel and
increase public confidence in police with respect to maintenance of
peace and order and a feeling of safety from crime'.[17] The scheme
believes that contemporary community problems can be resolved with
the help of a decentralized and personalized approach on the part
of the police and by involving the citizens in the process of policing
themselves.[18]

Community Policing in the State of Himachal Pradesh

In November 2000, a scheme of community policing was also introduced in Himachal Pradesh. The major objective of this scheme
was to mobilize the support of the public and ensure active public
participation in reducing the crime rate and maintaining law and
order. This scheme was considerably successful and has set a good
example.[19]

Community Policing in Ludhiana

The police department of Ludhiana introduced the scheme of community policing on 12 October 2002. Under this scheme, community
groups comprising 30 members each were formed in 400 beats, and the
members of this group were made to sit and discuss various problems

---

[17] Vinita Pandey. 2014. 'Community Policing for Conflict Resolution
and Community Resilience'. *International Journal of Social Work and Human
Services Practice* 2, no. 6, p. 229.

[18] Andhra Pradesh Police. 2007. 'Community Policing', Blog, 30 September.
Available at http://andhrapradeshpolice.blogspot.com/2007/09/community-
policing.html, accessed on 24 August 2019.

[19] Himachal Pradesh Police. Available at http://admis.hp.nic.in/himpol/,
accessed on 22 March 2018.

of the city every fortnight or once a month. Further, each group comprising a beat officer, who was associated with the resource centre, was given the duty of policing the community.[20]

Community Policing Initiative in Kolkata, West Bengal

The community policing initiative has also been introduced in the city of Kolkata, and it involves both civil society and the police personnel. Under this initiative, various programmes are organized such as drug awareness programmes, health check-ups for street children of the city, and weekly blood donation programmes.[21] The main aim of the initiative is to involve the public in dispute resolution and ensure a speedy justice delivery system in a cost-effective manner. The initiative also aimed at ensuring a reconciliatory situation for the parties to have a long-lasting solution and also develop a sense of belongingness with the state as well as the nation.

Mohalla Committee Movement Trust, Mumbai

The word 'mohalla' is a Hindi word that means locality. The Mumbai police formed the Mohalla Committee Movement under the initiative of J.F. Riberio, the then CP, Mumbai. After the 1992–3 Hindu–Muslim communal riots, which paralysed Mumbai and killed around 1,000 people, it was felt that a citizen–police committee is an urgent requirement.[22] Now, mohalla committees have become an integral part of the civil society structure of Mumbai. The committees work on the simple principle, 'Give people some power and make them responsible for it'. The primary duty of the members of these

---

[20] Official website of the Government of Punjab. Available at http://punjabgovt.nic.in/news2007/march/march_14.htm, accessed on 22 March 2018.

[21] S. Mohanty and R.K. Mohanty. 2014. *Community Policing as a Public Policy: Challenges and Recommendations*. Newcastle upon Tyne: Cambridge Scholars Publishing, p. 94.

[22] 'Handling Communal Riots'. Available at http://www.india-seminar.com/1999/483/483%20rai.htm, accessed on 22 March 2018.

committees is to maintain cordial relations between different communities, especially between Hindus and Muslims.[23]

Community Policing Initiative in Pune City

Pune introduced the initiative of community policing in 1992 in the form of mohalla committees to prevent future communal flare-ups and to restore public confidence. Around 30 mohalla committees were set up throughout the city of Pune. The members of these committees work with the police to maintain law and order in the city. Further, during festivals and other occasions, these mohalla committees call for meetings so that peace and communal harmony are maintained in the respective localities. Every beat officer holds a meeting of the mohalla committee in his beat once a month and the senior inspector of police of the police station concerned holds a meeting at least once in three months, which is attended by the ACP and other police officials.[24]

Criticism and Community Policing

The concept of community policing gained impetus in a number of countries in the world in the 1970s and the 1980s. Its aim was to identify the gaps between people and the police force. Towards this objective, many countries such as England, Canada, Germany, Japan, and Singapore started exploring alternative ways to the professional and bureaucratic method of policing. Surprisingly, in India, this has been an ancient practice and dates back to the Mauryan era. It included the involvement of communities to safeguard the their rights and interests. It involved more and more public participation.[25]

[23] Mohanty and Mohanty. *Community Policing as a Public Policy*, p. 95.

[24] Mohanty and Mohanty. *Community Policing as a Public Policy*, p. 95.

[25] 'Community Policing in India: Evolution and Various Models'. Available at https://www.gktoday.in/gk/community-policing-in-india-evolution-and-various-models/, accessed on 11 March 2019.

Moral policing or vigilantism is increasing day by day where these so-called vigilante groups try to enforce the code of morality without any kind of legal authority. Few groups like Bajrang Dal, Sri Ram Sena, and Anti-Romeo Squad[26] in India have become the moral police in the name of safeguarding Indian traditions and not the crimes taking place. Not only citizens but also the police are involved in such activities, for instance, the launching of 'Operation Majnu' by the Ghaziabad police in 2011.[27]

Many are of the opinion that though the idea of community policing is good in prevention of crime and protection of people, it has given rise to moral policing that is mostly aimed at females embracing 'Westernization' in the country, at couples in public places, and even at interfering in the personal life of people and invading their privacy. This needs to be checked by the police so that it does not create public nuisance and disturbances in the name of gender, caste, religion, and traditions in the country. The police and the public both need to come together and understand what needs to be done and what should not be done. There is a need to conduct training and awareness programmes by the police for the citizens who can help in building the community policing culture but without interfering in anybody's personal life and privacy.

* * *

The police constitute the internal defence mechanism of any country and their duty is to protect the nation by maintaining law and order. The police are like the white blood corpuscles of the body politic in all countries across the world and not just in India. Today, terrorism

[26] Lalmani Verma. 2017. 'Anti-Romeo & Love Jihad: Experiments in moral policing in Uttar Pradesh', *Indian Express*, 24 March. Available at https://indianexpress.com/article/explained/anti-romeo-love-jihad-experiments-in-moral-policing-in-uttar-pradesh/, accessed on 24 August 2019.

[27] Headlines Today Bureau. 2011. 'Ghaziabad Police launches "Operation Majnu", hound couples in Park', Indian Today, 30 November. Available at https://www.indiatoday.in/india/north/story/operation-majnu-ghaziabad-police-young-lovers-147309-2011-11-30, accessed on 24 August 2019.

has become one of the biggest threats to mankind and not a single country is untouched by it. It is increasing at a considerably fast rate across the world.[28] Terrorists groups have become too dangerous, and thus it has been a tough and challenging job for the security forces to detect, arrest, and punish them. They are a group of severe anti-social elements and are spread across the world and are not confined to a specific place, region, or country. The activities of these terrorists are growing day by day and the occurrence of increased violence and crimes including international terrorism, assassination of people, renowned as well as general public, smuggling of narcotics, and bombing in different states have challenged the police and other national security forces across the globe. The biggest challenge is faced by the police force in almost all nations as they carry a negative image among the public. There is a general lack of trust, confidence, and respect between the police and the public, and this has resulted in various incidents of open hostility between them. It has often been observed that the police have failed in differentiating between a law-abiding citizen and anti-social elements or those who break laws. Though the major duty of the police is to protect the public and maintain law and order, in reality, the police functions in an atmosphere of lack of trust, cooperation, and goodwill from the public for whom they have been appointed.

The only solution that has proved to be beneficial for both the police and the public is the concept of community policing. This has helped to improve the negative and tarnished image of the police considerably and reduced the doubts among the public on the duties of the police. The feedback that the police receive from the public and the image created among the public about the police is actually the result of the behaviour of the police. This is because the police do not interact with the general public and keep them at a distance. Hence the public has developed a negative image about the police. If the police function along with the public by associating with the latter, then people will get an idea about what actually happens in the police department, how

---

[28] 'Policing Central and Eastern Europe'. Available at http://www.ncjrs.gov/policing/fri149.htm, accessed on 25 March 2019.

it works, and what necessary help it requires from the public to reduce crimes and also punish criminals. Thus, community policing is a step forward in inculcating a sense of trust among the public and helping them to maintain law and order and prevent crimes. Such a scheme has also helped the police to improve its image considerably among the public.

CONCLUSION

The police system, as seen in many countries (especially in the developing nations), is based on the model that existed during colonial rule. The model of police system designed during that period was for helping trade and commerce to flourish and ensuring a stable government. During this period, policing was portrayed as militaristic and was only accountable to the colonial power. One of the best examples of colonial power and misuse of the police was in the form of the Indian Police Act, 1861, enacted by the then British colonial rulers. This act is still highly militaristic and draconian, and it needs immediate changes and reforms. It also needs to get rid of all clauses irrelevant to the present time so that democracy and human rights are upheld in the country. This act has become outdated and the Government of India has still not taken any serious steps in amending it or replacing it with a new and better legislation in the biggest democracy in the world.

The citizens of this country needs a sense of security. To this end, the police need to be citizen friendly, address to the needs and grievances of citizens, and help maintain law and order reducing crimes. Thus, there is a need for an effective, efficient, professional, and honest police force in the country. But in reality there are many crimes that the police force is committing such as arbitrary arrests, interrogation without any reason, custodial violence, ban on movement, and unnecessary troubling innocent citizens in the name of law. Such crimes are increasing day by day because of the fact that the Indian Police Act does not have any effective provisions to take actions against the police personnel. In such a scenario, a need for reforms was felt and various committees and organizations—the NHRC, the NPC, and the National Crime Records Bureau (NCRB)—were formed. These committees and organizations gave many suggestions and recommendations for reforming the police system, but till date nothing has been implemented. The need for police reform is self-evident and urgent.

The CoI provides fundamental rights to citizens, and among these, the right to life and personal liberty is an important one. Thus the human rights of every citizen of this country are fundamental rights. Violating these rights and depriving anyone of his/her right to life and personal liberty by the police and armed forces are serious matters of concern, which need to be addressed immediately and urgently. Besides the Government of India, it is also the duty of state governments in India to enact and amend laws concerned with the police with a citizen friendly approach, since the police and public order are state subjects.

After studying the organization and administrative structure of the Indian police force, it has been observed that it is highly complex organization in every state and is headed by a DGP. But in the case of metropolitan cities, the CP heads the force. Several aspects of the police administration, their organizational structure, work culture, training, politicization, accountability, magisterial control, corruption, brutality, and so on, have been discussed and reviewed. Various reforms have been suggested with respect to the functions, recruitments, training, personality and soft skill development, and so on, among the police personnel so that there is a better connection and communication between the police and the public, which will further help in reducing crimes and upholding the human rights of every individual of the country. Since India has ratified the ICCPR and the CRC, it is very important that the human rights of citizens are not violated. Thus the police and other security forces need to adhere to the provisions of these international protocols and conventions.

The IHRL on the right to protection against torture and other cruel, inhuman, and degrading treatment and punishment is *jus cogens* and is guaranteed under various international conventions and enactments such as the UDHR, the ICCPR, the CRC and the CAT. Though India has not yet ratified CAT, it has other international commitments for prohibiting and preventing torture and other inhuman and degrading treatments towards any individual as it has ratified the ICCPR and the CRC. It also has a duty to enact legislations and reforms so that proper infrastructure and initiatives are in place to prevent torture.

As far as criminalization of torture and other inhuman, cruel, and degrading treatment and punishment is concerned, there is a big gap in India as per the guidelines and provisions of the UDHR, the ICCPR, the CRC, and CAT. The Supreme Court of India has developed a series of guidelines for prohibiting torture and has also provided institutional mechanisms for dealing with the nuisance of torture and other forms of custodial violence as there are no particular laws in the country against torture and such degrading treatment. The Supreme Court of India has interpreted the provisions that are related to protection against torture as provided by the UDHR, the ICCPR, and CAT, and it has evolved a human rights policy by making the right to protection against torture a part of the fundamental rights guaranteed under Arts 14 and 21 of the CoI. This is based on the principle of fairness and natural justice. The Supreme Court and the high courts have further included the right to reparation (the right to fair relief and compensation) keeping in view the cases of torture and custodial violence, arbitrary arrests and illegal detention, forceful disappearance, and so on. In spite of evolving such principles and forming new fundamental rights, the Supreme Court of India is not entitled to enact legislations and penal laws as per the international framework and principles, as it is the government that has to enact laws. Hence, the Supreme Court has directed the Government of India to enact laws for ensuring unbiased investigation and prosecution.

Now, the right to protection against torture and custodial violence and other cruel, inhuman, and degrading treatment and punishment; the right to reparation; and the right to judicial remedy are the laws of land. Every citizen is entitled to equal and fair protection under these laws.

Providing a sense of security to ordinary citizens and attending to their grievances depends on the establishment of an efficient, honest, and a professional police force. But it is a fact that such a police force is rare to be seen in India. This has been proved by the findings of various commissions and committees, various complaints received by the NHRC, stories and incidents as reported by the media, and the experiences faced by citizens. Hence, the urgent and immediate need for reforms in police is evident.[1]

The Government of India as well as the state governments have to take into account all the crimes and custodial violence committed by the security forces, introduce reforms in the police system, and also enact new laws and amend the age-old police act and other relevant acts. Further, the central government should take the initiative and encourage state governments to bring reforms in the state police forces and other security forces of the state. This can be done through guide-lines, rules, standards and regulations, new and relevant policies, and so on, to prevent torture and other custodial violence and related crimes.

The role of the NHRC, State Human Rights Commissions (SHRCs), and the PHRA is to provide guidelines for the police and security forces and recommend reforms to the government, but little had been done since the government is not bound to follow their directions and rec-ommendations. Although the recommendation for setting up human rights courts in every district of the states has not been taken up by the government, the provision for ensuring the right to reparation as recommended by the NHRC and the recommendation for ensuring fairness, justice, and equity by the PHRA have been successful.

There are many laws that have been enacted by the government such as the Unlawful Activities Prevention Act (UAPA) and the MCOCA to prevent unlawful activities, terrorist activities, and so on. But these have not proved to be citizen friendly, functioning instead as abusive laws under which many innocent people have been subjected to tor-ture, cruel treatment, forceful arrests, and detention and disappearance. These laws gave unrestrained powers to police officers, which has proved to be an insult to the biggest democracy. But these laws can be made citizen friendly, and this can be done by the removing the immu-nity clause for security personnel, the extended preventive detention

---

[1] Human Rights Solidarity. Available at http://www.hrsolidarity.net/mainfile. php/2005vol15no05/2448/, accessed on 25 March 2018.

clause, and the exceptional evidence standards that include admissibility of confessions made before a police officer. If these amendments are done, then these laws will be citizen friendly and citizens will, in turn, feel a sense of security.

The Government of India has taken various steps and measures towards eradicating custodial violence and torture. One such step was the introduction of the POT Bill in 2010, but the bill was criticized considerably as it was very narrow and restrictive in its approach and also ignored the important provisions of CAT. Hence, India needs to take some more relevant and useful measures for ensuring the ratification of some significant international conventions such as CAT, Optional Protocol to CAT, Optional Protocols to the ICCPR (I and II), the Rome Statute, and the Additional Protocols (I and II) of the Geneva Conventions.

Besides ratifying international conventions related to the prevention against torture and the enactment of laws, there is also a need to bring in reforms in the police system. Towards this objective, there were many committees and commissions that were formed such as the Administrative Reforms Commission (1966), the NPC (1977), the Gore Committee on Police Training (1971), the Ribeiro Commission on Police Reforms (1998), and the Padmanabhaiah Committee (2000). In spite of these steps undertaken, the quality and efficiency of the operations of the police is deteriorating day by day. Hence, it is very important for the government to implement the recommendations given by the aforementioned committees so that an effective, citizen friendly, and transparent system is created.

Reforms in the police system can be further brought in by creating a friendly system and establishing a relationship between citizens and the police. This was introduced in India in various states in the form of community policing. The participation of the public in assisting the police in detecting and preventing crimes has proved to be very beneficial and has built trust between the police and the public.[2] This initiative and system of community policing should be introduced in

---

[2] Marian FitzGerald, Mike Hough, Ian Joseph, and Tariq Qureshi. 2002. *Policing for London*. Cullompton: Willan.

each and every state and union territory in India by the government. In this way, a good society can be built along with a responsible and accountable police system. However, it should be kept in mind that community policing does not turn into moral policing as there is a very thin line between the two. While working for the community, the police should safeguard citizens from crimes and prevent any crime in the society/locality rather than interfering in people's personal lives in the name of community policing.

The Government of India thus needs to take initiative and introduce reforms in the police system since the central government has the power and can also encourage state governments to bring in reforms in the state police forces.

However, as compared to the international standards of the police and other security forces, India has a long way to go in relation to reforms, both institutional and legal, so that fairness and impartiality in police administration, prison administration, and the criminal justice deliverance system is ensured.

APPENDICES*

Appendix A1: Crime Statistics and Data on the Indian Police Force

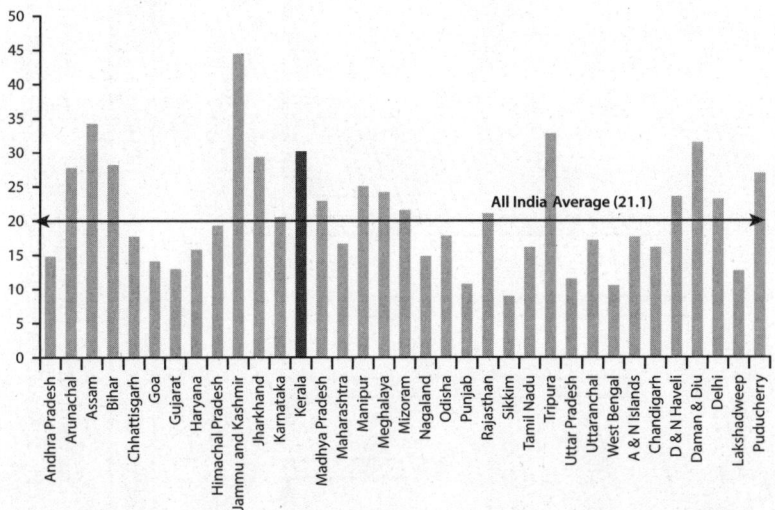

Figure A1.1   State-wise Crime Rate, 2002 (Number of Crimes per 100,000 Population)
Source: Crime Statistics. Available at http://www.keralapolice.org/crimestat.html, accessed on 21 February 2018.

* Appendix A2 and onwards contains text reproduced from various official documents and therefore follow the source spelling conventions.

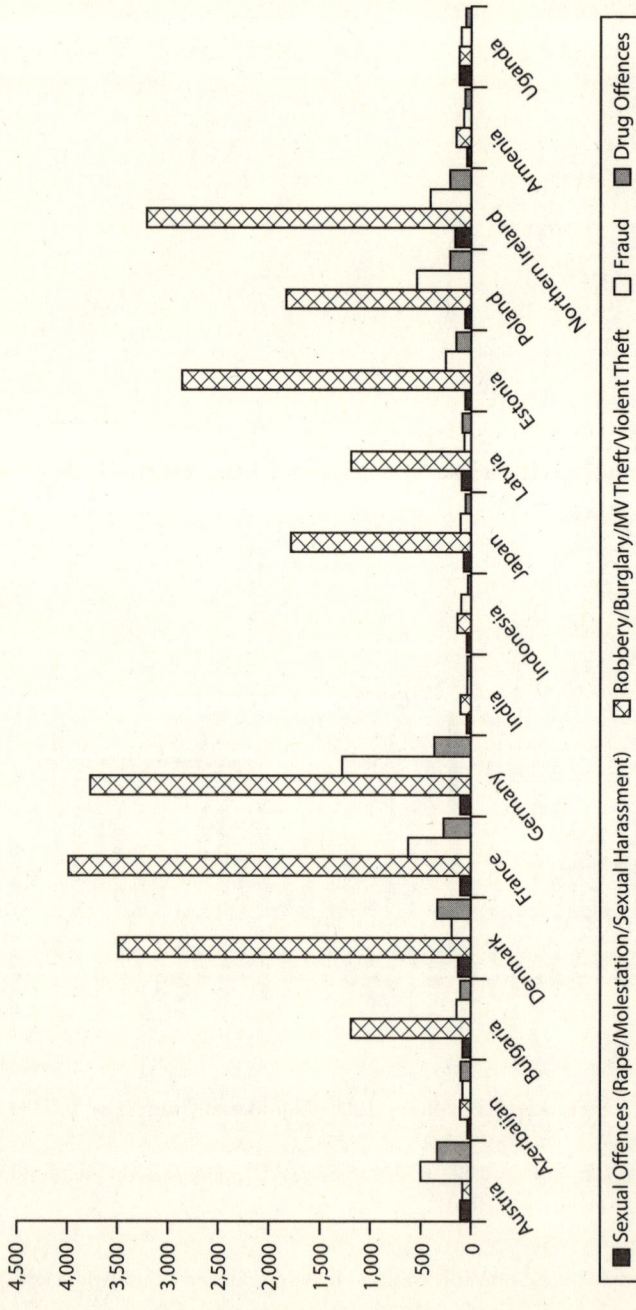

Figure A1.2 Country-wise Crime Rate, 2003 (Number of Crimes per 100,000 Population)

Source: Crime Statistics of India. Available at http://www.keralapolice.org/crimestat/8.html, accessed on 21 February 2018.

Table A1.1   Human Rights Abuse by Police and Type of Enquiry (2009–13)

Year	No. of Complaints Registered	Departmental Enquiry	Magisterial Enquiry	Judicial Enquiry
2009	54,873	24,302	611	481
2010	58,438	21,563	326	268
2011	61,765	21,144	282	246
2012	57,363	19,490	352	252
2013	51,120	14,928	247	655
Total (2009–13)	283,559	101,427	1818	1902

Source: Crime in India Reports (2009–13), NCRB.

Table A1.2   Types of Criminal Action Initiated in Cases of Human Rights Abuse by Police (2009–13)

Year	No. of Complaints Registered	No. of Police Personnel Sent for Trial	No. of Police Personnel Whose Cases Were Withdrawn	No. of Police Personnel Convicted	No. of Police Personnel Acquitted
2009	54,873	1,279	132	43	99
2010	58,438	1,107	141	53	152
2011	61,765	1,229	475	47	392
2012	57,363	1,147	633	42	116
2013	51,120	1,250	412	53	101
TOTAL (2009–13)	283,559	6,012	1,793	238	860

Source: Crime in India Reports (2009–13), NCRB.

Table A1.3   Actual Police Strength in Relation to Area, Population, Case Load, and Per Capita Expenditure (2009–13)

Year	Teeth to Tail Ratio	Police per 100 sq. km	Police per 1 Lakh Population	Case Load Per Capita Police Force	Case Load per Investigating Officers	Per Capita Expenditure
2009	1:07	49.2	133	2.3	46.5	203,842
2010	1:07	49.9	133	2.4	46.4	200,899
2011	1:07	52.4	137	2.5	41.3	298,625
2012	1:07	52.9	138	2.5	39.4	332,867
2013	1:07	54.7	141	2.6	40.5	335,125

Source: Crime in India Reports (2009–13), NCRB.

Appendix A2: Code of Conduct for the Police[1]

The code of conduct for the police in the country was adopted at the Conference of the Inspectors General of Police in 1960. This was later approved by the Government of India and circulated to all the state governments. The National Police Commission (NPC) examined the subject and recommended changes in Clause 12 of the earlier code. The final code as recommended by the NPC and accepted by the Government of India and circulated to all state governments is reproduced as follows:

1. The police must bear faithful allegiance to the Constitution of India and respect and uphold the rights of the citizens as guaranteed by it.

2. The police should not question the propriety of necessity of any law duly enacted. They should enforce the law firmly and impartially without fear or favour, malice or vindictiveness.

3. The police must recognise and respect the limitations of their powers and functions. They should not usurp or even seem to usurp the functions of the judiciary and sit in judgement on cases to avenge individuals and punish the guilty.

4. In securing the observance of law or in maintaining order, the police should as far as practicable, use the methods of persuasion, advice and warning. When the application of force becomes inevitable, only the irreducible minimum of force required in the circumstances should be used.

5. The prime duty of the police is to prevent crime and disorder and the police must recognise that the test of their efficiency is the absence of both and not the visible evidence of police action in dealing with them.

6. The police must recognise that they are members of the public, with the only difference that in the interest of the society and on its behalf they are employed to give full time attention to duties which are normally incumbent on every citizen to perform.

---

[1] 'Police Organization in India', Commonwealth Human Rights Initiative.

7. The police should realise that the efficient performance of their duties will be dependent on the extent of ready cooperation that they receive from the public. This, in turn, will depend on their ability to secure public approval of their conduct and actions and to earn and retain public respect and confidence.

8. The police should always keep the welfare of the people in mind and be sympathetic and considerate towards them. They should always be ready to offer individual service and friendship and render necessary assistance to all without regard to their wealth and/ or social standing.

9. The police should always place duty before self, should maintain calm in the face of danger, scorn or ridicule and should be ready to sacrifice their lives in protecting those of others.

10. The police should always be courteous and well mannered; they should be dependable and impartial; they should possess dignity and courage; and should cultivate character and the trust of the people.

11. Integrity of the highest order is the fundamental basis of the prestige of the police. Recognising this, the police must keep their private lives scrupulously clean, develop self-restraint and be truthful and honest in thought and deed, in both personal and official life, so that the public may regard them as exemplary citizens.

12. The police should recognise that their full utility to the State is best ensured only by maintaining a high standard of discipline, faithful performance of duties in accordance with law and implicit obedience to the lawful directions of commanding ranks and absolute loyalty to the force and by keeping themselves in the state of constant training and preparedness.

13. As members of a secular, democratic state the police should strive continually to rise above personal prejudices and promote harmony and the spirit of common brotherhood amongst all the people of India transcending religious, linguistic and regional or sectional diversities and to renounce practices derogatory to the dignity of women and disadvantaged segments of the society.

Appendix A3: Article 50 and Article 246 (Seventh Schedule) of the Constitution of India

The Constitution of India
(Article 50)
Separation of judiciary from executive.—**The State shall take steps to separate the judiciary from the executive in the public services of the State.**

Seventh Schedule
(Article 246)
List II—State List

1. Public order (but not including the use of any naval, military or air force or any other armed force of the Union or of any other force subject to the control of the Union or of any contingent or unit thereof in aid of the civil power).
2. Police (including railway and village police) subject to the provisions of entry 2A of List I.
3. Officers and servants of the High Court; procedure in rent and revenue courts; fees taken in all courts except the Supreme Court.
4. Prisons, reformatories, Borstal institutions and other institutions of a like nature, and persons detained therein; arrangements with other States for the use of prisons and other institutions.
5. Local government, that is to say, the Constitution and powers of municipal corporations, improvement trusts, districts boards, mining settlement authorities and other local authorities for the purpose of local self-government or village administration.
6. Public health and sanitation; hospitals and dispensaries.
7. Pilgrimages, other than pilgrimages to places outside India.
8. Intoxicating liquors, that is to say, the production, manufacture, possession, transport, purchase and sale of intoxicating liquors.
9. Relief of the disabled and unemployable.
10. Burials and burial grounds; cremations and cremation grounds.[2]

---

[2] Entry 11 omitted by Constitution (Forty-Second Amendment) Act, 1976, sec. 57, (w.e.f. 3 January 1977).

12. Libraries, museums and other similar institutions controlled or financed by the State; ancient and historical monuments and records other than those [declared by or under law made by Parliament] to be of national importance.

13. Communications, that is to say, roads, bridges, ferries, and other means of communication not specified in List I; municipal tramways; ropeways; inland waterways and traffic thereon subject to the provisions of List I and List III with regard to such waterways; vehicles other than mechanically propelled vehicles.

14. Agriculture, including agricultural education and research, protection against pests and prevention of plant diseases.

15. Preservation, protection and improvement of stock and prevention of animal diseases; veterinary training and practice.

16. Pounds and the prevention of cattle trespass.

17. Water, that is to say, water supplies, irrigation and canals, drainage and embankments, water storage and water power subject to the provisions of entry 56 of List I.

18. Land, that is to say, rights in or over land, land tenures including the relation of landlord and tenant, and the collection of rents; transfer and alienation of agricultural land; land improvement and agricultural loans; colonization.[3]

21. Fisheries.

22. Courts of wards subject to the provisions of entry 34 of List I; encumbered and attached estates.

23. Regulation of mines and mineral development subject to the provisions of List I with respect to regulation and development under the control of the Union.

24. Industries subject to the provisions of entries 7 and 52 of List I.

25. Gas and gas-works.

26. Trade and commerce within the State subject to the provisions of entry 33 of List III.

27. Production, supply and distribution of goods subject to the provisions of entry 33 of List III.

---

[3] Entries 19 and 20 omitted by the Constitution (Forty-Second Amendment) Act, 1976, sec. 57 (w.e.f. 3-1-1977).

28. Markets and fairs.[4]
30. Money-lending and money-lenders; relief of agricultural indebtedness.
31. Inns and inn-keepers.
32. Incorporation, regulation and winding up of corporations, other than those specified in List I, and universities; unincorporated trading, literary, scientific, religious and other societies and associations; co-operative societies.
33. Theatres and dramatic performances; cinemas subject to the provisions of entry 60 of List I; sports, entertainments and amusements.
34. Betting and gambling.
35. Works, lands and buildings vested in or in the possession of the State.[5]
37. Elections to the Legislature of the State subject to the provisions of any law made by Parliament.
38. Salaries and allowances of members of the Legislature of the State, of the Speaker and Deputy Speaker of the Legislative Assembly and, if there is a Legislative Council, of the Chairman and Deputy Chairman thereof.
39. Powers, privileges and immunities of the Legislative Assembly and of the members and the committees thereof, and, if there is a Legislative Council, of that Council and of the members and the committees thereof; enforcement of attendance of persons for giving evidence or producing documents before committees of the Legislature of the State.
40. Salaries and allowances of Ministers for the State.
41. State public services; State Public Service Commission.
42. State pensions, that is to say, pensions payable by the State or out of the Consolidated Fund of the State.
43. Public debt of the State.
44. Treasure trove.

---

[4] Entry 29 omitted by the Constitution (Forty-Second Amendment) Act, 1976, sec. 57 (w.e.f. 3-1-1977).

[5] Entry 36 omitted by the Constitution (Seventh Amendment) Act, 1956, sec. 26.

45. Land revenue, including the assessment and collection of revenue, the maintenance of land records, survey for revenue purposes and records of rights, and alienation of revenues.
46. Taxes on agricultural income.
47. Duties in respect of succession to agricultural land.
48. Estate duty in respect of agricultural land.
49. Taxes on lands and buildings.
50. Taxes on mineral rights subject to any limitations imposed by Parliament by law relating to mineral development.
51. Duties of excise on the following goods manufactured or produced in the State and countervailing duties at the same or lower rates on similar goods manufactured or produced elsewhere in India:—

     a. alcoholic liquors for human consumption;
     b. opium, Indian hemp and other narcotic drugs and narcotics;

     but not including medicinal and toilet preparations containing alcohol or any substance included in sub-paragraph (*b*) of this entry.

52. Taxes on the entry of goods into a local area for consumption, use or sale therein.
53. Taxes on the consumption or sale of electricity.
54. Taxes on the sale or purchase of goods other than newspapers, subject to the provisions of entry 92A of List I.
55. Taxes on advertisements other than advertisements published in the newspapers and advertisements broadcast by radio or television.
56. Taxes on goods and passengers carried by road or on inland waterways.
57. Taxes on vehicles, whether mechanically propelled or not, suitable for use on roads, including tramcars subject to the provisions of entry 35 of List III.
58. Taxes on animals and boats.
59. Tolls.
60. Taxes on professions, trades, callings and employments.
61. Capitation taxes.

62. Taxes on luxuries, including taxes on entertainments, amusements, betting and gambling.

63. Rates of stamp duty in respect of documents other than those specified in the provisions of List I with regard to rates of stamp duty.

64. Offences against laws with respect to any of the matters in this List.

65. Jurisdiction and powers of all courts, except the Supreme Court, with respect to any of the matters in this List.

66. Fees in respect of any of the matters in this List, but not including fees taken in any court.

Appendix A4: Summary of the Ribeiro Committee's Recommendations

First Report (October 1998)

1. A Security Commission should be set-up in each State consisting of the Minister in charge of Police as the Chairman, the Leader of the Opposition, the Chief Secretary of the State, a sitting or retired judge nominated by the Chief Justice of the State's High Court and three other non-political citizens of proven merit and integrity as members. These three citizens should be chosen by a committee to be set-up by the Chairman of the NHRC, which has taken much interest in the establishment of this proposed institution.

2. The name of the Commission should be 'The Police Performance and Accountability Commission.' (PPAC).

3. The four non-political members of this Commission excluding the Chief Secretary, should hold office for three years after which they will be replaced by persons of equal merit chosen in the same manner.

4. The Commission will have advisory and recommendatory powers for the present. The State's DGP will be its Secretary and Convener.

5. The Commission will oversee the performance of the Police and ensure that it is accountable to the law of the land. Its functions

will be as spelt out by the NPC in para 15.48 of their report. In addition, it will ensure that no premature transfers of officers of the rank of SP and above are made without prior clearance from the Commission and that transfers are made only by the authority competent under the rules to do so.

6. Besides the Commission, a District Police Complaints Authority will be set up in each Police District as a non statutory body to examine complaints from the public of police excesses, arbitrary arrests and detention, false implications in criminal cases, custodial violence, etc and to make appropriate recommendations to the Police Performance and Accountability Commission, as well as to the Government and to the State or National Human Rights Commission. The Principal District and Sessions Judge, the Collector of the district and the SSP should constitute this authority.

7. In every State, a Police Establishment Board should be constituted with the DGP and his four senior-most officers, borne on the IPS cadre of the State but who are immediately junior to the DGP, as members to monitor all transfers, promotions, rewards and punishments as well as other service related issues. The Board should be given the legal authority to discharge its duties by amending the relevant Rules.

8. Rules should be framed by the Government on transfers, tenures, promotions, rewards and punishments and the police authorities designated to administer these rules. Any departure from these norms and rules will be brought to the notice of the PPAC.

9. The DG of Police will be selected by the Chief Minister of the State from a panel of three names prepared by a Committee headed by the Chairman of the UPSC and consisting of the Union Home Secretary, the Director of Intelligence Bureau, the State's Chief Secretary and the State's incumbent DGP. This selection committee may consult the CVC before drawing up a panel. The DGP will have fixed tenure of three years. He can be removed within the period of tenure only on the recommendations of the PPAC and for specified reasons, made in writing to the Government.

10. The investigation wing of the Police will be insulated from undue pressure if the DGP is selected in the manner prescribed above and given a tenure and also if the PPAC discharges its role of overseeing police performance and ensuring accountability. All investigating officers should be specially trained in scientific methods of investigation and not utilised for law & order duties except in small rural police stations where it may not be possible to strictly demarcate the two important police functions. The investigating officers should not be shifted to law and order or other duties for five years at least.

Second Report (March 1999)

1. The NPC had recommended that there should be a State Security Commission at the centre. There is no need for such an institution at the central level. In case of CBI, the Supreme Court has already given directions. The IB is an intelligence organization and the BSF and the CRPF are para-military outfits which do not involve themselves with local politics and politicians.

2. The Central Police Committee as recommended by the NPC in its Seventh Report should be constituted.

3. The old Police Act of 1861 needs to be replaced by a new Police Act.

4. The Vohra Committee had recommended the establishment of a Nodal Cell in the Ministry of Home Affairs to deal with the problem of nexus between crime syndicates, political leaders, government functionaries and others. It is learnt that such a cell is already operative but how far it has succeeded in its endeavour is not known to our Committee.

5. The recommendations of the Law Commission about insulating the investigative functions of the police from its law and order work should be implemented urgently.

6. The recommendations of the NPC about recruitment, training and welfare of the constabulary should be implemented.

7. The minimum educational qualifications for recruitment to the level of Constable should be Higher Secondary.

8. The NPC had recommended the reorganisation of the hierarchy of the police, with an increase in the strength at middle levels of ASI/SI/Inspector to be offset by reducing numbers at the lower levels of constabulary. This would improve promotion opportunities of lower ranks. We endorse the recommendations of the NPC.

9. Every State should establish an independent Police Recruitment Board and entrust to it the task of recruitment of all non-gazetted ranks.

10. A qualitative change in the training being imparted in police training institutions is imperative to improve performance and behaviour of the police.

Appendix A5: Summary of Recommendations Made by the Padmanabhaiah Committee on Police Reforms

1. There should be a greater recruitment of Sub-Inspectors instead of Constables. Recruitment to constabulary should be restricted till a teeth-to-tail ratio of 1:4 is achieved as against present ratio, which ranges from 1:7 to 1:15 in different states.

2. Constables should be recruited young. Boys/girls, who have passed 10th Standard examination and are below 19 years in age should be eligible to appear in a common competitive qualifying examination. The successful candidates should be put through a rigorous 2-year training programme and qualify for appointment as constables only after passing a final examination.

3. The existing constabulary should be retrained to enable them to imbibe right attitudes to work. Those who do not successfully complete training should be compulsorily retired.

4. A Police Training Advisory Council should be set up at the centre and in each state to advise the Home Ministers on police training matters.

5. The eligibility criteria for recruitment to the level of Sub-Inspectors should be 12th class pass and an upper age limit of 21 years. They should be recruited on the basis of a common

written qualifying examination. The successful candidates must pass a final examination after undergoing a 3-year training programme. 50% of vacancies of Sub-Inspectors should be filled by direct recruitment and 50% reserved for promotions.

6. A constable should be classified as a 'skilled worker' in view of the skills required and risks involved in the job.

7. All promotions should be subject to completing the mandatory training programmes and passing of promotional examinations.

8. The Indian Police should adopt the philosophy of community policing. The Government of India should support this by bringing out a handbook on the subject, providing training inputs and funding pilot projects.

9. Lack of a proper tenure policy for posting of officers at different levels and arbitrary transfers have been used by politicians to control and abuse the police for their own ends. To deal with this problem, following action is required:

    a. A body headed by the Chief Justice of the State High court as Chairman, State Chief Secretary and an eminent public person as members should be constituted to recommend a panel of two names for appointment to the post of the Director General of Police.

    b. A police Establishment Board, consisting of DGP and three other members of the police force selected by him, should be constituted to decide transfers of all officers of the rank of Deputy Superintendent of Police and above.

    c. The minimum tenure of all officers should be 2 years.

    d. Another Committee under the Chief Secretary, with Home Secretary and the DGP as members, should be constituted to hear representations from police officers of the rank of Superintendent of Police and above alleging violation of rules in the matter of postings and transfers.

10. To deal with the problem of corruption in the police, which leads to the criminalisation of the force, the committee has recommended a more serious enforcement of the code of conduct and simpler but more effective procedures for removing corrupt officers.

11. Since police work cannot be organized on an 8-hour shift basis, police personnel should be given a weekly off and compulsorily required to go on earned leave every year. Holiday homes may be constructed for police personnel.

12. Investigation should be separated from law and order work. In the first phase, this separation should take place at police station level in all urban areas. An Additional Superintendent of Police should be exclusively responsible for crime and investigation work.

13. Sections 25 and 26 of the Indian Evidence Act should be deleted and confessions made to police officers of the rank of Superintendent of Police and above should be made admissible in evidence.

14. Every police station should be equipped with 'investigation kits' and every sub-division should have a mobile forensic science laboratory.

15. The police leadership, through proper manpower and career planning, improved training, effective supervision and by inculcating a sense of values amongst the members of the force, can play an important role in encouraging specialisation, promoting professionalism and increasing morale in the force.

16. There is an urgent need to encourage specialisation in various aspects of policing.

17. In each district, there should be a crime prevention cell manned by officers who have specialised in crime prevention work.

18. To deal with cyber crime effectively, police capabilities in various areas need to be developed. Capabilities of some police institutions, like the National Police Academy in the field of training, CBI in investigation, Intelligence Bureau in cyber surveillance and the National Crime Records Bureau in cyber technology/forensics should be enhanced.

19. The present classification of offences into cognizable and non-cognizable made 150 years ago is not very relevant today. The Law Commission of India should review the entire classification and the powers of the police to investigate.

20. The concept of VIP security has been grossly, blatantly and brazenly misused. The entire concept of personal security needs a careful review and dismantling.

21. Certain offences having inter-state, national and inter-national repercussions should be declared 'federal offences' to be investigated by the Special Crimes Division of the CBI, which should function under the administrative control of the Ministry of Home Affairs.

22. Taking into account the wide ramifications of the terrorist crime, there have to be different norms regarding the burden of proof, degree of proof and the legal procedures in regard to trial of terrorist cases. There is a need for a special and a comprehensive law to fight terrorism.

23. There should be a national counter terrorism coordinator to prepare a comprehensive counter-terrorism plan and budget.

24. A statutory independent Inspectorate of Police should be set up to carry out annual as well as thematic inspections of the police force and to report to the state government whether the police force is functioning efficiently and effectively.

25. A non statutory District Police Complaints Authority (DPCA) should be set up with the District Magistrate as the Chairman and a senior Additional Sessions Judge, the District Superintendent of Police and an eminent citizen nominated by the DM as members. Investigations into public complaints against the police should in the first instance be done by the police department itself. Those who are not satisfied can approach the DPCA.

26. There should be a mandatory judicial inquiry into all cases of alleged rape of a woman or death of any person in police custody.

27. The Government of India should establish a permanent National Commission for Policing Standards to lay down norms and standards for all police forces on matters of common concern and to see that that the State Governments set up mechanisms to enforce such standards.

28. The release of central grants for modernisation or up gradation funds should be dependent upon compliance by state governments with certain basic issues, like each state having a manpower and career planning system, a transparent recruitment, promotion and transfer policy and meeting certain minimum standards for training.

29. The Police Act of 1861 should be replaced by a new Act.
30. The State Government must give high priority to the allocation of resources to the police.
31. There should be a permanent National Commission for Police Standards and (NCPs) to set standards and to see that State Governments set up mechanisms to enforce such standards.
32. There is need for comprehensive reforms in criminal justice administration. Public would soon lose faith in the criminal justice system unless the other components of the systems are also thoroughly overhauled simultaneously.

INDEX

INDEX

ABOUT THE AUTHOR

Joshua N. Aston is an associate professor as well as the Associate Dean (Law) and is also a member of the executive team, School of Business and Law, Edith Cowan University, Western Australia. He is the author of the acclaimed text *Trafficking of Women and Children*. Aston obtained his Doctorate from Symbiosis International University, India, and Masters in International Criminal Law from the University of Sussex, United Kingdom.

His educational background in the area of international criminal law has given him a broad base from which he branches into specific areas by analysing the impact of actions of States at the national level and how this impacts in the international sphere. His focus has remained however on human rights violation which is very topical for the modern civil society. This interest has spurred him to work on issues of modern slavery in which he actively publishes. Through his work in the areas of human rights and international criminal law, he is continuously challenging the status quo and his academic writing is compelling and posits the need to change situations for a better and humane world.